The New Order of the Oceans
The Advent of a Managed Environment

THE NEW ORDER OF THE OCEANS

The Advent of a Managed Environment

Edited by GIULIO PONTECORVO

New York Columbia University Press *1986*

Library of Congress Cataloging-in-Publication Data

The New order of the ocean.

Includes bibliographies and index.
1. Marine resources conservation—Law and legislation. 2. Marine law. 3. Marine resources conservation. I. Pontecorvo, Giulio, 1923–
K3485.4.N49   341.7'62   86-6804
ISBN 0-231-05870-5

Columbia University Press
New York   Gildford, Surrey
Copyright © 1986 Columbia University Press
All rights reserved

Printed in the United States of America

This book is Smyth-sewn.

Contents

Contributors   vii

Foreword   xi
ELLIOT RICHARDSON

Part I. **The New Regime of the Oceans**

1. *Opportunity, Abundance, Scarcity: An Overview*   1
    GIULIO PONTECORVO

2. *Division of the Spoils: Hydrocarbons and*   15
    Living Resources
    GIULIO PONTECORVO

3. *Concepts and Realities in the New Law of the Sea*   29
    OSCAR SCHACHTER

    A Note: Military Uses of the Ocean and the Law of   60
    the Sea Conference
    GIULIO PONTECORVO

Part II. **Resources: Science and Technology**

4. *Ocean Science: Its Place in the New Order*   65
    of the Oceans
    DAVID ROSS

5. *Minerals of the Deep Sea: Myth and Reality*   85
    MARNE DUBS

Part III. **Voices of the New Regime**

6. *Historical Background of the Evolution of the*   125
    Exclusive Economic Zone and the Contribution
    of Africa
    FRANK X. NJENGA

7. *Law of the Sea: The Latin American View*   158
   ANDRÉS AGUILAR MAWDSLEY

8. *A Southeast Asian Perspective*   199
   HASJIM DJALAL

Part IV. **Unfinished Business**

9. *The United States and the Law of the*   219
   Sea Conference
   THOMAS A. CLINGAN, JR.

10. *The Unfinished Business of the Law of the*   238
    Sea Conference
    JONATHAN I. CHARNEY

Index   265

Contributors

JONATHAN I. CHARNEY is a professor of Law at the Vanderbilt University School of Law. He is a member of the American Law Institute, the American Society of International Law, and the Panel on Ocean Uses. During the Law of the Sea negotiations he served as a member of the United States Advisory Committee on the Law of the Sea. In that capacity he attended many of the sessions of the Conference on the Law of the Sea. He has published extensively on international law and the Law of the Sea in such journals as: *The American Journal of International Law, The British Year Book of International Law, Duke Law Journal, Foreign Affairs, Law and Contemporary Problems,* and *Ocean Development and International Law.* He has also served as a consultant to governments and has participated in various committees and professional programs.

THOMAS A. CLINGAN, JR. is professor of Law and Marine Affairs at the University of Miami. He served as vice-chairman of the U.S. delegation to the Third United Nations Law of the Sea Conference, and as chairman of the English Language Group of the conference drafting committee. He has also served as Deputy Assistant Secretary of State and Ambassador for Oceans and Fisheries Affairs. He has written numerous articles and papers on the subject of the Law of the Sea.

Dr. HASJIM DJALAL is the Indonesian ambassador to Canada. He earned his B.A. (1956) in political science from the Academy for the Foreign Service in Jakarta, and his M.A. (1959) and Ph.D. (1960) in foreign affairs from the University of Virginia. Some of his other affiliations have been as member of the Indonesian Continental Shelves Commission (1961–1983), director of Legal and Treaty Affairs in the Department of Foreign Affairs (1977–1979) and as head of International Law Division of the Legal Directorate in the Department of Foriegn Affairs in Jakarta (1969–1972).

MARNE A. DUBS is currently in private consulting practice on the evaluation and management of technology and new ventures with principal clients in the oil, mineral, and chemical industries. He was previously corporate director of technology for the Kennecott Corporation and manager of the Kennecott Consortium's manganese nodule project.

He has served on the National Advisory Council on Oceans and Atmosphere, as expert on the U.S. delegation to the Law of the Sea Conference, and as chairman of the Undersea Mineral Resources Committee of the American Mining Congress. Currently he is on the Advisory Council on Marine Affairs at the University of Rhode Island and also on the Advisory Board of the Center for Oceans Law and Policy at the University of Virginia.

He has a broad background in research and development and engineering. Prior to Kennecott, he worked at Union Carbide on the creation, utilization, and commercialization of new technologies, particularly in cryogenics and ocean operations. At Kennecott he was involved in new business development and research activities other than ocean activities. He also worked at the Standard Oil Company (Ohio), which acquired Kennecott, to inventory and evaluate all of their technology.

ANDRÉS AGUILAR MAWDSLEY is, at present, Permanent Representative of Venezuela to the United Nations, with the rank of Ambassador; member of the Advisory Committee for Foreign Affairs of Venezuela; member of the Human Rights Committee, established under the International Covenant on Civil and Political Rights; Fellow *(Individuo de Número)* of the Venezuelan Academy of Political and Social Sciences; Associate Member of the Hispano-Luso-Americano Institute for International Law and of the *Institut de Droit Internationel;* Chairman of the Venezuelan Delegation to the Third United Nations Conference on the Law of the Sea and Chairman of the Second Committee of this Conference in all of its sessions, with the exception of the Third Session.

DR. FRANK X. NJENGA is the Director of the Political Department of the Organization of African Unity (OAU) in Addis Ababa, Ethiopia. He was the Kenyan Representative in the negotiations of all three Law of the Sea Conferences, serving as Vice Chairman of the Second Committee and Chairman of the Negotiating Group on the Seabed. Dr.

Njenga introduced the concept of the exclusive economic zone in 1970, and has published several articles on the Law of the Sea.

Prior to his position with OAU, Dr. Njenga served on the Permanent Mission of Kenya to the United Nations and on the Ministry of Foriegn Affairs of Kenya. He taught international law at the University of Dire Dawa, and is a member of the United Nations Law Commission.

GIULIO PONTECORVO is a professor of Economics at the Graduate School of Business, Columbia University. He has served on the Department of State Advisory Committee on the Law of the Sea, several National Academy of Science committees, and the Advisory Committee on Economics for the Food and Agricultural Organization.

Currently, Professor Pontecorvo is director of the Center for Business and Government Studies, which includes the Center for Food Policy Studies and the Center for International Business Cycle Research, at Columbia University. He is chairman of the Senior Advisory Committee for the Program in Marine Affairs at Woods Hole Oceanographic Institution, and serves on the executive board of the Law of the Sea Institute, and the Advisory Committee of the Lamont-Doherty Geological Observatory.

He has published widely on the economics of fisheries and marine resources.

ELLIOT L. RICHARDSON is the former Ambassador-at-large and Special Representative of the President to the Law of the Sea Conference. He is currently a senior resident partner in the Washington office of Milbank, Tweed, Hadley and McCloy.

He has also served as Secretary of Commerce, Attorney General of the United States, Secretary of Defense, Secretary of Health, Education and Welfare, and Under Secretary of State. Dr. Richardson has published numerous articles on government, law, and foreign policy.

Dr. DAVID A. ROSS is a marine geologist at the Woods Hole Oceanographic Institution in Woods Hole, Massachusetts. From 1980 to 1985 he was director of the Marine Policy and Ocean Management Center at that Institution and presently is Sea Grant Coordinator and chairman of the Geology and Geophysics Department. He has been involved in several of the Law of the Sea Conference meetings and was also twice on the U.S. delegation to the Intergovernmental Oceanographic Commission. Dr. Ross has had marine science or marine policy programs with Egypt, Saudi Arabia, Iran, Colombia, and Ecuador. He has published numerous scientific articles and has written or edited nine books.

OSCAR SCHACHTER is Hamilton Fish Professor Emeritus of International Law and Diplomacy at Columbia University. A graduate of Columbia Law School, and a member of the Bar of New York, his career has included U.S. government service and positions in international organizations. He was a legal adviser at the United Nations from 1946 to 1966 and later a director of the United Nations Institute for Training and Research. During much of this period, he also taught at Yale Law School and for short periods at other universities. Since 1975, he has been on the law and political science faculties at Columbia. His professional honors include election to the Institut de Droit International in 1965, the presidency of the American Society of International Law (1968–1970) and the Manley Hudson Medal for achievement in International Law (1981). He has been an editor of the American Journal of International Law since 1959 and its coeditor in chief from 1978 to 1984. His publications treat many aspects of international law and international institutions and two of his books *Sharing the World's Resources* (1977) and *International Law in Theory and Practice* (1985) are especially pertinent to the Law of the Sea.

Foreword

ELLIOT L. RICHARDSON

IN THE CLASSIC STORY about the blind men and the elephant, each of the blind men touches a different portion of the animal and comes up with a radically different version of what it must look like. Given the complexity of the Law of the Sea negotiations and the diversity of the backgrounds, interests, and points of view of the authors represented in this volume, it might have been anticipated that their versions of the process and its outcome would be no less divergent than the blind men's descriptions of the elephant. These observers, however, are clearly talking about the same creature. Since Professor Pontecorvo would, I know, disclaim having imposed his own views, this remarkable result can only be accounted for by the fact that the authors have in common both a broad base of knowledge and a high degree of objectivity. And for this the editor, having selected the contributors, deserves a large measure of credit.

This is not to say, of course, that everyone who participated in those extraordinary negotiations will completely concur in every judgment or every interpretation of events. Indeed, I myself find it hard to resist the temptation to take issue with one or another point of emphasis or detail. But this is a foreword, not another chapter; an appreciation, not a book review. Besides, whatever I might add or subtract would not significantly alter the composite picture that emerges from the book in its entirety.

Read as parts of a comprehensive whole, the essays portray an astonishingly ambitious effort. In terms of scope, duration, number of participants, the improvisation of new kinds of negotiating devices, and success in enlisting consensus, the history of multilateral negotiations has never seen anything like it. Already precedent-setting in so many other ways, the Law of the Sea Convention broke still another record when it was closed for signature on December 10, 1984: it had then been signed by 159 states and other entities. With twenty ratifications as of June 21, 1985, it will enter into force when it has been ratified by forty more countries.

As Jonathan Charney points out in his essay on the unfinished business of the Law of the Sea Conference, the Convention left a number of issues to be dealt with at a later stage. Some are delegated to the competent international organizations; others are to be resolved either through one of the Convention's prescribed dispute-settlement mechanisms or by invoking its relatively simple amendment procedures. The Preparatory Commission, which was created to pave the way for the Convention's entry into force, is now drafting rules and regulations that will close loopholes and eliminate ambiguities in the deep-seabed mining provisions. In so doing the Commission will make the regime more workable and better able to attract investment. But the net effect of Professor Charney's delineation of matters that the Convention did not definitively address is to throw into sharp relief the extraordinary range of what it did accomplish.

Like themes differently developed by different composers but still recognizably the same, certain basic ideas recur throughout these essays. Taken together, they account both for the otherwise improbable circumstance that the Third United Nations Conference on the Law of the Sea was convened at all and for the equally remarkable fact that it did not lapse into incoherence.

One such theme is the impact of new technology. In the years leading up to the convening of the Conference, the evolution of science and engineering was rapidly extending to greater water depths the ability to recover oil and gas from the continental shelf. It was also enabling sonar-guided factory ships to destroy entire fishery stocks. In still more innovative forms it was on the verge of bringing within reach of commercial exploitation the manganese nodules that had long been known to litter the ocean floor in enormous quantities and at vast depths. The norms of international law that ripened in the mercantile climate of the seventeenth century were no longer adequate to cope with the competing claims generated by twentieth-century R&D. As Professor Pontecorvo observes, "A political/legal solution had to be found that was more inclusive, that accommodated the needs of many more nations and that reflected the complexities of the ocean management problems that had emerged after the second world war."

The second recurring theme grows out of the first. It concerns the clash between the interests of maritime states in navigational freedom and the interests of coastal states—and developing countries generally—in the conservation and exploitation of oceanic resources. But for the Conference participants' wide recognition that economic realities required workable rules, the outcome could easily have been chaos. There emerged instead the Conference's most innovative compromises, notably the exclusive economic zone, whose evolution is illuminated here by Andres Aguilar and Frank Njenga, two of the leading participants in the process.

The Conference's most controversial resource-related issue, deep-seabed mining, still evokes sharply contrasting ideological themes. In the early years every encounter between the rhetoric of the New International Economic Order and the dogmas of *laissez faire* capitalism tended to produce dissonance if not cacophony. Each successive Conference session, however, brought clearer understanding of the facts, and with it came the moderation that always accompanies realism. This trend has been extended since the Conference ended, and it is reflected in contributions by Marne Dubs and Hasjim Djalal. Although the former chaired the American Mining Congress committee on deep-seabed mining and the latter represented Indonesia in the Conference committee that dealt with this subject, the old themes are much muted in their essays. Both are critical of this country's shortsightedness. Mr. Dubs predicts that under the rules and regulations being formulated by the Preparatory Commission:

Most of the ills of the treaty, from an openminded private investor viewpoint, will be sufficiently ameliorated that it will be a satisfactory vehicle for private investment. Contracts will be granted by the authority which may be subject to less change and fewer bureaucratic difficulties than operating in many of the developed countries and most individual developing countries. Unfortunately the United States will not be part of that process and has forfeited its opportunity to help forge the real seabed treaty.

Dr. Djalal makes essentially the same point:

The United States would realize in due course that the protection of its interest in seabed mining would be far more secure under a generally internationally agreed regime as formulated and negotiated in the Convention rather than under a unilaterally formulated national legislation or any kind of mini-treaty outside the context of the Law of the Sea Convention. . . . [T]he seabed mining regime under the Convention was far more workable and secure than an opposing seabed mining regime under unilateral legislation or mini-treaty.

In contrast to the discord generated by seabed mining, the rule of law promoted harmony. A commitment to this goal, as distinguished from any narrow national interest, gave the Conference a sense of purpose. The authors unanimously acknowledge its force. But that is scarcely surprising; all of them, in various capacities, devoted months and years to the effort to extend the rule of law over more than two-thirds of the earth's surface. Eloquent passages evoking this theme surface at many points in these chapters. Its relevance for the United States is highlighted by Thomas A. Clingan:

The United States has been traditionally perceived as advancing the rule of law in international affairs. It has supported negotiated solutions to problems and it has supported peaceful conflict resolution. If there is, in the rejection of the treaty, a shift in policy in this regard, then that fact is not only a cause for concern but it is puzzling as well. . . . Clearly, the U.S. believes it can protect its ocean interests by a projection of economic and military strength. But it is strange, in the view of the history referred to, that it does not see the advantage of achieving rules of international law that solidify these national goals.
If the rule of law is the unifying theme, the connective tissue is the concept of "the package deal." Recognizing that no comprehensive agreement was possible that did not give something to all parties— and that fragmentation of the components would frustrate this purpose—the leaders of the Conference saw the necessity for tying them together. What this means in terms of the extent to which the Law of the Sea can be regarded as defining customary international law is an issue discussed by many of the authors. So too is its counterpart: in what respects will a nonparty to the Convention be entitled to pick and choose among its benefits? Although the authors who address this issue do not attempt definitive answers, they do illuminate the extent to which the Law of the Sea Convention, although not yet in force, has already transformed international law. They also reveal the potential prejudice to the full enjoyment of freedom of navigation and overflight that could be incurred by any country that attempts to claim the full benefits of the Convention without adhering to it. As Oscar Schachter points out, "The political costs of the use of force would be much less

if the naval power could rely on a clear and generally accepted treaty provision. These considerations indicate that a maritime power that does not adhere to the 1982 convention will be giving up important benefits."

Even more remarkable in some ways than the substantive achievements of the Law of the Sea Conference were its procedural innovations. Touched on at many points in this volume, such devices as the single negotiating texts and the multiple uses of working groups were indispensable means of developing consensus. Their systematic analysis should yield insights that will help to guide future multilateral efforts to create the institutional arrangements necessary to coping with the complex realities of an ever more interdependent world.

One of the Law of the Sea Convention's best kept secrets, meanwhile, is its virtually total endorsement by the Reagan administration. In a statement made during the December 13, 1984, UN General Assembly debate on the LOS resolution, a spokesman for the United States said:

The U.S. . . . views the 1982 Convention on the LOS (Law of the Sea) as a major accomplishment in the development of international law relating to the oceans. . . . The U.S. takes this opportunity to reiterate its commitment to cooperate with the international community on the development of international law relating to the oceans. This cooperation extends to a vast number of important principles contained in the 1982 Convention on the LOS.

In fact, the administration's objections to the Convention concern fewer than 10 of some 450 articles. All 10 deal with deep-seabed mining, the one part of the treaty unlikely to have any practical significance for a long time to come. As the writers represented here amply demonstrate, this is an anomaly that has already been costly to the United States in terms of international leadership; it could cause future harm to important domestic concerns as well. If, in addition to its more general value, the book hastens the day when this country takes a more enlightened approach to the calculation of its national interest, it will have made a major additional contribution.

Preface

This book grew out of a University Seminar, "On the Uses of the Oceans," conducted at Columbia from 1972 to 1982. The seminar was partially supported by the Arkville Erpf and Exxon Foundations, and to them, my thanks.

The intellectual debts are to the many speakers and participants who collectively contributed to the awareness and understanding of the underlying causes and the details of the proximate issues that confronted the Law of the Sea Conference.

Further thanks go to those who labored so long to bring order and international cooperation to the new order of the oceans. This group is well personified by the dedication of the late Bernardo Zuleta (former Under-Secretary-General and Special Representative of the Secretary General to the Third United Nations Conference on the Law of the Sea) who, if he had not passed away, would have been a contributor to this enterprise.

Giulio Pontecorvo
Morningside Heights

The New Order of the Oceans
The Advent of a Managed Environment

PART I
The New Regime of the Oceans

1.
Opportunity, Abundance, Scarcity: An Overview

GIULIO PONTECORVO

THE WHO, how, and why of the uses of the oceans are at the heart of western economic and political development. Tracing the history that leads from the European vision of a dark unknown sea, to the Dutch rationalization articulated in the legal writings of Grotius, of the preference for freedom of the seas in order to gain access to resources and markets, and from Grotius to the Truman Declarations and the series of Law of the Sea Conferences in the second half of the twentieth century, requires an extended excursion into Western economic development, an excursion that is quite beyond us here. Yet to understand today's struggle over control and use of ocean space and resources we need insight about the role of the oceans in this historical process.

To this end we will employ two artificial constructs: a simple model which describes the role of the oceans in economic development and an arbitrary division of this history into three time periods. These constructs are the tools required to provide a glimpse of the dominant economic forces embedded in five centuries of economic and political development. The model used here is limited to economics and technology and the process of interaction between them. Therefore, it does not allow for transitory political events or any impact international law may have on economic structure or behavior prior to, or as a consequence of the Law of the Sea Conference and the subsequent treaty.

The model links overseas investment and the European demand for goods. It hypothesizes that the opening of the western ocean in the fifteenth century created for Europe an investment opportunity that was extensive and highly profitable—one that on the average promised higher rates of return than were available internally in Europe; an investment opportunity that attracted European capital and labor for the next five centuries. The engine that drove the system involved the interaction of potential and actual higher rates of return on overseas investment, the extension of geographic limits to European outreach and changes in technology that, as existing opportunities were exploited, continually expanded the investment horizon.

What was true of capital was also true of labor, as higher wage rates, better working environments, and especially a looser set of social constraints on individual advancement pulled European labor overseas. In the first two time periods, i.e., opportunity and abundance, the model operated in a world where the supply of capital and labor were short relative to the supply of the broadly defined resource land.

The initial investment possibilities involved direct exploitation of minerals, fish, furs and other staples, and of exotic products such as sugar, spices and tobacco. In this environment the oceans were the means of access to the higher rates of return on capital and labor, and these higher rates of return were in part a function of the richer, previously unexploited resource base and the products that were complimentary to European output. Also overseas there was greater relative flexibility in the structure of economic activity and the organization of production, which contributed to lower overhead costs and also to the high level of expectations about the rate of return on overseas development. Thus the initial impetus to movement overseas was the expectation of high rates of return on the set of relatively easily exploited investment opportunities for which the technology was at hand in the sixteenth and seventeenth centuries. The ocean was the means of access to riches and the process was in part self generating since the supply of available investment opportunities abroad was extensive, and simultaneously European demand was fed by the declining real prices of goods, which tended to become more abundant over time.

The second simplifying construct is the division of this history into three time periods: from the fifteenth century to the period of Grotius, from the time of Grotius till the beginnings of the twentieth century and from before World War I to date. In this division dates are symbols not *de facto* conditions, yet at these turning points one can distinguish the beginnings of a different direction in the course of events and a different role for the oceans in the process of expansion and development.

The demand pull investment model applies to the first two periods:

opportunity and abundance. A difference between these two periods is how the ocean was regarded, either as the private property of nation states or as the agent that provided freedom of access. The first two periods also differ in the number of nations involved in significant utilization of the oceans. The third period—relative scarcity—requires a more complex model and a different analytical approach that includes in its analysis limited access to resources and the need to manage ocean space and resources in order to accommodate both the increased number of national claims and changes in supply conditions.

Events

Prior to the seventeenth century the prevailing view of the oceans was that they constituted an extension of the European nation states just emerging from the medieval world order. The papal bull of Alexander VI in 1493 and the subsequent treaty of Tordesillas (1494) divided the world and its oceans between Spain and Portugal. At the time little was known of the dimensions and complexity of this ocean space and even less was known of the difficulties of using and managing it. In the sixteenth century the voyages of discovery and the ability of the Spaniards to exploit the mineral treasure of the New World contributed to the positive expectations about the profitability of overseas investment and impressed the countries of Western Europe with the importance of initiation of an investment/exploitation process, a process that quickly became competitive among nations.

Up to the seventeenth century, the struggle among the British, Dutch, French, Portuguese and Spanish was over ownership of the seas. It was Grotius who saw the economic advantage for a small country in distinguishing between freedom of the seas and control of the seas in the sense of ownership of property. In a competitive world freedom of access was cheaper than paying the costs of ownership and protection of a wide array of distant assets.

The question of the cost of exploiting new economic opportunities was closely linked with the form of economic organization used, primarily by the Dutch and British, to carry out overseas development. In the seventeenth century the corporate form was being adapted from its medieval uses in town and university governance to become the business firm, an economically efficient and flexible instrument for organizing economic ventures. Given a charter by the state the "semi-private" firm of the seventeenth century assumed the risks and cost of the development of trade and commerce. This permitted the nation to capture the energy and preferences of individuals and economic groups and so pursue, on a quasi-public, quasi-private basis many economic alternatives at minimum cost to the state in both money and organization.

Thus it was no mere coincidence that Grotius wrote *Mare Liberum* while an attorney with the Dutch East India Company. In 1604 he was employed by the Company to defend the action of one of their captains who took a Portuguese galleon as a prize in the Straits of Malacca. Grotius' defense argued that the concept advanced by the Portuguese that Eastern Waters (the East Indies) were private property was wrong and that the seas were free to all nations, *mare liberum*. Grotius' views on the oceans (just a part of his broad work on international law and the legal basis for resolution of the religious struggles of the period) did not take hold at once, but over time the *de facto* condition of freedom of the seas gained in strength by the action of states and private companies operating under the corporate charters which created them as both private corporations and as agents of the state.

Given this form of mercantile economic organization from the early fifteenth to the middle of the nineteenth century, the basic functional relationships in the model were: positive expectations about the return on future investments, high returns to capital and labor on existing activity, a continuously evolving technology, and concomitant increases in aggregate demand for final output. The expanding opportunities described by the simple investment pull model were exploited by the corporations and the state and the activity of these two sets of agents dominated the economic, political, and military uses of the oceans. The technology was primarily the continuous but slow evolution of the sailing vessel into a cheaper and more reliable commercial and military transportation and protection system. This system could be used to exploit economic opportunities throughout the world. Regardless of where economic activity took place, the ocean transportation network with its growing ancillary services—insurance, finance, protection in ports of entry and from theft on the high seas—was the crucial link between resources, goods and markets. At the same time the technological improvements in sailing vessels led to geographic extension of and increased productivity in fishing.

Transition

The transition from the open ocean system, the two periods of opportunity and abundance, to today's world of increasing relative scarcity that requires management at both the national and international levels has taken a century—and the process is by no means complete. Modification of the open ocean system began after the middle of the 19th century. Two developments in technology central in initiating the transition were the tramp steamer, which by the end of the century evolved into the steam trawler, and the railroad. The railroad allowed the exploitation of resources far from the coast. Equally important were the political and economic implications of railroads for the organization of nation states, especially those with large land masses and those who had been colonial outposts with their economic and political life centered at tide water.

From the time of Henry the Navigator, Columbus, and da Gama, to the end of the nineteenth century, the problem had been how to gain access to the resources and markets available throughout the world. Economic, political and physical limits have moved this century toward the problem of how to distribute the available supply of ocean resources and regulate the use of its space. In this century space and resources have become heavily utilized and problems of conflict in use and crowding in heretofore open space have become important. One may say the world is having to learn to drive in traffic.

These twentieth-century developments may be described as the introduction of new limits on economic and political behavior. The concept of "limits" is complex—it includes economic, political and despite the common wisdom, of much less importance, physical limits. The political limits that encroach upon the open ocean system derive from the organization of new nation states that both seek to internalize their own resources and to obtain a share of the shrinking international commons. The economics of this process involves, as part of the market development resource exploitation process, the continuous transfer, to the new nations, of evolving western technology of all sorts, i.e, political, military, economic, legal, etc., and also the raising of national consciousness throughout the world about the value of resources, including the value of knowledge, especially scientific knowledge. The world simply has become more "industrialized," and coupled with the associated demographic growth these forces have increased the pres-

sure on ocean resources and space and forced the political/legal issue
of international control of uses of the oceans.

Yet despite the accumulating evidence on the decline of the open
ocean system, the rationale of Grotius' defense of his client the priva-
teer captain persisted as the conventional wisdom until the end of
World War II when the concept of the open ocean was shattered by the
impact of technological change, the perception of the possibility of
short-run supply-side limitations, the emergence of many new nation
states, the effect of rising levels of income and population on aggregate
demand and the political development of the conservation movement.

One illustration of the process of transition from the earlier more
abundant spacious world to today's more restricted one is in the history
of the last one hundred years of fisheries development. It was possible
and reasonable for as astute an observer as the British scientist Thomas
Huxley to say at the fisheries exhibition of 1883: "I believe that the cod
fishery, the herring fishery, the pilchard fishery, the mackerel fishery,
and probably all the great sea-fisheries are inexhaustible; that it is to
say that nothing we can do seriously affects the number of fish."

Even at that time this view of abundance was not universal. Huxley's
contemporary, the economist Alfred Marshall, was more cautious, despite his understanding of the functional relationships between the
supply of any commodity, including fish, and its market price.

As to the seas, opinions differ. Its volume is vast, and fish are very
prolific; and some think that a practically unlimited supply can be
drawn from the sea by man without appreciably affecting the numbers
that remain there; or in other words, that the law of diminishing
returns scarcely applies at all to sea fisheries; while others think that
experience shows a falling off of the productiveness of those fisheries
that have been vigorously worked, especially by steam trawlers. The
question is important, for the future population of the world will be
appreciably affected as regards both quantity and quality, by the available supply of fish.

By 1899 there was much broader appreciation of conservation problems so when the King of Sweden invited those interested in the North
Sea and Baltic fisheries to discuss marine problems the nations responded and in 1901 the first major international body concerned with
marine conservation, the International Council for the Exploration of
the Seas (ICES) was formed. This development and discussion of the

"trawler question" in England were among the first indications that in Marshall's phrase "diminishing returns" did apply to ocean resources and space.

One hundred years have elapsed between Huxley's statement that the supply of fish was, relative to human fishing effort, essentially infinite, and the realization in the 1970s and 1980s that the existing mix of the catch of the fish in the seas is at or near its sustainable biological limit. For one hundred years the wolf of diminishing returns was driven from the door by a combination of extensive (geographic extension) and intensive fisheries development. Of course the wolf can still be kept at bay by moving to still abundant but less acceptable marine organisms further down the food chain, the widespread development of aquaculture and other means, but these latter possibilities represent potential investments that may take place in an institutional and economic environment that differs significantly from the period of open access, elastic supply and less specialized technology. The movement away from simple harvesting to more capital and energy intensive processes is a movement in both degree and kind, a shift in the underlying production arrangements.

Finally as evidence of the difficulty of perceiving what was transpiring in the oceans let us note with interest the investment decisions taken by the Eastern bloc, especially the USSR, Poland and East Germany in the 1950–60s and early 70s. The decision to invest heavily in long distance pulse fishing fleets rested on several assumptions and the need to provide supplementary support for agricultural production. The revealed assumptions are that to those decision makers the oceans were still the world of Grotius and Huxley, i.e., that it was possible to freely fish anywhere on the high seas and that the supply of fish would not be adversely affected by the utilization of large scale capital intensive twentieth-century fishing technology.

The Law of the Sea Treaty

By the end of World War II the steam trawlers that raised the specter of diminishing returns in Marshall's mind were transformed into long distance pulse fishing fleets capable of taking entire fish populations in a given area in one season. The offshore drilling rig opened up the hydrocarbon resources of the continental shelves and the possibility

As noted, from the 1930s to date national positions have evolved and changed. There has been extensive bilateral and regional negotiations on specific Law of the Sea issues, governments have reorganized internally to meet the problem of dealing simultaneously with the full range of ocean issues and the United Nations has mobilized its resources in order to manage the negotiations which have continued for over ten years, and which have, after a prolonged and unique struggle in international diplomacy, resulted in a treaty.

Intentions and Results: Coastal State Authority

The process of negotiation from 1973 to 1984 is reasonably described as a long-playing diplomatic fugue. Essentially all the nations in the world were actively represented in the negotiations along with their interests both real and imagined and their objectives both broad and narrow. The process of negotiations was organized in three principal committees, each dealing with a share of the key issues. Beyond the three committees, detailed legal questions were debated and resolved in subgroups upon subgroups, some with wonderful names (Margineers, the Land-Locked and Geographically Disadvantaged, the 77, etc.) and the negotiations even produced a nonedible biscuits formula and a nonpotable "Irish formula." With so many themes played for so long, what were the underlying proximate problems that forced the pace of the negotiations?

The first issue, the premise accepted by all states, was that the recent history crudely illustrated by table 1.1 made it necessary to establish a regime of law to permit the peaceful use of ocean space and resources. Changes in technology and the level of economic growth had rendered the preexisting body of law inadequate. A political/legal solution had to be found that was more inclusive, that accommodated the needs of many more nations and that reflected the complexities of the ocean management problems that had emerged after World War II.

The second issue was that the Conference was constrained by the military concerns of the two superpowers. While there was no conspiracy of silence, in the drafting of the treaty articles the military concerns of the USSR and the United States were largely accepted by the negotiators. Thus the treaty defined the nonmilitary problems and issues.

The third substantive issue was the distribution of income among the nations. Income distribution problems are among the most intractable and complex in economics. In order to understand how economic welfare is changed by any shift in the pattern of the international distribution of income one must consider not only the observed income distribution among nation states but also the internal distribution within each nation. A further complication is that a given change, e.g., the introduction of a new source of basic minerals that at a low price in world markets will make all nation states better off, may benefit some of the developed states more than some of the less developed ones. Is the resultant increase in inequality in distribution, but with everyone better off, an optimal result or should all changes in the direction of greater inequality be opposed regardless of how much better off all might be? It is not surprising, given the different ideological preconceptions of all parties to the negotiations, that the negotiators were trapped by these problems.

Difficulties inherent in the income distribution problem and direct national political and economic pressure on the negotiators combined to produce the key economic result of the Law of the Sea negotiations, the acceptance of coastal state control of resources in the extended economic zone. The acquiesence in coastal state control (*de facto* ownership) means that for the foreseeable future, the economic consequences of the treaty will weigh on the side of increased inequality in the distribution of income among the nations of the world.

Over a decade ago in a discussion of fishery problems a British observer, Austin Laing, eloquently pointed out the ultimate implications of coastal state preference: "Fundamentally, therefore, the practical conflict has been a question of pace: preference moves more slowly than priority but, given continued coastal state growth, both eventually mean exclusive exploitation by the coastal state. Again in practice, if not in theory also, exclusive exploitation must give rise to exclusive jurisdiction. Hence preference, priority and exclusive jurisdiction belong to a single continuum or almost an inexorable line of development."[1]

The difference between what is intended and what results take place is a continuing paradox in human affairs. Today we find an enormous gap between the original intent of the LOS negotiations and the results, the initial idealism embodied in the concept of the "common heritage of mankind" and the economic realities incorporated in the Law of the Sea Treaty.

Here we cannot analyze the failure of idealism; we can only note the result and comment briefly on the process that led to that result. Initially all were idealistic but the test of this idealism came early in the negotiations, perhaps too early for all to understand the implications of the test. The test involved the Richardson proposal of 1970. This proposal was a compromise that provided for both coastal state rights and international revenue sharing of the income generated in the extended economic zone. The Richardson proposal was the result of an intense internal struggle in the United States among the State, Interior, and Defense departments. In addition the proposal was influenced by congressional pressure and lobbying by the oil industry. The proposal, which was approved by President Nixon and presented to the delegates to the UN Seabed Committee meeting in Geneva in 1970, was focused on the key economic issue of Coastal State rights. It called for no national claims to seabed resources beyond 200 meters (compared to today's 200-mile limit). From 200 meters to the continental margin the coastal state would act as a trustee for the international community in the exploitation of resources. The revenues from economic activity in the zone were to be shared between the coastal state and an international authority. (Today there is no revenue sharing in the resource zone.) Beyond the trustee zone an international authority would regulate resource exploitation. The political failure of this compromise opened the door for coastal state preference and the resulting increased inequality in income distribution. In the "should have been category" it would have been far more fruitful for the conference to have fully explored the economic implications of a broad international revenue sharing plan rather than to have engaged ten years later in a bitter ideological dispute over what is so far an empty economic box— deep-sea mining.

Capitulation to the coastal state made geography the key to the redistribution of assets, primarily hydrocarbons and fish stocks on the continental shelves. Contrary to the ideological positions at the Conference, geography made "winners" and "losers" out of both developed and developing states. Certain Latin American states had early on seen the benefits to themselves of coastal state preference and they, plus others including Canada, the USSR and the United States, all benefited from the transfer of assets from the international commons to the Coastal State. But assets are not income—they are only potential sources of income, and each state must efficiently manage its newly acquired assets if it is to generate net income. Let us note that thus far in their east coast fisheries Canada and the United States have failed to do so and thus the measurement of the worldwide redistribution of income that has taken place is difficult. However, despite any difficulties in measurement, the amounts involved in the redistribution process are very large and they will have a significant impact on the relative economic position of nations.

Finally it is fair to point out another aspect of the failure of idealism, the link between the difficulties inherent in the distribution of assets and income and the way the negotiations were handled. The complexities of the legal drafting process were acknowledged by all participants at the negotiations and acted on. At the same time individual states did bits and pieces of the economic analysis required to understand the economic implication of decisions. However, economic analysis, couched as it must be in probability terms, was not part of the common mode of discourse of the negotiators (primarily diplomats and lawyers) and therefore was not easily introduced into the drafting process. Further there was no overall or worldwide view of the economic implications of the treaty available to the nations. By and large delegates were forced to depend on the economic positions advanced by specific economic interest groups in their own country, a circumstance which tended to push aside the larger economic issues.

But the end is not yet, as the issue of international income distribution is endemic, and it may affect the future of military activity, as well as trade and commerce. The military issue and freedom of transit in the pursuit of trade and commerce were broadly agreed upon, and protection against interference with commerce was built into the treaty. Yet both cases, freedom for the military and free transit for commercial purposes, should not be considered completely closed issues or as problems solved once and for all. In the short run no threat appears to the existing interpretation of the articles as negotiated. Yet in the long run, when coastal states are outside the process of negotiation and are more likely to be under pressure from domestic economic and political interests to act unilaterally, there is the possibility of change, a paradigm shift that would impose restrictions on the military and taxes or charges on trade and commerce. Suffice to say one reason tolls on commerce and restrictions on military activity will be thought about by coastal states is that the process involves for them an increase in income at the expense of other nations.

These activities may involve charges for the cost of providing safety at sea, pollution damage actual or potential, etc. Regardless of cause or method, changes of this kind will benefit a particular coastal state that dominates a narrow waterway, or such restrictive actions may be the policy of a regional block-seeking conflict avoidance, or action by many states to indirectly tax the activities of a limited number of richer ones.

Professor Charney points out in essay 10 that there is much unfinished business directly related to the work of the Law of the Sea Treaty itself. There is also the potential unfinished business not yet articulated but which is inherent in national policies, the ongoing efforts of ocean scientists and the application of new technology to the uses of the oceans.

NOTE

1. A. Laing, in Giulio Pontecorvo, ed., *Fisheries Conflicts in the North Atlantic: Problems of Jurisdiction and Enforcement* (Cambridge, Mass.: Ballinger, 1974).

2.
Division of the Spoils:
Hydrocarbons and Living Resources

GIULIO PONTECORVO

THREE PROBLEMS in the redistribution of income were imbedded in the negotiations over the Law of the Sea Treaty.[1] Of these three the potential threat to trade and ocean commerce implicit in the retreat from a regime of freedom of the seas is, for the future, a concern for all nations. Implementation of this threat may take many forms: various user fees, pollution prevention charges, charges imposed for the costs of providing safety at sea, etc. All such charges are taxes which would increase the cost of international trade and in turn tend to reduce by different amounts the income of all nations. But there is a limited set of countries, e.g., those controlling narrow waterways who will benefit from the imposition of charges. Hopefully, these potentially destructive actions will be prevented by the legal safeguards provided in the treaty.

The second problem, deep-sea mining, involved a decade of acute political trauma and complex legal negotiation over an activity whose current present value, in economic terms, is at best near zero. Nevertheless the negotiators were forced to develop an elaborate management structure and involved regulatory procedures for an industry that is yet to be. It was felt by many, following the 1967 Pardo speech on the common heritage of mankind and the wealth of the deep sea that sea mining was the crucial income distribution issue. Once this issue became central in the political and legal consciousness of the negotiators it had to play itself out.

This diplomatic drama might have been avoided in two ways: by a realistic economic examination of the proposed deep-sea mining industry within the larger context of the world's mineral industry to ascertain the level of income that could reasonably be expected to flow from deep-sea mining, and by charging an up front fee for the privilege of participating in the mining phase of the negotiations or for engaging in mining activity. The fees and subsequent income taxes on any earnings from deep-sea mining could then have been used for income redistribution purposes. In the absence of careful economic evaluation of the potential economic yield from sea mining the focus in the negotiations was on legal issues of regulation and control of the yet to be organized industry and political issues. In this framework sea mining visibly and military concerns invisibly tended to overshadow other issues.

It should be emphasized that the debate over deep-sea mining was driven basically by political, not economic considerations. Thus the investment opportunity presented by deep-sea mining is very different from those discussed using the demand pull investment model of essay 1. If as suggested there had been a charge for participation in the negotiations or in engaging in mining then the nations would have had to face the economic problems (the cost of development of the needed technology, price changes for final products as a result of increased supply from sea mining, employment effects, etc.), involved in adding to the world's supply of minerals at some undetermined cost. But once expectations were raised by the mere presence of physical supply in the oceans, whether it had any economic value or not, it became politically necessary to participate to protect each nation's interest. Furthermore pursuit of this political objective contributed significantly to other irrelevant and distracting debates such as the argument over the transfer of technology.

Common Property

Political concern over the hydrocarbon and living resources of the continental shelves and margins, was publicly articulated by the Truman Proclamations in 1945. In the period between 1945 and the treaty negotiations the well-organized international energy companies became increasingly concerned about keeping national rather than international control, over the energy resources of the shelves and margins. To achieve this end they obtained support from the U.S. government for their position, and while there was extended debate in the United States, publicly and among government agencies (Interior, State, Defense) and also at the United Nations in a *de facto* sense the broad outlines of agreement on coastal state control of the resources of the shelf was in place, early in the negotiations, essentially by 1975. This was also true of fish stocks most of which are found on (above) the continental shelves.

It was the transfer of these two assets, hydrocarbons and living resources, to the coastal state that is the core of the income and wealth redistribution that has taken place, as a result of the Law of the Sea Treaty. This paper presents the monetary impact of the asset transfers involving fish populations. However these remarks also apply to hydrocarbons, and it is the sum of the net present value of these two resources that represents the aggregate international redistribution of wealth and income.

The exploitation of fishery resources throughout the world has produced considerable theoretical biological knowledge of the population dynamics of fish stocks, practical experience in fisheries management for purposes of conservation of the stocks and a body of economic analysis and empirical studies all of which contributes to understanding the implications for all nations of the LOS treaty decisions on fisheries.

However, before inquiring about the amounts by which the income of nations has been augmented or diminished by the transfer of ownership of fish stocks we must comment on what is known as the *common property problem*. (A fish stock may be thought of as a specific related population of fish, e.g., the cod stock on Georges Bank. If a stock is fished it may be thought of as an asset that yields income, the market value of the catch.)

Under Extended Fisheries Jurisdiction (EFJ) the redistribution of assets, fish stocks, is a transfer of wealth from the international commons, where it was available to all nations, to a coastal state. This wealth transfer will result, in most cases, in an income transfer as the fish stocks (wealth) yield a flow of income, the yearly catch of fish. If the coastal nation observes appropriate biological regulation of fishing effort, the stock is managed properly, this income flow should be perpetual.

Today the world's catch of ocean fish of the types currently utilized is at or near the biological limit, approximately 70–75 million metric tons.[2] Under EFJ, the redistribution of fishery wealth and income is therefore a redistribution of a fixed or nearly fixed total world catch. The transfer of a substantial part of these assets from the international commons to a limited number of coastal states, when the world catch is at a limit, must therefore create "winners" and "losers" as the coastal state may reserve for its own fishermen the catch that was formerly available to fishermen from other countries.

In any plan for income redistribution, it is always easier to redistribute out of a growing level of income so that while some may win others at least do not lose. It is, therefore, a considerable achievement that the treaty negotiators reached agreement on fisheries despite the actual and potential losses suffered by some states, primarily Japan and the USSR.

Below the level of nation-states lies the impact of the international income (wealth) transfers on the individuals and business organizations that make up the fishing industry. Unfortunately there are no easy conclusions about the impact of the wealth transfers at the individual level. For example, under the EFJ the United States is a "winner," yet we cannot conclude that her fishermen, relatively wealthy compared to fishermen in some lesser developed states, are better off as a result of the transfer. Prior to extended fisheries jurisdiction, the fish off the coast of the United States were the common property of all who fished those waters. EFJ permitted the United States to largely eliminate the foreigners and the resource, the population of fishes, became the common property (wealth) of the United States. Many U.S. fishermen saw the profit opportunity presented by driving out the foreigners, and more men and vessels entered U.S. fisheries. However, as is true with any common property resource with easy entry, the returns per individual, which rose at first, have more recently tended to sink back to where they just cover costs. So that today we find more fishermen employed catching approximately the same amount of fish as before but with no or very little increase in the average income per fisherman. Therefore, the conditions under which each coastal state manages its fish stocks, its ability to effectively rationalize the common property problem and other taxes, quotas, subsidy issues, etc., all influence the returns to individuals and business firms and prevent any general conclusions involving all nations about winners and losers at the individual level.

While we cannot draw broad conclusions about the change in the economic status of individuals and firms under EFJ, what we can measure is some of the wealth (income) transfers from the international commons to individual countries. Even here however transboundary stocks and the migratory species, tunas, etc., make any precise computation of total gains and losses difficult. But within this broader framework there lies a set of wealth transfers that are clearly defined and measurable. It is this set that we have as our illustration of the impact of the treaty decisions on the wealth of nations.

Biological Limits: Full Utilization

Table 2.1 gives an oblique view of income redistribution in fisheries. It shows how the world's catch of fish from all stocks was divided between developed countries and lesser developed countries. This is an approximation of the ideological division that existed at the Conference between the Group of 77 and the rest of the nations. This oblique view fits the principal ideological model, yet it fails to provide understanding of the dynamics of the worldwide yield from fishery resources and the impact of the treaty on the distribution of this yield.

There has been only approximately a 10 percent increase in aggregate output from the late 1960s to date and essentially there has been very little increase in catch since 1976. The world catch of fish, which grew rapidly from the end of World War II to the 1970s, has approached the limit of the current mix of catch, approximately 70–75 million metric tons per year. It is roughly true therefore that of the existing kinds of fish now being caught all that can be caught are caught. Unless the world chooses to greatly expand the exploitation of certain organisms, such as Antarctic krill, which heretofore it has regarded as unattractive,

Table 2.1.   Nominal World Catches
(millions of metric tons)

1982	Marine Areas	Inland Waters	Total
Developed countries	34	5	39
Developing countries (G-77)	33	4	37
Others	1	0	1
TOTAL	68	9	77

SOURCE: *1982 FAO Yearbook of Fishery Statistics*, p. 77, tables A1–A5.

the aggregate worldwide catch will not grow significantly, and under EFJ, for several reasons, it may even decline somewhat.

A second key point is that it is not the division between the Group of 77 and the developed states that matters in the distribution of income from the catch of the fish in the sea. What matters is how the fish populations are distributed geographically and how efficiently each state manages the stocks that it has, or it gains by the redistribution process; e.g., in the early 1970s Peru, with its anchoveta fishery, had landings that averaged over 7.5 million metric tons, 10 percent of the world's catch. By the end of the decade this catch had declined (a variety of causes was involved including overfishing, the unstable nature of the resource itself, a clupiod population, and the impact of el niño) to half of its previous level. Yet during the same time period the Mexican catch increased around threefold. This variation in catch by country emphasizes the need to focus on individual nations rather than categories of nations to ascertain who won and who lost in the extension of national jurisdiction over ocean space and resources.

A further dimension in the performance of individual states in managing fisheries that is of worldwide importance in determining the impact of EFJ on the world supply of fish protein involves the rate of utilization of the stocks. In the LOS treaty there is a moral commitment to "full utilization" of fishery resources so that the maximum amount of protein the ocean can produce under current conditions is produced. Extension of fisheries jurisdiction has created ambiguities and subjects fulfillment of this moral commitment to the preference of the coastal state.

Consider a fishing ground with two fish stocks, A and B: B is the most abundant and A is a predator population that feeds on B. The consumers in the adjacent coastal state eat A but reject B as inedible. In an open fishery (prior to EFJ) both A and B will be caught and the total supply of fish protein will be the sum of the catch as fishermen from the coastal state catch A while fishermen from other countries (fishing in the open fishery), where B is acceptable to consumers, will catch both A and B. When EFJ comes into being the coastal state gains control of the fishery and drives out the foreigners. Fishermen from the coastal state will gain that share of A formerly caught by foreign fleets but since their consumers reject population B, only A will be caught. Full utilization of the yield from A is consistent with the preferences of the owner of the resource, the coastal state, and represents to the coastal state full utilization of the resource, yet the world loses the yield from population B.

Circumstances of this kind are important in several fisheries such as the Georges Bank case discussed below. Today in many international fisheries negotiations some restrictions on maximizing the output from the aggregate bio-mass (all the stocks in an ecological system) are apparent. Some of the worldwide loss from the exercise of coastal state preference can be overcome by education of consumers in the coastal state to gain acceptance of Stock B, joint ventures with foreign fishermen, appropriate fees that allow foreigners to fish, etc. But these negotiations are complex and it will take time for these "offsets" to achieve full utilization of both A and B.

Georges Bank: An Illustration of the Transfer of Wealth and Income

Georges Bank is unique; it is one of the most valuable fishing grounds in the world.[3] In basic biota it is estimated to be more productive than most other areas. This high productivity extends up the food chain where proportionately it yields more cod, haddock, and various kinds of flounder and shellfish than any adjacent fishing area in North America. It has been estimated that the bank will provide a substainable yield of about 125,000 tons of highly valued fish and shellfish (primarily cod, haddock, yellow-tail flounder, other flounder, scallops, lobster) per year given the post-EFJ mix of the catch.

This high level of biological productivity attracted the long-distance fishing fleets of many nations, and in the late 1960s and early 1970s the catch on the bank was distributed among Canada, Mexico, Ireland, Italy, Poland, Romania, Spain, USSR, USA and Japan.[4] This catch included quantities of squid and several kinds of hake, species that are seldom purchased by North American consumers and therefore tend to be ignored by North American fishermen. Since Georges Bank lies within the area encompassed by EFJ it came, in 1977, under coastal state jurisdiction. (The phrase "coastal state" is slightly incorrect; it should be "coastal states," since Canada and the United States currently share the ownership of the bank.)

What is significant in measuring the impact of the new order of the oceans on nation states is that EFJ gave control of the bank and its rich resources to the two highly developed states of North America. All other previous users of the bank may no longer fish there or if they are allowed to they must pay for the privilege, catching only what kind and in what quantity the new owners allow. Furthermore, since the new owners' market for fish consists primarily of fresh and frozen high quality processed sea food this is what their fishermen catch. Some of what was formerly caught by others, the squid and hake, is today left in the ocean.

Finally one can note with some sadness that by inadequate management the new owners have largely dissipated the gains from their newly acquired asset. The coastal states now own an extremely valuable asset, but the income from that asset has been spread in the manner noted above among additions to capital and labor that are redundant—in the sense that the additions are not necessary to catch the available 125,000 tons, and therefore production is inefficient; a kind of featherbedding has taken place. This result, the normal condition for an inadequately regulated valuable common property resources uses up the net yield from the resource to pay the redundant factors of production and so tends to spread the income gains from acquisitions of the asset, to employment rather than employing the redundant labor and capital elsewhere to incease national income. In this sense the fishery is partially a form of unemployment insurance rather than an efficient productive industry. Regardless of the present degree of inefficiency in production, we can estimate (quantify) the net returns from the resource and the abundant fish on the bank, and thus measure the potential gain to the coastal state both in its wealth (the value of Georges Bank as an asset) and in the increase in national income (the value of the catch).

The average value of the U.S. catch on Georges Bank for the years 1981–83 was approximately $155.1 million in current dollars (table 2.2). Numerous economic studies of fisheries suggest that in the case of common property resources of high value with free entry that on the average all the agents exploiting the resource make a return just equal to their costs of production. If we assume that 25 percent of the capital and labor is redundant, i.e., the catch could be caught by the remaining 75 percent of fishermen and vessels, the income to the unnecessary 25 percent represents the net yield from the fishery. Since this net yield will presumably, with adequate biological management of the stocks, continue in perpetuity then the value of the asset (the fish stocks on

Table 2.2. Average Georges Bank
Total U.S. Catch, 1981–1983
(metric tons)

SPECIES	CATCH
Cod	34,595
Haddock	13,474
Silver hake	1,372
Yellow-tail	15,306
Flounder (NS)	14,315
Red and white hake	1,293
Pollack	5,777
Redfish	2,316
Herring	9
Lobster	1,215
Sea scallops	6,386
Misc.	7,350
TOTAL	103,408

The total value of the above catch was calculated as follows:

$1500/ton × 103,408 tons = $155,112,000

SOURCE: U.S. Dept. of Commerce, "U.S. Catch by Species Group From Georges Bank 1904–1983." National Oceanic and Atmospheric Administration, National Marine Fisheries Service, Northeast Fisheries Center, Woods Hole Laboratory, Woods Hole, Mass. 02543.

Georges Bank) becomes as with any asset (stocks, bonds, farms, office buildings, etc.) one might invest in, the discounted net present value of the perpetual income stream.

The numerical estimates presented here should, for many reasons, be regarded more as indexes of relative magnitudes rather than exact measures. These results provide a metric that suggests the relative orders of magnitude of the economic value of the redistribution of assets and income for the international commons to the coastal state.

The average 1981–83 U.S. landings (excluding Canadian landings) from Georges Bank of fin fish (9 principal species) and shell fish (2 species: lobsters and sea scallops) were 103,408 metric tons per year. For the same period, price data for Georges yielded an average price of approximately $0.68 per pound. At $0.68 per pound the catch was worth $1,500 per metric ton ($.68 × 2204.6); 103,408 metric tons (average 1981–83 catch) at $1,500 per metric ton yield, a value of $155,112,000 ($155.1 million) for the U.S. catch on Georges.

We have already pointed out that under common property conditions which results in inefficient production the value of the catch ($155.1

Table 2.3.   1981–1983 Data, Georges Bank

Circumstance	Value of Catch ($ million)	Net Yield from Fisheries
Today's inefficient fishery cost of production = 155.1	155.1	0 × 155.1 = 0
Catch could be landed using 90% of today's capital and labor. 10% are redundant.	155.1	.10 × 155.1 = 15.5 million
Catch could be landed using 75% of today's capital and labor.	155.1	.25 × 155.1 = 38.8 million
Catch could be landed using 67% of today's capital and labor.	155.1	.33 × 155.1 = 51.2 million
Catch could be landed using 50% of today's capital and labor.	155.1	.50 × 155.1 = 77.6 million

million) is also equal to the cost of catching it and the income of fishermen and the return on capital utilized. Therefore the total cost of production is also approximately $155.1 million. We have asserted that production is inefficient: how inefficient? Rather than attempt to answer that question precisely let us look at several possibilities which will allow the establishment of a range of values.

If production is 10 percent inefficient we say that 90 percent of the capital and labor currently employed could catch the 103,408 metric tons. The same relationships hold for the other levels of inefficiency specified 25, 33, and 50 percent. Table 2.3 indicates these results.

Thus while the gross yield was $155.1 million the net yield from the fishery may range from 0 approximately today's circumstance to $77 million if half the average annual capital and labor employed during 1981–83 was redundant. Most empirical analysis of fisheries suggest that the appropriate answer to the question of "how inefficient" lies in the 25 to 33 percent range.

At this point it is possible to answer the question of what is the value of Georges Bank? If one could buy Georges Bank, own it outright, and control all fishing, what would one pay for it? Here we assume that with reasonable biological management of the stocks the current yield 103,400 metric tons will continue in perpetuity and also that initially the price of fish and the cost of production will not change. If we assume a ten-year period of ownership and use a rate of discount of 10 percent the net present value of the Bank ranges, as indicated in table 2. 4, between $105 million and $525 million.

Table 2.4. Present Value Georges Bank Based on U.S. Landings
(10 percent discount rate; 10-year investment horizon)

Redundant Capital and Labor	Estimated Net Yield From Georges Bank ($ million)	Present Value of Georges Bank ($ million)
10%	15.5	105
25%	38.8	262
33%	51.2	346
50%	77.6	525

If estimates of the redundant capital and labor of roughly 30 percent are realistic the analysis yields a current net present value of the Bank of approximately $300 million. Therefore the impact of extended fisheries jurisdiction is to transfer from the international commons to the United States, an asset worth today (with a ten-year time horizon and a 10 percent discount rate) approximately $300 million. This is the value a prudent investor, reasonably certain that the physical yield was protected by the conservation measures now in place, would pay for the asset.[5]

Furthermore we are quite certain that the existing mix of catch from the bank cannot be increased. We also know that the demand for high quality fish protein increases with the growth of population and the level of personal income. We have every expectation that both will continue to increase in the United States and Canada. Thus we have a relatively fixed supply of fish and in the long run increased demand for this fixed supply. The price of fish will rise and so will the value of the asset, Georges Bank. We can reasonably expect that in the 1990s the present value of the bank will be significantly higher than today and that the value of the bank will continue to increase in the future. In addition, this increase in value, as a result of increases in the price of fish, will be augmented further as increases in productivity (technological change) act to reduce the cost of catching fish.

This illustration using the fisheries of Georges Bank just hints at the magnitude of the economic legacy of the movement toward closed seas embodied in the Law of the Sea Treaty. The legacy involving fisheries and hydrocarbons is very substantial indeed. Georges Bank is a small fraction of the area of the world's continental shelves where most of the fish stocks and hydrocarbons are found.

The method utilized to measure the value of Georges Bank can be applied to fishing grounds throughout the world. Using this approach the gains and losses from EFJ can be calculated for all nations with substantive fishing industries. However, for two reasons, it is at this time premature to make such calculations. The output from any fishing ground will tend to have a substantial year-to-year variation; e.g., while it was indicated above that the expected catch from Georges Bank was 125,000 metric tons of the existing mix of fin and shell fish this catch may under normal conditions vary from 100,000 to 150,000 tons. Thus to allow for normal variance it is necessary to average the catch over several years. Furthermore this average value must be far enough away in time from the late 1970s to allow for the full impact of EFJ on the pattern of fishing activity. The coming of EFJ was not an instant once and for all change. It has required extended international negotiations over historical fishing rights, concern over other foreign policy issues such as the U.S. reaction to the situation in Afghanistan, etc. Currently we are observing a rearrangement of fishing effort throughout the world and this rearrangement must proceed further before precise measures of the value of the new distribution of the catch should be devised.

Nevertheless, the rearrangement process is underway. In 1975 the USSR caught 9.0 million metric tons: 1.17 million in the northwest Atlantic, which was 13 percent of the total Russian catch. In 1981 the Russian catch was 8.7 million tons of which .11 tons, 1 percent, was in the northwest Atlantic. Similarly the USSR catch in the northeast Pacific as a percent of its total catch declined from 6 percent in 1975 to almost zero in 1981. The USSR compensated for the loss of catch in the northwest Atlantic and the northeast Pacific by shifting fishing effort primarily to the northeast Pacific. Poland and the German Democratic Republic show roughly similar patterns of change during this period. In the case of Japan, given her close political connections with North America, the changes are less pronounced but they are measurable; e.g., the Japanese catch fell 50 percent in the northeast Atlantic and 16 percent in the northeast Pacific, describing a process that is still underway. On the basis of the same two year comparison the Canadian catch rose 38 percent, essentially all in Canadian waters, while Mexican landings went from .450 million tons to 1.469 million tons, a gain of 227 percent. Coastal state authority is steadily rearranging the pattern of worldwide fishing activity. This rearrangement will be largely worked out by the mid 1990s and then more precise measurements of gains and losses may be calculated.

On a regional basis the results are equally striking: in 1975 there were twenty-two countries fishing north Atlantic waters. By 1981 five countries no longer fished those waters and of the remaining seventeen, thirteen showed substantial declines in catch, while only the coastal states—Canada, Greenland, and the United States—showed large increases.

We may note that Georges Bank, with an annual yield of 125,000 metric tons based only on the U.S. catch, had in 1983 a value of roughly $300 million. In 1982 the worldwide catch of fish was estimated at 68 million metric tons. If we assume that the value of the worldwide catch was only twenty percent of the value of the catch on Georges (the worldwide catch includes fish for fishmeal, etc.) and that the other numbers in our illustration of Georges Bank are applicable, the value of the world's fishing grounds are in the trillions of dollars.[6]

The value of the world's fishing grounds is dwarfed by the value of the hydrocarbons on the shelves and margins. Unfortunately, our current ability to accurately measure the value of these hydrocarbons is very limited. Within the broad category of economic resources, i.e., those that can be exploited profitably today, "identified" hydrocarbon resources are those whose grade, quantity and quality are known or estimated from geological evidence. In turn, "identified" resources may be either "demonstrated" or "inferred," and demonstrated resources may be measured (by detailed sampling) or indicated by less than completely adequate sampling. Undiscovered resources may be classified as hypothetical or speculative depending on the probability that they exist.

The value of the hydrocarbons on shelves and margins should, of course, include the value in all these categories but today we cannot go beyond saying the value is very large. Today detailed economic estimates of the aggregate value of these assets simply cannot be taken seriously. In making useful estimates of value it is necessary to fall back on the category of demonstrated identified resources, which are economic, i.e., subject to profitable exploitation. Yet even within this narrow category only measures of gross value may be obtained. To calculate the net present value of this limited set of ocean resources requires estimates of the cost of production, the rate of utilization of the resource over time, and the present and future price of the output mix. As an example consider the Hiberina field, the largest oil find in North America in recent times. The Hiberina field lies about 200 miles off the coast of Newfoundland. It has demonstrated economic resources of about 13 billion barrels of recoverable high-grade crude as

compared with approximately 10 billion barrels at Prudhoe Bay. Today's
$15 per barrel OPEC price suggests a gross revenue of 195 billion dollars
from the field. Unfortunately we cannot translate this gross revenue
into a price for the asset without detailed knowledge of the cost of
lifting the oil, production plans, and price estimates.

Canada, with the oil at Hiberina and the gas fields at Sable Island
has gained valuable assets that will if they are exploited rationally
contribute significantly to the wealth and income of Canada.

If we could calculate the value worldwide of both the identified and
the undiscovered economic hydrocarbon resources then we would have
numbers far in excess of the trillions, which suggest the value of the
fish stocks.

Thus the economic impact of the movement to closed seas potentially
increases the assets and income of the coastal state by the sum of the
value of the resources of shelf and margin. This result is the initial
economic legacy of the changes embodied in the Law of the Sea Treaty.

NOTES

1. There are other issues which involve the distribution of income either
directly or indirectly, e.g., freedom of scientific research, etc.

2. *FAO Yearbook of Fishery Statistics*, 52:55. The figure of 67 million tons for
1981 is for "marine fishing areas." The world total for "inland waters" for the
same year is 8 million metric tons (p. 53). The total for the same year, i.e.,
marine + inland waters = 75 million metric tons (p. 50).

3. Georges Bank lies off the coast of Massachusetts, within the 200-mile
limit and close to the primary U.S. market for fish.

4. *Fisheries of the United States*, 1980, U.S. Department of Commerce. The
countries listed are actually for the year 1979.

5. The numbers used are for the value of Georges as an asset. Similar
estimates can be made for the contribution of the transfer to the flow of current
national income.

6. Assume the value of the worldwide catch is half that of Georges Bank,
i.e., 1500/2 = $750 per metric ton or that it is 20 percent of the value of Georges
1500/5 = $300 per metric ton. Utilizing the parameters of the Georges Bank
illustration, in the former case the value of the world's fishing grounds is of
the order of $103 trillion dollars, in the latter case, $41 trillion.

3.
Concepts and Realities in the New Law of the Sea

OSCAR SCHACHTER

THE NEW, AND STILL EMERGING, Law of the Sea is complex in structure, rich in concepts. Much of it is now written law, a *lex scripta* which is also often customary law or intelligible only in the light of custom. It includes stated and unstated postulates and many intricacies of rules and procedures. Nearly every legal question leads into a web of competing considerations and it is easy, almost unavoidable, to become entangled in detail. That is why a broad conspectus, placing ideas and trends in perspective, may be helpful, even to experts. It is the aim of this essay to contribute to that broad view.

The central concern is the Law of the Sea, but even as we focus on the law we must consider the clash of interests and the tensions that led to the legal "solutions" and will lead to new difficulties. Hence our analysis takes us beyond the law into sociohistorical trends, political forces, and economic and technical factors that have shaped the law. At the same time we are mindful that the Law of the Sea has its own relative autonomy as a regime governing state conduct. It may be in continuing flux but it is also a force for stability, imposing order on the multifarious activities in ocean space. Despite the conflicts and unsolved problems that still remain, the new Law of the Sea is an impressive achievement. The comments that follow are meant to show why this is so and also to suggest the way to the next stage of development.

This essay is divided into four sections. It begins with an analysis of freedom of the seas, its historical role, inadequacies, and reasons for its partial erosion. The second section seeks to convey an idea of the

This essay was drawn from a lecture given as part of the general course at the Hague Academy of International Law.

complexity of the structure of the Law of the Sea, with its diverse legal formulas and classifications, interrelated treaties and pervasive linkages between conventional and customary law. In the third section, I discuss the balancing of rights between coastal and maritime states in regard to navigation, fishing, marine research and environmental protection. The last section deals with the concepts of *res communis* and the common heritage in the light of present controversies and future problems.

The Erosion of Freedom in the Oceans

In the international law we now call traditional the principle of freedom of the seas had a preeminent place. It was viewed as one of the foundation stones of the edifice begun by Grotius and as the crowning achievement of modern international law. Extolled as "noble," the principle had less than noble origins. Grotius formulated the conception of maritime freedom when, as a young lawyer for the Dutch East Indies Company, he defended the seizure of a Portuguese treasure-ship by his client's vessel.[1] The famous tract *Mare Liberum* was his brief in defense of pillage; he won his case. But that judicial victory would have meant little were it not for the ambitions of the rising British and Dutch empires and the power of their fleets. Their vessels freely seized Spanish and Portuguese treasure ships and put an end to the Iberian claims of dominion (as well as to the Papal Bull granting such dominion).[2] The new maritime powers did not press their own claims of dominion (though some jurists advised them to do so), concluding that their interest was better served by freedom of navigation.[3] This did not seem inconsistent to the British with their belief that "Britannia rules the waves." Like other legal ideals, the concepts of freedom of the seas and of *res communis* can be seen as grounded in the interest of great powers.

However this did not exclude their other justifications. As a normative principle freedom of the seas was in accord with the perceived characteristics of the ocean space, particularly their indivisibility and availability. It seemed clear that states could not divide up the seas and maintain distant borders. As Grotius put it: "The sea, since it is as incapable of being seized as the air, cannot be attached to the possessions of any particular nation."[4] Except for a narrow belt of territorial sea close to the shore, it was not practicable for states to claim and hold on to vast expanses of ocean far from their shores. Second, and more important, there seemed to be ocean enough for all. Remember that, until recently, the two main uses of the ocean were navigation and fishing. Use for navigation by one state did not diminish such use by others; the oceans could not be used up by shipping. In that sense, their benefits were jointly available. The same perception held for fishing since it was long taken for granted that the fish in the seas were continuously replenished and generally available to all who could catch them.

From these two premises, two conclusions followed. The first was that the seas must be inappropriable, that is, not subject to sovereign claims by states. The second was that the oceans should be freely accessible to all. Like a public park, the oceans were a collective good. It seemed right that they should be a "commons" with free access and use that did not impinge on the rights of others. At least it seemed right until historic developments cast doubt on the basic premises. Those developments were a consequence of scientific and technological advance, of the growth of population and consequential pressure for food and energy and of intensified nationalism of countries sensitive to economic exploitation by foreigners. How these factors influenced events cannot be described in detail here but it is worth recalling the main elements. They are still significant in the continuing transformation of the Law of the Sea.

Viewed from a lawyer's perspective, the first notable action in derogation of the *res communis* was the claim by the United States in 1945 to full sovereignty over the continental shelf. That claim expressed in the Truman Proclamation has been generally seen as the start of the process of territorial expansion in ocean space.[5] The shelf was claimed by the United States as an extension of the land-mass of the adjacent state and thus naturally appurtenant to it. Over a decade or so, the U.S. position was adopted by others and then embodied in the 1958 Geneva convention on the continental shelf. It did not give rise to controversy since the extension of national authority over the shelf did not impinge very much on the traditional uses of the seas—fishing and navigation. Only sedentary fish, such as oysters, were shelf resources. What was important as technology developed were the hydrocarbon resources, oil and gas, that were found and exploited on the shelf. These resources are still the most valuable of the resources of the sea. This is the main reason for the concern of states over the delimitation of the shelf.

Although the appropriation of the shelf by coastal states did not appear to challenge the freedom of the seas, it had an influence on the claims made in the 1940s and 1950s by some coastal states to exclusive rights to fish or to engage in whaling in a 200 mile zone off their coasts. Claims by Chile (later joined by Ecuador and Peru) to exclusive fishing rights were a response to increased whaling activities in the South Pacific by Norway and Japan.[6] In due course, the demands for preferential and exclusive fishing zones spread to other coastal countries and were more vigorously expressed.

The coastal states used force in some cases, resulting in the "cod wars" between Iceland and the United Kingdom and the "tuna war" between Ecuador and the United States. The term "war" is an exaggeration, yet the fact that force was used by weaker against stronger powers showed the way the wind was blowing. The world was reminded that protection of coastal fisheries was a natural response to the fishing technology that vastly increased the catch of fish and threatened biological reproduction levels. The long-held assumption of unlimited supplies of fish could no longer be sustained; overfishing and depletion were evident in many areas. This coincided with a large increase in the demand for fish because of various factors, including the use of fish for animal feed and the general increase in population and income levels in many countries. More and more fishing effort was directed at fewer fish. The poorer coastal countries and also some of the richer countries became increasingly resentful of foreign fisherman in "their" coastal waters.

The situation can also be described in terms of the economists' concept of the "common pool" problem.[7] The problem arises whenever accessible but exhaustible natural resources are available freely. Fishermen, having no property rights, take no account of the opportunity cost in not leaving the stock for future exploitation. Hence exploitation occurs at a higher level of output than would be optimal for a single fisherman. As the resource is depleted, an incentive is created to harvest more quickly. Thus, unless fishermen are forced to factor in the external costs of their operation (especially depletion) they continue to fish in a way incompatible with long-range economic benefits. One way of meeting this problem is to establish exclusive rights in a national entity that would by regulation internalize the external costs so as to control excessive exploitation.

As a consequence of these factors, demands for special rights of protection for coastal states were followed by claims of preferential rights. Such rights were embodied in treaties and given judicial imprimatur in the fisheries cases involving Iceland decided by the International Court in 1974.[8] In a rather short period of time (for international law), preferential rights evolved into exclusive rights over a fishing zone generally of 200 miles. These zones became the 200-mile exclusive economic zones in which coastal states exercised "sovereign rights" over all resources. In the course of the ten-year period of negotiation of the UN Convention on the Law of the Sea, the principle of the exclusive economic zone was gradually given legal force by unilateral acts of coastal states while it received acceptance as a major principle of the new convention.

What is striking about this process is that the powerful maritime states, originally opposed to erosion of the freedom of the seas, came to accept the exclusive zones initially proposed by a few small and weak countries. Many legal scholars strongly supportive of the freedom of the seas, and opposed to broad extensions of national authority in international waters, criticized the excessive nationalism of developing states. Some deplored the "democratization" of international law-making through UN conferences in which small states could outvote the larger "more responsible" states. They considered that international law was greatly weakened when the assertions of extended jurisdiction by coastal states were not effectively resisted by the more powerful long-distance fishing countries (such as the United States, the USSR, Japan, Great Britain, and France).

Why, one might ask, did these maritime powers not use force to maintain their rights? A plausible answer is that restraints on the use of force to vindicate fishing rights were influenced at least in part by the legal prohibition against force plus the political assessment that action against coastal states would provoke much opposition in "third world" countries whose support was desired in other respects. Perhaps more significant than this general political consideration was the pressure within some of the larger countries for protection of their own fisheries in nearby coastal waters. In the United States, for example, the domestic fishing industry pressed to eliminate Japanese, Russian, and other long-distance, high technology fishing fleets from U.S. coastal waters and a 1976 U.S. law declared a 200-mile fishing zone.[9] Thus it cannot be said that the developed states were outvoted or outmaneuvered by the poorer states. In fact the triumph of the poor over the rich in regard to the exclusive zones is much less than was claimed. Major beneficiaries of the 200-mile exclusive zone include several large developed countries such as the United States, Canada, Australia and the Soviet Union. The United States, for example, added about 3 million square miles to areas under its jurisdiction (the largest "territorial" expansion in its history); Individually Canada and Australia added almost as much.

Another irony is that only a small number of the developing countries, those with long coastlines and abundant offcoast living resources, can benefit from the exclusive economic zones. Many of the poorer countries that supported the exclusive economic zones gained little from them since they had short (or no) coasts and few offcoastal resources. Nonetheless, these "geographically disadvantaged countries" (as they came to be called) supported the extension of jurisdiction by others largely because of political and ideological consideratons that transcended their immediate self-interest. Foremost among those considerations was the intensified nationalism of the third world countries in the 1960s, a nationalism directed particularly against the economic exploitation by foreign capital in those countries. Perceived as "neo-colonialism" and economic imperialism, the activities of transnational enterprises were attacked as a curtailment of the sovereignty of the host states over their natural resources. Socialist and nationalist aspirations found common ground in the assertion of state authority over foreign enterprise. They joined as well in repudiation of classic market principles, perceiving in free trade and free capital movements the power of the rich to exploit unfairly the natural resources of the poor.

These political ideas were readily transferable to the offshore resources. The traditional freedom of fishing was seen as the counterpart of free capital movements, enabling the foreign fleets of the richer countries to profit from the resources of poorer states. The technological advances in fishing lent support to the charge of unfair exploitation. No longer were the foreign fleets mere fishermen hunting fish; they had become large aggregates, equipped with sonar and radar, harvesting fish through new devices, and processing them through factories at sea. The depletion of some stocks was proceeding at a rapid rate and under the principle of freedom to fish adequate regulation was almost impossible. These conditions were seen as the counterpart of the more general impact of unfettered economic freedoms on the poor. Thus, most developing countries, with or without coastal resources, could identify with the demand for extended sovereign rights over the rich coastal waters as a response to overexploitation by long-distance fishing fleets.[10] They did not see any great difference between the sovereign claims over the continental shelf (initiated by the Truman proclamation) and the claims to the superjacent waters. Both areas were viewed as appurtenant to the land territory and therefore rightly included in the sovereign domain of the adjacent states. Virtually all of the developing states saw the demand for the extension of sovereignty into the oceans as an aspect of the wider demand for economic self-determination and the "permanent and inalienable sovereignty over natural resources" and, as we mentioned earlier, some of the major developed states shared political and economic reasons for enlarging their own sovereign domain to exclude (or regulate) the competitive foreign exploiters.

While fish resources were most prominent among the concerns of coastal states, other interests were also pertinent. Once again, consider the historical context. During the 1960s and 70s, an increasing awareness of environmental damage affected governmental decisions. Dramatic oil-spills attributable to the expanded traffic in petroleum and the huge tankers focussed attention on the dangers of pollution to living resources of the sea, especially in coastal regions.[11] Adding to the concern was the spread of "open registry" oil tankers under "flags of convenience" that were seen as only minimally regulated. In short, freedom of navigation no longer seemed as cost-free as it had been. The navigation of one state could now deprive others of uses of the oceans. Regulation of vessels for environmental protection was seen as necessary.

Also of significance was the extraordinary extension of military technology to the oceans. Naval power expanded through submarine fleets, the use of diverse detection devices and the placement of destructive weapons on the ocean bed. The coastal waters of countries all over the world became areas of military concern and were actually or potentially new environments for great power rivalry. The coastal states understandably had a strong interest in asserting control over these waters and the underlying seabed.[12] This interest extended to scientific research and exploration for resources since these innocent activities could not always be distinguished from military uses. In this respect as in the others the freedoms prized by the larger naval powers were seen by coastal states as a potential cover for actions threatening their independence. The demand for jurisdictional authority of the coastal states was strengthened by the growing importance of covert naval power.

It might be thought that all of these concerns relating to the use and abuse of offshore areas could have been met by international rules and international institutions. Many international lawyers believed that an international regime could have provided adequate regulation of the coastal zones and brought about more rational and equitable management of the resources. Some felt that freedom of the seas remained the best assurance of efficient use and that abuses could be met by treaty rules. But in the concrete historical setting, these alternatives had little political appeal. Most states of the world, rich and poor, believed they could rely best on their own authority; few were prepared to entrust important decisions on resources and security to an international organization or a legal system. The United Nations and related international organizations were seen more as political arenas for diplomatic exchange and debate and less as efficient operational agencies. Control by sovereign states had more appeal on the political level and seemed more likely to be effective than international authority. The obvious exception to the nationalist trend was the acceptance of an international authority for seabed mining. That exception reflects, of course, the inability of most states to exploit the resources of the seabed, but here too they abandoned the principle of freedom for the radically different conception of international management of a common heritage.

It is interesting to note that the extension of national authority over the most valuable regions of the oceans proceeded on the basis of contiguity, rather than on the basis of occupation or prescription. International lawyers in the past tended to minimize the significance of contiguity as a principle of territorial acquisition.[13] Lauterpacht, on the contrary, saw it as a more likely factor in future acquisitions.[14] He proved to be right when geographical propinquity and continuity were widely accepted as a basis of entitlement for extension of sovereign rights and jurisdiction over the shelf, the 200-mile economic zone and archipelagic waters. We have already sketched the political and economic reasons for this development but it is important also to see how they found a legal (and in a sense, an equitable) basis in geographical contiguity. At least for the uninhabited areas of the world, geography appeared to offer a more acceptable basis for acquisition than such possible alternative principles as economic efficiency or social need. Although contiguity does not avoid competing claims (as shown by the many offshore territorial disputes) it has an objective and "natural" quality in comparison to entitlements based on historical antecedents or economic and social values.[15] It does not ask that "nature be refashioned" for particular interests and it is substantially in accord with the majority perception that past imperialism and present neocolonialism should yield to claims of national sovereignty.

However, contiguity has obvious limits. By its very nature, it dissipates with distance. No state can be contiguous to distant areas of the seas. An attempt to draw boundary lines outward from every coastal state would produce a tangle of overlapping claims. Nor could most coastal states exert effective power in far-off maritime areas. If there ever is to be an enclosure of the high seas, it would occur by action of the great powers (a result envisaged in Orwell's *1984*). We cannot rule that out as a future possibility but at the moment it appears unlikely. Whether the USSR and the United States are capable of dividing the oceans between them by agreement (as Spain and Portugal sought to do in a treaty of 1494 following the papal grant to them) is open to conjecture but there appears to be little practical reason for them to seek such vast extension of authority at the present time. Less remote is the gradual accretion of jurisdictional authority by the coastal states entrusted with less than full sovereignty over the exclusive economic zones and certain other areas. Such "creeping jurisdiction" has been predicted by some as a probable consequence of a weak international structure to safeguard rights of navigation and of overflight in respect of areas where coastal states have been given extensive rights over resources and, in some cases, wider jurisdiction over vessels. This prediction rests largely on the success of the coastal states in establishing the wider territorial sea, the exclusive economic zone and certain other areas of authority. However, that recent experience does not demonstrate that the major powers with strong interests in maritime and air navigation will yield their legal rights in freedom of transportation to the coastal states. Indeed, their strong military position and their fairly precise legal entitlement recognized in the 1982 Convention suggest that they will not give way to creeping jurisdiction. The principle of freedom of the seas, reduced though it be, still remains a viable legal principle regarded by the major and many of the smaller powers as of vital interest to them.

The Complex Structure of the New Law of the Sea in Treaty and Custom

The UN Convention on the Law of the Sea concluded in 1982 is the largest and most comprehensive multilateral treaty concluded by states. It contains 320 articles in the main part and 119 additional articles in the 9 annexes. It applies to all the nonland surface of the world and on its face at least it offers a legal answer to almost any question that may be asked. Even today, before it has entered into force, it has become the main written authority on the Law of the Sea. Every lawyer will begin his examination of the law on any specific issue by consulting that Convention, but he would be unduly optimistic to expect that the treaty would readily answer all questions or even many of them.

The complexities of the Convention and the related body of customary law are a major reason for this. One might begin by noting, as a perceptive delegate has pointed out,[16] that the Convention recognizes 57 kinds of legal persons and 58 legal sea areas.[17] As legal answers vary with person and area, these facts are alone awesome, but much more complexity results from the great diversity of formulas to describe the relations of the parties (and other legal persons) in regard to areas, activities, and things. A list shows 59 sets of such legal relations.[18] Moreover, these legal relations are superimposed on each other; hence the same area or activity may be the subject of overlaying legal relations.

A reading of the Convention also reveals a bewildering array of clauses that qualify the exercise of rights and powers by states. For example, sometimes the states "must take account of," elsewhere they must "act on the basis of"; their action in some places must "be in conformity with"; elsewhere "without prejudice to" or simply "appropriate." We have reason to believe that these terms, reached after years of negotiation, reflect different intentions but we have no precise guide to these intentions in the Convention or in the travaux preparatoires. (We will comment on the latter below.) Should one assume that such differences in language are of minor significance? It would probably be foolish to do so until a body of interpretation arises. Whatever the differences may mean in particular circumstances, one important characteristic of the Convention emerges from a reading of these diverse modifiers and qualifiers of state action. As Allott has pointed out,[19] the Convention rarely confers unfettered discretion on states to act as they please even in areas of sovereign authority. The powers given are not "freedoms." They are authorizations to act subject to limits. True those limits are described in many formulas that are uncertain in meaning, but degrees of uncertainty are not quite the same as complete discretion. Moreover the elaborate system of dispute settlement (with both binding and nonbinding compulsory procedures) may in time reduce the areas of uncertainty.

The structure of the Convention is also complicated by the numerous linkages among various articles. This reflects the general "package deal" theory of the negotiation and also the many different package deals on more specific subjects. As the preamble declares, the drafters were "conscious that the problems of ocean space are closely interrelated and need to be considered as a whole." One can readily see why governments that negotiated this complex interrelated text would now resist attempts by nonparty states to pick and choose among its provisions. The prohibition of reservations (article 309) is an expression of this attitude. In practice international lawyers will have numerous opportunities to search out the interconnections among various articles. Such links are sometimes made explicit but are often left to interpretation. They require analysis of articles belonging to different parts of the Convention (for example, article 76 defining the continental shelf and article 134 [4] on limits of the seabed). They also call for close examination of articles in the same part where the many compromises reached are reflected in different provisions on the subject (as for example in the part on straits or the economic zone).

In addition to the internal linkages, the Convention has numerous connections with other treaties and with customary law. Consider, for example, the relations with the four Geneva conventions of 1958. The premise of the 1982 convention is that the Geneva conventions have become obsolete in many respects, yet there is no explicit statement

customary law when that provision is conditioned on conformity to other rules of the Convention, including dispute settlement, which has not been accepted by the nonparty.

It might be asked at this point how the foregoing comment can be reconciled with the notion of the treaty as an expression of the intentions of its drafters and the governments ratifying it. I do not mean to exclude such intentions from the body of material relevant to the meaning and application of the conventions. That material insofar as it can be elicited remains in principle an admissible source of authority. However, the ascertainment of intent is extraordinarily difficult in the case of a Convention negotiated by about 150 states over more than a decade in a context of package deals and bargaining by numerous groups. UNCLOS III was marked by the creation of negotiation bodies and working groups. Mediators and go-betweens proliferated, carrying drafts and interpretations from one group to another. Can we speak of a "common intent" on any but the most general level? Obviously there were many intentions, and numerous drafts formulated, modified, replaced and in the end adopted.

Unlike most other international conventions, the 1982 Convention has no comprehensive clearly identifiable body of travaux preparatoires. Yet it cannot be said it has no travaux (as is the case of the Rome EEC treaty and some other conventions). There are, for example, the successive drafts of the negotiating texts and the summary statements of the chairmen of the Conference and of its major committees. In addition, Conference documents with prepared texts and amendments are voluminous but rarely afford any clear indication of common intent. The absence of summary records of committees creates a large gap in the process of giving meaning to the drafts and the attitudes toward them. Unofficial statements made at the time of debate and thereafter cannot be considered as travaux preparatoires in the usual sense though they may throw light on the positions taken and on the intent of the negotiators.[22] They will almost surely be referred to for their evidentiary value even if they reflect partisan and self-serving positions. The unofficial retrospective "legislative histories" that will appear in due course may have a greater measure of objectivity than most contemporaneous accounts but they too cannot be expected to be free of particular biases and parochial judgments. One hopes that as in the best historical writing, the unofficial histories will seek to meet exacting criteria of evidence and exhibit a generous measure of humility in presenting opinions as to common intent. But just as "scientific" scholars adhering to positivist tenets have reached generalized conclusions that go much beyond the evidence on hand, the historians of the Law of the Sea negotiations will sometimes allow their own conceptions to influence their generalizations. As Namier said of historians in general, those writing on the Law of the Sea are also likely "to imagine the past and remember the future." That too, may have its merits.

The Balance of Rights Between Coastal and Maritime States

The extension of national authority over large areas of ocean space, sometimes characterized as an "enclosure movement," has been accompanied (as we noted earlier) by numerous limitations and qualifications on such authority. One can attribute this to the "package deal" sought by the UN negotiating conference and to the many subsidiary package deals achieved in respect of particular sections of the new Convention. In perhaps a deeper sense, the legal structure of rights and their limits can be seen as reflecting the "incorrigibly plural" character of the world today and the felt need to reconcile conflicting interests in a balanced structure. One may discern, not only the attempted reconciliation of competing national wills, but also the recognition of a common interest in the use and conservation of a global resource. The limits imposed on state power are meant, at least in some cases, to serve that global interest.

In this light, the formulation used in some sections of the 1982 Convention—that states should exercise their rights with due regard to the rights and duties of other states—is more than empty rhetoric. It is a principle that can be invoked to challenge claims of plenary authority based on sovereign rights. The International Court of Justice reminded us in the Iceland Fisheries Case of the principle in article 2 of the Geneva convention on the high seas that freedom of the seas "shall be exercised by all with reasonable regard to the interests of all other states in their exercise of freedom." The Court noted that this was a principle of customary law and it considered Iceland's interference with United Kingdom fishing as an infringement of the principle.[23] The 1982 Convention includes a similar principle in the articles relating to sovereign rights of the coastal state over the exclusive economic zone.[24]

This highly general principle, with which no one can quarrel, is given more concrete meaning in many of the sections of the new Convention. It is most conspicuous, and also most important, in respect of the rights of passage and the competing rights of jurisdiction over the territorial sea, the exclusive economic zone and the archipelagic sea lanes. In regard to the territorial sea, for example, the customary right of innocent passage has been clarified considerably in the new Convention. Its provisions now specify in some detail the activities that are not innocent (article 19) and the subjects that can be regulated by coastal states and those that cannot be regulated (article 21). The Convention has gone significantly beyond the traditional customary law by according a right of transit passage through many international straits and archipelagic waters, a right free of many of the restriction imposed on innocent passage.[25] The rights of coastal states in regard to such transit passage have been limited to safety of navigation, pollution, fishing and customs, fiscal, immigration and sanitary regulations. Even more important a coastal state may not suspend transit passage in a strait; it may not require a submarine to surface; and it must allow overflight by planes. This new transit right was a major objective of the maritime powers and its inclusion in the 1982 Convention was regarded as an essential feature of the package deal. However, the issue has now shifted to whether this right is customary law. The United States, not wishing to become a party to the new Convention, now asserts that the right of transit has become customary law through practice and *opinio juris,* independently of the Convention.[26] The claim is disputed. At present, the attitude of most coastal states involved (that is, those with jurisdiction over international straits) is that treaty adherence is a condition of transit rights through straits.[27] An issue of this kind cannot be decided on the basis of the general principle of due regard for rights of others since the question in controversy is whether there is a right of unimpeded passage under general international law.

The problem of balancing competing rights under the principle of "due regard" for others also arises with respect to the right of navigation in the exclusive economic zone. It is in connection with the exclusive economic zone (EEZ) that the Convention refers to the due regard principle (articles 56 and 58). It also has a general provision that addresses the conflict in rights between the coastal state and other states regarding the EEZ. That provision stipulates that such conflicts should be resolved "on the basis of equity and in the light of all relevant circumstances, taking into account the respective importance of the interests involved to the parties as well as to the international community" (article 59). This formula is still so broad as to appear to offer little guidance for specific decisions. It does recognize, however, that an evaluation of the "importance" of the interests involved is required and that "equity" is relevant. Equity, in this context, would have to extend beyond geographical factors (such as those involved in delimitation disputes) and consider economic and social aspects. It would require consideration of the relative degree of harm that might result from the exercise of a right. Hence, conservation and environmental measures by a coastal state might be justified on grounds of equity to prevail over navigation by high-risk vessels. On the other side, regulation by the coastal state that appears to be without reasonable ground would not be equitable to shipping. Such regulation might also be contrary to the general interest of the international community in world trade and transportation.

The criteria for deciding between competing claims of coastal and shipping countries will have to be given more determinate content in particular cases. This could occur through use of the dispute settlement machinery provided in the Convention (article 297). The use of conciliation and adjudicatory mechanisms would allow such disputes to be resolved in accord with the standards of the Convention applied to particular circumstances. Generally such disputes would require a balancing of rights with decisions that both sides can tolerate. Such decisions are likely to turn on the specific facts rather than on general principles or rules. But it may be expected that over time, the decisions will exhibit patterns that can be formulated as rules of conduct. In this way, the principle of "due regard" will acquire more content. It is obviously important that dispute settlement procedures be utilized as contemplated by the Convention. However, states that are not parties are not bound by such provisions and they cannot invoke them. True they may have recourse to procedures outside of the Convention such as applying to the International Court on the basis of special agreements or acceptances under the optional clause but this may not be accepted by others. It is ironic that a country like the United States, concerned over protection of its rights of navigation and therefore strongly in favor of mandatory dispute settlement, will not be able to take advantage of the Convention's provisions (which responded to its aims) because of its rejection of the Convention on other grounds.

Relevant to the competing claims of navigation and coastal authority is a conceptual controversy over the legal status of the EEZ. One view strongly urged by the maritime powers is that the zone is part of the high seas though subject to the specified resource authority of adjacent coastal states. An opposing view holds that since it is an area in which extensive sovereign rights are recognized, it is inappropriate to characterize it as the high seas. I cannot see that this conceptual controversy will help greatly in resolving particular disputes. The Convention itself spells out the relevant rights on both sides, and whether the areas are characterized as high seas or a special type of resource zone will not in itself contribute to a decision as to which rights should prevail in a particular case. It is possible, however, that disputes will arise on issues not covered by the rights spelled out in the Convention. In such cases, a decision may be influenced by the status of the area as high seas or not.

The resource rights of coastal states are also subject to the rights of other states in other respects than rights of passage. A substantial number of articles impose obligations on the coastal states in regard to conservation and sharing of living resources. Included in such obligations is a broad duty to ensure that living resources are not endangered by overexploitation. This is an obligation owed to the international community and as such can be treated as an obligtion *erga omes*. I would consider this an obligation of customary law as well as a duty under the Convention. Coastal states that do not have the capacity to harvest the entire "allowable" catch of fish in their zones have an obligation to give other states access to the surplus. It is somewhat debatable whether this obligation can have much significance since the coastal state itself determines what is the allowable catch and whether there is a surplus.[28] Moreover a coastal state may contract with foreign vessels to harvest the allowable catch and in that way avoid declaring a surplus for other states. Should there be a surplus, the coastal state would be obliged to allow neighboring states that are landlocked and geographically disadvantaged access to the fish resources. It also would have a qualified obligation to allow fishing by states whose nationals have habitually fished in the zone or have conducted research concerning the fishing stocks in question. These provisions are somewhat more complicated than this summary indicates. They are indicative of the general effort to introduce some measure of equitable sharing to the exploitation of the resources of the EEZ. It must be said, however, that the coastal state is given so much discretion to determine the factors that yield the optimum utilization that it seems doubtful that surpluses will be declared. It is more likely that states which cannot harvest all the fish in the zone will contract with or license foreign fishermen to exploit the area. Such bilateral arrangements would not seem to be contrary to the letter of the treaty but they may be inconsistent with the intent to give access to developing or geographically disadvantaged countries.

Another package deal relates to scientific marine research in the EEZ and on the continental shelf. It includes 26 articles (part XIII), many of them quite complicated. The basic rule is that the consent of the coastal state is necessary for such research. However, the coastal state is required to give its consent in normal circumstances if certain conditions are met. The reference to normal circumstances would allow the coastal state to exclude research carried out by nationals of a hostile regime. Among the conditions to be met is a requirement that research be exclusively for peaceful purposes and "to increase scientific knowledge for the benefit of all mankind" (article 246). This latter condition is further implemented by a general obligation of the researching state to make its results internationally available. However such international dissemination is qualified by a provision that allows the coastal state to prevent dissemination of material related to resource development. In fact, the coastal state is allowed to exclude research entirely if it is of direct significance for exploration or exploitation of natural resources, living or nonliving. Several other grounds for denial of consent are also stated. In addition the researching state must give detailed information to the coastal state and to allow the latter to take part in the research free of charge.

The broad grants of authority to the coastal states are to some degree balanced by the general obligation to grant consent in normal circumstances for scientific projects. Coastal states are also required to establish rules and procedures to ensure that consent will not be denied or delayed unreasonably. The researching states benefit from an "implied consent" provision (article 252), which allows a research project to proceed without the express consent of the coastal state six months after filing an application if the coastal state did not reply in four months. This provision will have practical value.

Researching states may avail themselves of the dispute settlement procedures in part XV of the Convention. However, the procedures for binding dispute settlement by arbitration or adjudication do not apply to two important categories of coastal state action in respect to research, namely (a) exercise of a right or discretion by the coastal state, (b) orders for suspension or termination of research.[29] In view of the extensive discretionary grants to the coastal state the exception is significant. On the other hand, the nonbinding conciliation procedures remain available and may be unilaterally initiated by an aggrieved party. That provides some safeguard against arbitrary action. More important, of course, will be the actual practice and agreements of coastal states in respect to marine research. It remains to be seen whether their apprehensions over resource exploitation and potential military use will lead them to impose severe restrictions on "innocent" research.

Another complicated balancing of rights in the Convention relates to protection of the marine environment especially in respect to pollution caused by vessels. The rights of the coastal state to deal with foreign flag vessels are spelled out and grounds for action against the vessel are clearly specified. The coastal state rules relating to pollution control must conform to "applicable international rules and standards established through a competent international organization or general diplomatic conference."[30] This is a safeguard against domestic laws that may be extreme or unfair. The coastal state may take enforcement action in situations described in the treaty. If a polluting vessel has left its waters, the coastal state may request another state in whose port the ship has stopped to investigate the violations and impose penalties if warranted. On the other hand, the flag state has the right to request that proceedings in the coastal state be suspended so as to allow the flag state to take legal action. But the coastal or port state need not suspend its proceedings if it relates to a case of major damage or if the flag state has repeatedly violated its obligations in regard to pollution by its vessels, (articles 218, 228). These environmental provisions tend to favor coastal state authority vis-à-vis flag states and it may prove difficult to impose legal restraints on a coastal state that has evidence of violations by foreign flag vessels. There are of course good reasons to accord priority to coastal state interests in deterring pollution and enforcing the rules as long as they are reasonable. Some of the articles provide a measure of protection for the flag states against arbitrary action or harsh enforcement by the coastal states. It is fair to say that the rights of both sides are reasonably protected by the Convention, at least on paper.

In referring to rights "on paper," I come back to the question raised earlier of creeping jurisdiction by coastal states. The new Convention, as we saw, includes broad grants of discretionary authority to the coastal states in the EEZ enabling them to limit the exercise of rights by other states. In most situations, the obligation to balance rights will fall on the coastal state in the first instance. Whether it acts in an unreasonable or discriminatory manner will depend more on political and economic considerations than on the legal rules in the Convention. Some of the coastal states may be under pressure to use their authority over ocean space to extract political or economic advantages from other states that utilize their offshore areas. A protectionist position on the part of the coastal states may also be a response to adverse actions by other states in fields unrelated to the sea. The disputes that are likely to arise may be settled by agreement or just remain unresolved (which is the more common way states have for coping with difficulties). It would be preferable in many cases if the dispute settlement provisions could be utilized as envisaged by the new Convention. As we noted above some important kinds of disputes are excluded from the binding arbitral and adjudicatory procedures but they are covered by mandatory nonbinding conciliation.[31] It remains to be seen whether conciliation will be used for such disputes and whether, when used, they lead to a further specification of reciprocal rights and duties.

We must note once again that states such as the United States which will not adhere to the Convention will lose the advantages of the dispute settlement obligations. Moreover it remains uncertain whether such nonparty states will be able to claim the benefit of many of the new rules (such as those on research and pollution control) while rejecting the application of the interrelated rules of the Convention on dispute settlement. The claim that the new rules on the EEZ are customary law will be weakened by the domestic laws of coastal states that claim exclusive jurisdiction over resources but do not embody the limitations found in the Convention. Such domestic laws would constitute evidence of state practice at variance with the treaty rules limiting coastal state authority. It may therefore be difficult for a nonparty to maintain that the specific treaty rules on the EEZ are customary law even if the EEZ is generally accepted as a customary rule.

A maritime state that cannot rely on the new Convention as a party may therefore have difficulty in obtaining its benefits. It is doubtful that political, economic or even military measures by nonparty maritime states will prove effective if a large part of the world denies their legal rights. The past experiences of the United States in meeting the seizures of U.S. vessels by Ecuador and Peru indicates how little economic and political pressures helped. The concentrated interest of a coastal state in its zone tends to prevail over the more diffuse interests of a global maritime state. Gunboat diplomacy to enforce rights against a coastal state in regard to resources or pollution is problematic. Naval powers are more likely to use force to ensure passage through strategic straits but coastal straits states are probably well equipped today with precision guided missiles to resist such force effectively.[32] While bilateral arrangements may be worked out, changes in regimes (witness, the change in Iran) may render such arrangements of dubious value if the legal right of passage is not accepted. The political costs of the use of force would be much less if the naval power could rely on a clear and generally accepted treaty provision. These considerations indicate that a maritime power that does not adhere to the 1982 Convention will be giving up important benefits.

The Common Heritage Beyond National Jurisdiction

The most controversial and publicized issue in the Law of the Sea concerns the legal status of the seabed beyond national jurisdiction. The specific question at issue is whether a national state has the legal right today to engage in mining in that area and to acquire the mineral resources just as it has the right to catch fish on the high seas. Those countries, which assert that right (notably, the United States), maintain that in the absence of its agreement to do otherwise, a state is free under customary law to exploit the mineral resources of the seabed. The right, it is argued, is embraced within the recognized principle of freedom of the seas in the areas beyond national jurisdiction. It is subject only "to a duty of reasonable regard to the interest of other states in their exercise of these and other freedoms recognized by general principles of international law."[33]

The opposing position is that the seabed beyond national jurisdiction and the minerals on it are "the common heritage of mankind" and have been declared as such by declaration of the UN General Assembly adopted by a large majority of states (including the United States) without any negative votes. (However, 14 states abstained in the vote.)[35] On this view, the area can only be exploited lawfully pursuant to an international regime adopted by a generally accepted treaty. It is contended by proponents of this position that the UN Convention of 1982 has established a generally accepted legal regime, which on entry into force, will govern all mining activities in the area through a Seabed Authority.[36]

The debates in the United Nations and in other forums on the controversy have brought out a number of overlapping arguments on both sides, some legal others political. To clarify the issue, it is neccessary to distinguish the different questions raised.

One of the principle questions concerns the status of the seabed under customary international law prior to recent developments. Three main positions have been expressed:

1. that the seabed, like unclaimed land, is *res nullius* and therefore subject to national appropriation.

2. that the sea and the seabed constitute a legal unity and that both are *res communis*, not subject to appropriation by any state or person but open to access and use by all.

3. that no customary international law applied to the seabed inasmuch as there was and could be no exploitation; consequently no state practice, let alone custom, existed prior to the UN Declaration of 1970.

The *res nullius* position rests primarily on the analogy of the ocean floor to unclaimed land that can be acquired through occupation and control.[37] It also finds a precedent in the exclusive rights to areas of the seabed exploited for sedentary fish, such as sponges. Despite these arguments, no government has claimed sovereign rights to the ocean floor beyond the limits of the continental shelf or EEZ. It has been suggested that governments are incapable of occupation and control over such areas but this is by no means evident. One cannot rule it out as a future possibility. For the present, however, the significant legal fact is the absence of any governmental claims to sovereignty over any part of the seabed.

The second position, which maintains that the seabed is *res communis*, free for exploitation by all, has two legal elements. One relates to the seabed itself, the other to the resources (minerals or living resources) that are found on it. With respect to the seabed, it rejects the *res nullius* argument by pointing to the absence of any territorial claims and to the assumption implicit in the doctrine of the continental shelf that the area beyond the shelf was *res communis*. Customary law, it notes, drew no distinction between the sea (i.e., the water) and the ocean floor. Consequently, the resources of the bed like those of the water can be "captured" by any state exercising its freedom of access and use. Customary law has never declared any resources immune from capture and in the absence of agreement states remain free to acquire such resources. States are only subject to the general obligation to pay due regard to the interests of other states in the exercise of their legal rights. On this view, the fact that manganese nodules were not exploitable until recently does not exclude them from the general rule regarding acquisition of resources. However, unlike fishing, mining would require exclusive rights to exploit a particular tract under license of a state or competent international authority.[38]

The third position rejects the legal unity of the sea and the seabed. It regards the ocean floor as distinct from land and sea and maintains that no state practice or custom could develop when exploitation of the area was impossible. Hence, customary law simply did not cover the seabed until states collectively expressed an *opinio juris communis* that the area was part of the common heritage and that neither it nor the resources on it could be exploited unilaterally. Under the new law that emerged with the Declaration of Principles of 1970, such exploitation could only take place lawfully in accordance with the rules of the international regime established by treaty. The essential feature of their position, insofar as customary law is concerned, is that the bed is so different from the water above it that the principle of freedom generally applicable to the sea cannot be considered as applicable to the bed in the absence of state practice and *opinio juris* specifically related to the seabed. The majority of states take this position and many legal commentators have agreed with it.[39]

The second legal issue in the controversy over the seabed concerns the legal significance of the "common heritage" principle. On the record the principle appears to have been accepted by all states. It is the main article of the unanimous Declaration of Principles Governing the Seabed. It has been affirmed time and time again by developed as well as developing states. In 1970 President Nixon declared it to be the United States position and proposed a Seabed Resources Authority which would collect royalties for "international community purposes" and developing countries.[40] Other developed states have similarly acknowledged their approval of the "common heritage" status of the seabed.[41]

However, affirmation of the principle has been accompanied by divergence as to the meaning of the common heritage and its mode of implementation. Positions have ranged from a regime of free access and exploitation to a system of international ownership and management. These differences, as we saw, have not been resolved. The new Convention contains a compromise system in which an international seabed authority would exercise regulatory authority and mining operations would be carried out both by an international enterprise and by individual firms awarded contracts by the authority. Since this part of the Convention has been rejected by several countries, the dispute about the interpretation of the common heritage remains. It raises the question whether the principle can be considered as accepted law when its essential meaning is in dispute.

Yet governments on the whole tend to treat it as an accepted principle albeit a principle that requires further specification and implementation. Despite the differences that relate to the system of exploitation, it is generally agreed that the "common heritage" precludes national appropriation and sovereign claims to any area of the seabed. This is virtually noncontroversial today as is the principle that all states have a duty to prevent environmental damage to the common seabed. We can also find general approbation of the idea that exploitation of the "common heritage" should benefit "all mankind" and be shared equitably. Opinion divides, as we saw, on what this means practically. Governments opposed to international management and to the seabed provisions of the Convention have favored some revenue sharing for the benefit of the less-developed countries. This was a feature of the United States proposal in 1970. The present U.S. legislation under which seabed mining by U.S. companies would be carried out contemplates a trust fund for international benefits.[42] The seabed mining law of the Federal Republic of Germany also includes a trust fund for the benefit of developing countries.[43] Although these provisions fall far short of those in the 1982 Convention, they do recognize a distributive obligation that is derived from the common heritage concept. Those who favor greater freedom of production for private companies maintain that this would in fact confer more benefits on "all mankind" than would a system of international management.[44] While this claim has not been accepted by the majority of countries, it shows at least that the minority group of technologically advanced states recognize that benefit-sharing in some measure is a requirement for seabed mining.

The record also shows that in general states have accepted the principle that seabed mining should be governed by an international regime that has received general approval. This is stated in the Declaration of Principles of 1970. The lengthy negotiations in the UN Conference on the Law of the Sea were its practical expression. The fact that the treaty which emerged was not fully acceptable to all states has frustrated that objective. But this does not mean that an international regime has ceased to be an essential element in the concept of the common heritage. The United States and others of the nonadhering states have not renounced their position that a generally accepted multilateral regime for the seabed is the appropriate means for giving effect to the common heritage idea.[45] The obligation to seek such an agreement through negotiations in good faith should therefore be considered as a continuing legal commitment despite the present impasse. Changing political and economic conditions may well lead to renewed negotiation.

A pertinent factor which had not been anticipated in the early period of the United Nations Conference is the lack of substantial economic incentives to carry on commercial mining operations. The reasons for this are that the land-based sources of the minerals in question are more than adequate to meet worldwide demand and the prices of those minerals are much too low to warrant the comparatively high-cost operations on the seabed. Obviously the minerals of the seabed have no real economic value as long as the same minerals can be obtained more cheaply on land. Moreover, estimates of future demand and supply do not show that the situation will change much during the next two or three decades. Another factor that will tend to discourage mining in the seabed beyond national jurisdiction is the discovery of commercially exploitable manganese nodules on the continental shelf in several areas. Should market conditions change so as to warrant mining of the nodules, it is likely that shelf areas under national control will be the main source of such nodules.[47] These economic and technical factors indicate that the much publicized promise of vast riches from the minerals on the deep seabed is far from realization. Indeed it makes little economic sense for either the international enterprise or private firms to engage in seabed mining beyond national jurisdiction.

In the absence of economic justification, political reasons for seabed exploitation have come to the fore. Arguments have been made that, even if not profitable, seabed mineral development is desirable to ensure safe sources of supply in the interest of national defense. Exploitation may also be begun to preempt valuable areas. Such preemptive efforts are likely to be protected by naval forces particularly when carried out by states not party to the Convention. Legal challenges are possible in the domestic court of a country receiving the nodules for processing but such challenges are unlikely to succeed where the national legislation has authorized the mining. The mining may also be challenged by a contentious proceeding in the International Court when jurisdiction can be based on an acceptance of compulsory jurisdiction or through a request for advisory opinion by the General Assembly. Such judicial proceedings may serve to avoid armed clashes but the use of force "in self-defense" by competing states cannot be ruled out. It may well be that the practical safeguard against armed hostilities is the hard fact that the manganese nodules in the deep-seabed do not have economic value under present market conditions. There is therefore good reason for both sides to proceed slowly and to prepare the way for further negotiation. It will not be the first time that economic adversity offers an opportunity for a negotiated solution.

Will an eventual solution for seabed mining (assuming it makes economic sense) reduce the significance of the common heritage principle in the Law of the Sea generally? Once a universally accepted regime is in place, reliance on the abstract conception of a common heritage for rules of conduct will be slight, and only marginal. However, its significance may be revived for uses of ocean space other than seabed mining. Such uses are still conjectural but we are often reminded of the possibilities.[48] Thermal energy conversion is one example; another is the use of waves and currents for energy. We are told to expect more and larger artificial islands and new types of underwater installations. These and other predicted developments will take place first in areas under national jurisdiction but it is not inconceivable that they will be extended to ocean space beyond those areas. When this occurs, claims of extended national authority will almost surely be made. A new series of "enclosure" movements will take place. To counteract this and the conflicts that will ensue, the conception of the common heritage may again play a role as a basis of international cooperation and an attractive alternative to competitive extensions of national jurisdiction.

Our analysis of concepts and realities indicates how difficult it is for the international community to adopt a comprehensive self-contained supreme law for a large area of international life. Virtually everything in the 1982 Convention has a relation to the practices and interaction of states over a long period of time. Those practices and interactions are in a continuous process of change; they cannot be stilled by a new text. True, the new text exerts its own power; it imposes standards and determines conduct to a considerable degree. It influences developments and is itself influenced and altered by new developments. We must expect it to be buffeted by outside forces and transformed by practice and interpretation. It will remain in motion, interwoven with the continuing changing body of customary law.

NOTES

1. The captured Portuguese vessel was sold in Holland but some stockholders of the East Indies Company objected to the company's action on grounds of Christian principles and law. Grotius, in a legal brief, supported the capture and sale under the law of spoils. Part of his brief later appeared as *Mare Liberum*. See A. Nussbaum, *A Concise History of the Law of Nations* (New York: Macmillan, 1947), pp. 97, 107; T. W. Fulton, *The Sovereignty of the Sea* (1911; reprint Millwood, N.Y.: Kraus, 1976), pp. 338 ff.

2. J. Verzijl, *International Law in Historical Perspective* (Leyden: Sijthoft, 1971), 4:8–20. J. Goebel, *The Struggle For the Falkland Islands* (New Haven: Yale University Press, 1927), pp. 47–58.

3. Fulton, *Sovereignty of the Sea*, pp. 366–67.

4. Grotius, *De Jure Pradae*, William, tr. (Oxford: Clarendon Press, 1950), ch. 12 sec. 1.

5. For historical account of continental shelf doctrine before and after Truman Proclamation, see R. Anand, *Legal Regime of the Sea Bed and the Developing Countries* (New Delhi: Thomson, 1975), pp. 31–75. See also S. Oda, Dissenting Opinion in Tunisia-Libya Case concerning the Continental Shelf *I.C.J. Reports* 1982, p. 157 ff. (paras 134–145).

6. Chile's claims to a 200-mile zone originated in the World War II shortages of fats and oils in Chile and the establishment of a new whaling industry in Chile. At the end of the war, European and Japanese whaling were extended and Chile's infant industry faced a shortage. It sought a 50-mile exclusive zone but its lawyers found a "precedent" in a "neutral" or "safety" zone of 300 to 500 miles declared by the United States and other Latin-American countries in October 1939 to exclude world war belligerent activities. This questionable

precedent led to the Chilean zone of 200 miles proclaimed in 1947. Ecuador and Peru followed suit in order to protect their fishing interests in anchovies and tuna (they did not mention whaling). The Chilean and Peruvian proclamations used language similar to the Truman Proclamation of 1945 and the governments presumably considered their action as consistent with international law and practice. See Hollick, "The Origins of 200-mile Off shore Zones," *American Journal of International Law* (1977), 71:494–500.

7. See R. Eckert, *The Enclosure of Ocean Resources* (Stanford: Hoover Institution Press, 1979), pp. 99–103; Friedman, "The Economics of the Common Pool," *U.C.L.A. Law Review* (1971), 18:855.

8. Fisheries Jurisdiction Case (United Kingdom v. Iceland) *I.C.J. Reports* (1974), p. 3.

9. Fishery Conservation and Management Act 16, U.S.C. sec. 1801–1857. See Burke, "U.S. Fishery Management" *American Journal of International Law* (1982), 76:24–55.

10. O. Schachter, *Sharing the World's Resources* (New York: Columbia University Press, 1977), pp. 41 ff.

11. R. M'Gonigle and M. Zacher, *Pollution, Politics, and International Law* (Berkeley: University of California Press, 1979).

12. D. O'Connell, *The Influence of Law on Sea Power* (Annapolis: Naval Institute Press, 1975), esp. pp. 72–78, 146–159; Treves, "Military Installations, Structures and Devices on the Seabed" *American Journal of International Law* (1980), 74:808–857.

13. See Max Huber opinion in "Island of Palmas Case 2," *Rep. Int. Arb. Awards*, p. 869. Waldock, "Disputed Sovereignty in the Falkland Island Dependencies," *British Yearbook of International Law* (1948), vol. 25.

14. H. Lauterpacht, "Sovereignty over Submarine Areas" *British Yearbook of International Law* (1950), 27:425–27.

15. See North Sea Continental Shelf Cases, *I.C.J. Reports,* (1969), pp. 30–31, for discussion of "proximity" and "natural prolongation" of shelf.

16. P. Allott, "Power Sharing in the Law of the Sea," *American Journal of International Law* (1983), 77:1, 9.

17. *Ibid,* pp. 28–29.

18. *Ibid,* pp. 29–30.

19. *Ibid,* pp. 26–27.

20. Proclamation and statement of President Reagan, March 1983. See *International Legal Materials* (1983), 22:464, U.S. State Dept. *Bulletin* (1983), no. 2075, pp. 70–71.

21. Charney, "Exclusive Economic Zone and Public International Law" *Ocean Development and International Law* (1984), 15:233–288; Grolin, "The Future of the Law of the Sea" *Ocean Development and International Law* (1983), 13:1, 9, 11.

22. Numerous articles written by participants in UNCLOS III throw light on the intent of the drafters. The series of articles in the *American Journal of International Law* begun by Stevenson and Oxman and continued by Oxman are especially valuable for a contemporaneous account of Conference discussion on specific drafts.

23. *I.C.J. Reports* (1974), pp. 22, 29.

24. Articles 56(2) and 58(3) use the words "due regard" in place of "reasonable regard."

25. UN Convention on the Law of the Sea, 1982, articles 37–44. The right of transit passage is limited to straits that are used for international navigation between two areas of the high seas or between two exclusive economic zones. There are some exceptions. For example the right does not apply where the strait is between an island and the mainland and there is an equally convenient route seaward of the island. Hence the Corfu Channel would not be subject to the right of transit passage. Straits governed by international treaties in force are also excluded from the straits subject to rights of passage. See J. N. Moore, "The Regime of Straits and the Law of the Sea," *American Journal of International Law* (1980), 74:77 ff.

26. J. L. Malone (Assistant Secretary of State for Ocean Affairs) in address to Law of the Sea Institute, September 24, 1984. State Dept. Release, Current Policy No. 617 (Sept. 24, 1984).

27. For references to statements rejecting nonparty rights, see Lee, "The Law of the Sea Convention and Third States," *American Journal of International Law* (1983), 77:541, especially p. 547 *n* 18. For arguments against nonparty rights see Note, "United States Activity Outside the Law of the Sea Convention" *Columbia Law Review* (1984) 84:1055–57.

28. See Oda, "Fisheries under the United Nations Convention on the Law of the Sea," *American Journal of International Law* (1983), 77:739 ff.

29. Article 297 (2) of 1982 Convention.

30. Article 211 (5) of 1982 Convention.

31. Adede, "The Basic Structure of the Disputes Settlement Part of the Law of the Sea Convention" *Ocean Development and International Law Journal* (1982), 11:125 ff; Sohn, "Peaceful Settlement of Disputes in Ocean Conflicts" *Law & Contemporary Problems* (1983), 46:195 ff.

32. Hazlett, "Straight Shooting," *U.S. Naval Institute Proceedings* (June 1982), p. 71; Pirtle, "Transit Rights and U.S. Security Interests in International Straits" *Ocean Development and International Law Journal* (1978), 5:482.

33. U.S. Deep Seabed Hard Mineral Resources Act of 1980, 30 U.S.C. sec. 1401 (a)(12).

34. GA Res. 2749 (1970) on Declaration of Principles governing the Seabed and Ocean Floor and the Subsoil thereof, Beyond the Limits of National Jurisdiction.

35. The abstaining states were nearly all members of the Communist bloc who later changed their position generally to support the principles of the declaration. Hence it is plausible to consider the declaration as generally accepted.

36. This position implies that mining by states outside the regime would be illegal. See statement of T. T. Koh, President of the Law of the Sea Conference in *Law and Contemporary Problems* (1983) 46:89. See also Biggs, "Deep Seabed Mining and Unilateral Legislation" *Ocean Development and International Law* (1980), 8:223 ff. Contra: E. D. Brown, "Freedom of the High Seas versus the

Common Heritage of Mankind," *San Diego Law Review* (1983), 20:521–560, especially pp. 534–537.

37. See T. Kronmiller, *The Lawfulness of Deep Seabed Mining* (Dobbs Ferry, N.Y.: Oceana, 1980), esp. pp. 204–206. For earlier position on same lines see Sir Cecil Hurst, "Whose is the Bed of the Sea," *British Yearbook of International Law,* (1923–24), 4:43 ff.

38. Miners' rights involving exclusive use of a defined tract for a limited period would be granted under license by states. It has been described as a "usufructuary right." See E. M. F. Goldie, "Customary International Law and Seabed Mining," *Syracuse Journal of International Law and Commerce* (1978–79), 6:173 ff. Whether states parties to an international regime would have to recognize such licenses is debatable. It has been suggested that as parties to the 1982 Convention they would be barred by the Treaty from such recognition. See Bailey, "The Future of Exploitation of the Resources of the Deep Seabed," *Law and Contemporary Problems* (1983), 46:72–73. For a contrary view see Oxman, *idem,* p. 78, and E. D. Brown, "Freedom of the High Sea."

39. See Letter of Group of Experts of Group 77, Off. Records UNCLOS III, 11:80–82 (1973). See also Biggs and writers cited therein.

40. S. Lay, R. Churchhill, and M. Nordquist, eds., *New Directions in the Law of the Sea* (Dobbs Ferry, N.Y.: Oceana, 1973), 2:751–68. See also F. Richardson in *Digest of U.S. Practice in International Law* (1978), p. 1018.

41. See Statement of representative of Fed. Rep. of Germany, Off. Rec. UNCLOS, 2:16; United Kingdom proposal in UN Doc. A/8421 (1971), pp. 18–19 and Annex; Japan proposal in UN Doc. A/Conf. 62/C.1/L9 (1974).

42. 30 U.S.C. sec. 1472 (1980); 26 U.S.C. sec. 4495. See also Note "United States Activity Outside of the Law of the Sea Convention" *Columbia Law Review* (1984), 84:1032 at pp. 1046–47.

43. See *International Legal Matters* 19:1330, 1335.

44. Malone, n. 26.

45. In 1984, the principal U.S. official concerned with the law of the sea suggested that "in the next six or eight years" negotiations to amend the seabed mining provisions of the 1982 Convention may well take place. See Malone, p. 5. For earlier statement on United States policy on international regimes, see statement of J. N. Moore before Senate Subcommittee on Minerals, Materials, and Fuels, 93 Cong., 2d Sess. p. 989 (1974).

46. See M. Dubs, "Comment on Future of Seabed Mining" in *Law and Contemporary Problems* (1983), 46:81–82.

47. See A. Pardo, "Ocean Space and Mankind," *Third World Quarterly* (1984), 6:569 ("deep seabed mining will take place. . . perhaps predominantly within the expanded legal continental shelf sanctioned by the new convention").

48. See British argument in the Anglo-Norwegian Fisheries Case, pleading, argument, documents. 2:428–30.

49. See Pardo, pp. 560–63, 570–72.

A Note:
Military Uses of the Ocean and the Law of the Sea Conference

GIULIO PONTECORVO

T HE MILITARY interests of the United States and the Soviet Union set limits on what the Conference could decide. The majority of nations accepted this military constraint with great reluctance, although the members of NATO and the Eastern bloc of course supported the military positions taken jointly by the United States and the USSR. Given acceptance by the Conference of the necessity of accommodating the military concerns of the superpowers it follows that the treaty that was finally articulated in 1982 covers the set of nonmilitary issues. This means that the legal rules applied by the treaty to all nations do not interfere in any essential way with the freedom of action of the military in the two superpowers. This military limitation on the treaty's coverage was not achieved easily and therefore the specifics of the issues debated are important as they contain the seeds of future concerns over military perogatives. An example of how this issue may arise involves the 1981 flip-flop by the United States on its position in favor of the treaty, a policy change that had the acquiescence of the Pentagon. The current U.S. position is that the protection of its military interests, made specific by commission and omission in the articles of treaty, is now, hopefully, safeguarded by customary international law.

The military rights of the superpowers were accommodated by the Conference, which equated their military activity with self-defense and thereby made it consistent with the original charter of the United Nations. All naval activity in the oceans in preparation for self-defense constituted a peaceful use of the seas and therefore was in accord with the UN charter.

This general position was not sufficient and hard bargaining took place over the issues of: transit (innocent) passage, the extended economic zone (EEZ), environmental concerns, and a distinction between scientific research and military activity in the EEZ, which favors the military at a potential cost to ocean science. The debate over both innocent and transit passage involved the rights of warships in straits and archipelagic seas, the question of overflight rights and the ability of submarines to travel through these passages while submerged. During the protracted negotiations over the treaty numerous attempts, ultimately unsuccessful, were made to give the coastal state at least some degree of control over foreign military transit. This was the basic tradeoff in the negotiations. The superpowers just would not accept any limitations on what they regarded as their military necessities. The pressure that was applied was the threat to leave the Conference if the military position on free transit was not resolved favorably. It is ironic that when the U.S. did leave the Conference it was over the, at best, marginal issue of deep-sea mining and it remains to be seen if that decision poses a threat to the original military trade-off.

After free transit, the next crucial military issue involved the legal status of the EEZ. Again, the military resisted the concept that the EEZ was sovereign territory, i.e., the military needed these zones to be treated as high seas so it would have the right to put various types of structures and a wide variety of electronic devices on the continental shelves of other countries. Again, this issue, the legal status of the EEZ and the rights of the coastal state therein were argued in a variety of ways and again, military activity was exempted from any coastal state control.

Ocean scientists sought unsuccessfully to obtain the same freedom. Since to the United States freedom of science, unlike military interests, was a negotiable issue, science came under a set of negotiated rules which gives considerable *de jure* and probably *de facto* control of scientific research to the coastal state if it should choose to exercise the full range of its options under the treaty.

What was true of transit and the EEZ is also true of environment concerns as naval vessels are exempt from treaty restrictions on vessel source pollution.

As this brief review suggests, the two superpowers gained their military objectives in the treaty. What may be in doubt is the potential problem presented by creeping jurisdiction. Once the treaty is either adopted or becomes part of customary international law, internal political pressures will build in some states to gradually acquire some or all of the powers and control over transit and sovereignty traded off under pressure during the treaty negotiations. Thus, potentially the military issues presumably settled by the treaty may gradually reappear as unfinished business.

Finally, it is interesting to note the change in the position of the USSR. The United States, with its naval power, was concerned with its freedom to exercise military power at least since the voyage of the Great White Fleet just after the turn of the century. The Russians historically relatively weaker as a naval force essentially up to the start of the treaty negotiations, preferred coastal state control of transit and the EEZ. The start of the treaty negotiations, together with the realization of their new naval strength on the part of the USSR, brought a major shift in the Russian position. They moved from their earlier restrictive position to the U.S. position of freedom of military action.

PART II
Resources: Science and Technology

4.
Ocean Science:
Its Place in the New Order
of the Oceans

DAVID A. ROSS

THE OCEANS, which comprise over 70 percent of our planet, are still a relatively unknown environment. Nevertheless they offer exciting potential for mineral and biological resources, a potentially safe disposal site for some human and industrial wastes, new sources of energy, control or modification of climate, a medium for transport of much of the world's trade, a military playground, and other potential not yet even considered. The study of the ocean necessary to achieve this potential is visualized by some countries as a form of power, by others as an opportunity, and by still others as a frustration because of their lack of marine science expertise. In any case, marine scientific research will be critical to those countries that wish to develop their new 200-nautical-mile Exclusive Economic Zone (EEZ) and other marine areas having potential. Those countries without marine science expertise will be at a disadvantage unless they develop such capabilities and/or develop cooperative efforts in scientific research and training with those countries that have such skills. The achievement of a country's marine objectives may often be more a function of national policy and politics than the ability to pose and solve the appropriate scientific or technical question.

Many scientists feel that marine research is approaching a very

Contribution No. 5706 of the Woods Hole Oceanographic Institution. Support for writing this essay was derived from the Pew Memorial Trust, the Woods Hole Oceanographic Institution's Marine Policy and Ocean Management Program and the Department of Commerce, NOAA, National Sea Grant College Program, under Grant NA 83-AA-D-00049 (E/L-1).

important crossroad. On one path are recent exciting scientific discoveries such as the deep-sea vents along oceanic spreading centers and their associated polymetallic sulfide deposits and exotic lifeforms or similarly our increasing understanding of air–sea interactions, and thus ultimately better climate prediction and even modification. These discoveries hold considerable promise for major advances in our use and exploitation of the ocean, that can also eventually impact on many other human endeavors. On the other path, however, are some aspects of the Law of the Sea (LOS) treaty that could severely reduce or restrict marine scientific research in large and important areas of the ocean. The challenge is to find an intermediate or new path that allows the continuation of important marine research, without scientists or countries becoming frustrated or diverted by the LOS treaty and other entanglements. Indeed, it may even be possible that the LOS treaty could yield positive benefits, but to achieve them and capitalize fully on present and new scientific discoveries will require innovative approaches toward marine research. *It is to everyone's advantage that the ocean is used properly.*

In this paper I would like to comment on various aspects of the LOS treaty for marine scientific research, their implications for scientists and developing countries, and then conclude with some suggestions for improving marine science opportunities for all. As a marine scientist, from a developed country, my views may well be biased. However, I have worked during much of my career with developing countries and hopefully have and can express a feeling as to some of their marine scientific expectations.

Background

During most of the early history of marine scientific research, essentially all of the ocean was free for exploration; restrictions, even after the first LOS Convention in 1958, were limited to the territorial sea and some types of continental shelf research. During these times the main restrictions on scientific research were technology, an occasional inability to formulate an appropriate hypothesis for testing, and infrequent financial constraints; political restraints were rare. Marine technology and science then clearly was not captive to national or international rules.[1] Unfortunately, some aspects of marine science may have been too successful, in particular the promotion of certain ocean mineral resources, especially manganese nodules and hydrocarbons. Anticipation of potential riches from the sea floor helped to encourage an international movement toward increasing ocean enclosure that culminated in the Third United Nations Conference on the Law of the Sea (UNCLOS III). At this conference ocean science was not generally visualized as a natural freedom of the sea or even a benefit, but rather as a threat toward resource development or as having important military implications. Scientific information, and the ability to use it, has an economic value which often cannot be fully used by developing countries. Thus often the case for science was lost in the north-south dialogue. Much could be written to show how poorly the presentation for science was made, but that is another story.

The present marine science conditions, resulting from the LOS negotiations and treaty, include coastal state permission for research as well as several very specific requirements (described in more detail in following sections) covering all portions of the coastal ocean. Individually none of these requirements have to be limiting; collectively, however, they will present a difficult path for a marine scientist to follow if he or she wishes to develop a marine scientific program with a foreign country. It may well be that the perceptions of these difficulties could do more to discourage scientists from working in foreign waters than the treaty itself. The EEZs of the world, it should be noted, include about 28 million square nautical miles or around 32 percent of the total ocean area. If all regions of the ocean that will have controls for marine science are considered, about 42 percent of the ocean is involved.[2] This region obviously includes many important areas of oceanographic study and most of the ocean's biological and mineral resources.

UNCLOS III and Marine Scientific Research

Formal negotiations concerning marine scientific research and other issues at UNCLOS III began in 1974, and eventually on April 30, 1982, a Law of the Sea Treaty was approved by a vote of 130 to 4.[3] The United States, Venezuela, Turkey, and Israel voted against it, and 17 other countries abstained; 60 nations must ratify the treaty for it to enter into force, 20 have done so by mid-1985.

The new regime for marine scientific research in much of the ocean will change the present way marine scientific research programs are developed and implemented. It should be stressed that it is irrelevant whether the treaty is eventually ratified by the necessary 60 countries or not, since most coastal countries have already adopted rules concerning marine scientific research in their EEZ.

Some of the history of the marine science negotiations during UNCLOS III has been published.[4] Many countries, including most coastal states, favored or even encouraged restrictions on marine research. The few supporters of marine science were the United States, the Soviet Union (until 1976), West Germany, the Netherlands, and sometimes Japan.[5] By supporters of marine science I mean those countries that supported relatively few, minor or no restrictions on marine science in the exclusive economic zone and further seaward regions. During UNCLOS III there was essentially a consensus concerning coastal state control over research in internal waters and the 12-nautical-mile territorial sea.

The LOS treaty has produced several distinct juridical regions for the ocean; these include: internal waters, territorial seas, straits used for international navigation, archipelagic waters, exclusive economic zones, the continental shelf beyond 200 miles, a region called "the area," and high seas. The treaty establishes boundaries between these juridical regions (or in some instances defines the method by which such boundaries are to be determined), the mixture of coastal state and flag state jurisdiction within each region, and the rules of conduct within each region. Several of these jurisdictions, such as the exclusive economic zone, archipelagic waters, and "the area" (figure 4.1) are new. Broadly speaking there is more restriction for essentially all uses of the ocean as one moves from the open ocean toward the coast; for science from essentially complete freedom on the high seas to absolute coastal state jurisdiction over foreign research in a coastal nation's internal waters.[6]

The treaty itself does not define the term marine scientific research; it does, however, say that "marine scientific research shall be conducted exclusively for peaceful purposes;. . . shall be conducted with appropriate scientific methods . . . , [and] shall not unjustifiably interfere with other legitimate uses of the sea" (article 240). A further comment is that coastal states "shall endeavour to adopt reasonable rules, regulations and procedures to promote and facilitate marine scientific research . . . beyond their territorial sea and to facilitate . . . access to

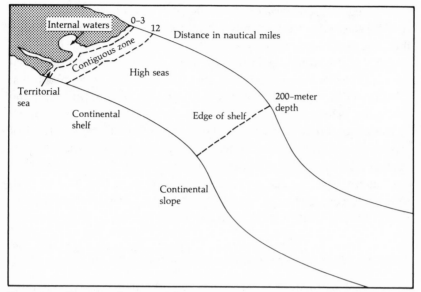

Figure 4.1. The major divisions of the ocean under the various 1958 conventions.

their harbours and promote assistance for marine scientific research vessels" (article 255). It also says that "states and competent international organizations shall promote and facilitate the development and conduct of marine scientific research in accordance with this Convention" (article 239). As positive as these articles may seem, all except 240 are nonbinding. What follows is a brief discussion of scientific conditions within each juridical region.[7]

Internal Waters

Internal waters include rivers, bays, lakes, and other marine areas landward of the base line from which the territorial sea is delineated. Within internal waters the coastal state exercises complete jurisdiction over who shall enter and conduct marine scientific research and under what conditions. These rules are similar to those in the 1958 convention on the territorial sea and contiguous zone.

Territorial Sea

The treaty establishes a territorial sea of up to 12 nautical miles in width. Within the territorial sea the coastal state has "the exclusive right to regulate, authorize and conduct marine scientific research, . . . [which] shall be conducted only with the express consent of and under the conditions set forth by the coastal State" (article 245). These provisions are also similar to those of the 1958 Convention on the Territorial Sea and the Contiguous Zone; a new aspect is the clear definition of a 12-mile width to the territorial sea. The treaty does not mention the mechanisms to get permission for research in a country's territorial sea or the conditions that a coastal state can impose. There is a right of innocent passage through the territorial seas; however, article 19, paragraph 2(j), eliminates "the carrying out of research or survey activities" as an accepted activity under innocent passage. On a positive side those countries signing the treaty will be restricted to no more than a 12-mile width for their territorial sea.

Straits Used for International Navigation

The establishment of 12-nautical-mile-wide territorial seas will have an important effect on 116 straits that are more than 6 but less than 24 miles wide, and that now will be included within the territorial seas of the adjacent states.[8] Examples include Bab el Mandeb (Red Sea) and the Strait of Gibraltar. Article 40 states that "foreign ships, including marine scientific research and hydrographic survey ships, may not carry out any research or survey activities without prior authorization of the States bordering straits." This, in effect, means that international straits less than 24 miles wide will be treated as territorial seas, as far as marine scientific research is concerned.

Archipelagic Waters

Several treaty articles will allow archipelagic states to define base lines for archipelagic waters, although the actual extent of these waters is not clear. An archipelagic state is one formed by one or more archipelagos, such as Indonesia and the Philippines; Hawaii and the Galapagos Islands are not candidates. An archipelagic state can exercise a similar jurisdiction over marine scientific research in its archipelagic waters as it does over such research in its territorial sea, i.e., essentially complete control.

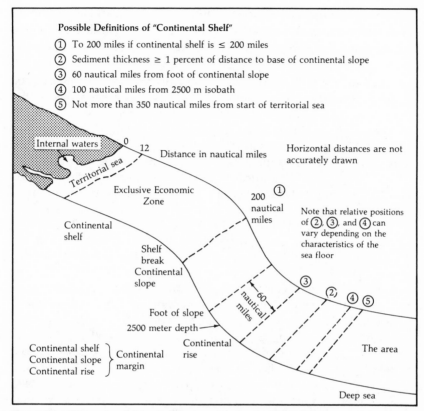

Possible Definitions of "Continental Shelf"

① To 200 miles if continental shelf is ≤ 200 miles
② Sediment thickness ≥ 1 percent of distance to base of continental slope
③ 60 nautical miles from foot of continental slope
④ 100 nautical miles from 2500 m isobath
⑤ Not more than 350 nautical miles from start of territorial sea

Internal waters
Territorial sea
0   12   Distance in nautical miles
Horizontal distances are not accurately drawn

Exclusive Economic Zone
Continental shelf
Shelf break
Continental slope
Foot of slope
2500 meter depth
Continental rise
Continental shelf ⎫
Continental slope ⎬ Continental margin
Continental rise ⎭

200 nautical miles ①
Note that relative positions of ②, ③, and ④ can vary depending on the characteristics of the sea floor
60 nautical miles
③   ②   ④ ⑤
The area
Deep sea

Figure 4.2. The major divisions of the ocean under the UNCLOS III treaty. The numbers in (b) refer to possible definitions of the continental shelf: 1) to 200 miles if the continental shelf is < 200 miles; 2) sediment thickness ≥ 1 percent of the distance to the foot of the continental slope; 3) 60 nautical miles from the foot of the continental slope; 4) 100 nautical miles from the 2500–meter isobath; and 5) not more than 350 nautical miles from the inner boundary of the territorial sea. Note that the relative position of 2, 3, and 4 can vary depending on the characteristics of the sea floor. (Horizontal distances are not accurately drawn.)

Exclusive Economic Zone

The exclusive economic zone is a new concept, it extends 200 nautical miles (370 kilometers) from the baseline from which the territorial sea is measured (figure 4.2). As such it includes all of the world's coastal waters and most of the geological continental shelves. The treaty, however, does not seem to apply to the Antarctic continent. Requirements for marine scientific research in a foreign country's exclusive economic zone (or on the continental shelf within its zone) include consent and an imposing set of requirements. There are six important conditions.

1. Consent is necessary and shall "in normal circumstances" be granted (article 246, paragraph 3). Consent can be denied if the project (i) "is of direct significance for the exploration and exploitation of natural resources, whether living or non-living"; (ii) "involves drilling into the continental shelf, the use of explosives or the introduction of harmful substances into the marine environment"; (iii) "involves the construction, operation or use of artificial islands . . . ;" or (iv) if the request of consent contains inaccurate information "or if the researching State or competent international organization has outstanding obligations to the coastal State from a prior research project" (article 246, paragraph 5). A coastal state's decision based on these four provisions is not reviewable by a third party (article 297, paragraph 2).

2. Specific information concerning the research must be supplied not less than 6 months before the start of the project. Research states or international organizations must provide descriptions of (i) "the nature and objectives of the project"; (ii) "the method and means to be used, including name, tonnage, type and class of vessels and a description of scientific equipment"; (iii) "the precise geographical areas in which the project is to be conducted"; (iv) "the expected date of first appearance and final departure of the research vessels, or deployment of the equipment and its removal, as appropriate"; (v) "the name of the sponsoring institution, its director, and the person in charge of the project"; and (vi) "the extent to which it is considered that the coastal state should be able to participate or to be represented in the project" (article 248).

3. Applicants for consent to conduct research must (i) "ensure the right of the coastal state, if it so desires, to participate or be represented in the marine scientific research project, especially on board research vessels. . . ;" (ii) provide preliminary and final reports, if the coastal state so requests; (iii) provide access for the coastal state to all data and samples for the project and "furnish it with data which may be copied and samples which may be divided without detriment to their scientific value"; (iv) provide, if requested, "an assessment of such data, samples and research results or provide assistance in their assessment or interpretation"; (v) ensure "that research results are made internationally available through appropriate national or international channels"; and (vi) "inform the

coastal state immediately of any major change in the research programme" (article 249).

4. "Communications concerning the marine scientific research
projects shall be made through appropriate official channels unless
otherwise agreed" (article 250). These official channels will probably
be foreign ministries or in the case of the United States its Department of State. The requirement of using "official channels" will
lessen the role of a scientist-to-scientist contact that so often has
been successful in developing projects. On the positive side, using
official channels should reduce ambiguity concerning responsibility
for granting the permission, an item which has caused troubles in
the past.

5. Coastal states can suspend research activities (i) if they are "not
being conducted in accordance with the information communi-
cated" (that is, the information requested in article 248), or if the
conditions specified in article 249 are not met; or (ii) if there is a
major change in the research project or activities (article 253). Coastal
states can stop the marine scientific research activities if such problems or changes "are not rectified within a reasonable period of
time" (article 253).

6. After permission to conduct research is granted, "land-locked
and geographically disadvantaged states" can request to receive the
information provided under articles 248 and 249. Land-locked or
geographically disadvantaged states may also participate when feasible in the project through qualified experts, although the coastal
state can object to their choice of experts (article 254). The potential
for a three-party conflict could be high, especially concerning states
having poor relationships (Pakistan and Afghanistan, for example).

The net effect of these and other conditions fall into three broad
categories. First and perhaps most important, concerns the *predictability*
of whether the actual expedition occurs and if the program will be
modified or changed during the sea-going part or afterwards. Without
adequate predictability scientists could well tend to avoid areas or
regions where expectations of success are relatively low. The second
concern is that of *flexibility* in the actual research. Quite often discoveries are made at sea that should be followed up. However, these may
require changes in the ship's course or in the research protocol. In
some instances these may require permission which, in turn, will
require time and delay perhaps leading to lost or missed scientific
opportunities. The last concern is that of the increasing *politicalization*

of the ocean. Decisions concerning scientific access may often be made on a political basis rather than on its scientific merits. Soviet scientists have indicated up to 100 refusals of entry to foreign parts in the past year and similar, though less frequent, refusals have been received by U.S. scientists.

Continental Shelf Beyond 200 Miles

The juridical continental shelf has a complex, essentially nonscientific definition (figure 4.2), and its outer edge occasionally may correspond to the outer part of the geological continental margin. In the treaty the juridical continental shelf can extend to at least 200 nautical miles or to the edge of the exclusive economic zone. When the continental shelf falls entirely within the exclusive economic zone the rules for marine scientific research are the same. Considerable confusion can (and will) occur in defining the outer edge of the juridical continental shelf when the continental margin (shelf, slope, and rise in the geological sense) extends beyond 200 nautical miles. The outer edge can be defined "by the foot" (a very poorly defined term) "of the continental slope" or the thickness of the sedimentary rocks (how this thickness is determined is not stated) (article 76, paragraph 4); in any case, the outer edge of the shelf shall not exceed 350 nautical miles from the territorial sea base line or 100 nautical miles from the 2500-meter isobath (article 76, paragraph 5) unless a plateau, rise, cap, bank, or spur extends beyond 350 miles (article 76, paragraph 6). The actual extent of the continental shelf beyond 200 miles cannot be determined at this time, but some estimates put it as high as 8 to 10 percent of the ocean.[9] The provision concerning sediment thickness is bound to cause confusion and allow for excessive claims.

The conditions for marine scientific research on the continental shelf beyond 200 nautical miles are the same as described for the exclusive economic zone *except* that a coastal state may withhold consent *only* in areas it has publicly designated as subject to exploitation or detailed exploratory operations within a reasonable period of time (article 246, paragraph 6). Scientific studies in the water column above the continental shelf and beyond the limits of the exclusive economic zone are not considered marine research on the continental shelf, and conditions are similar to the high seas.

"The Area"

The seabed beyond coastal state jurisdiction (that is, beyond the continental shelf when it extends past the EEZ) is defined as "the area." At present the treaty has no significant restrictions concerning marine scientific research in "the area" and "States' parties may carry out marine scientific research in the area" (articles 87, 143, and 256). The treaty also says that states "shall promote international cooperation in marine scientific research" (article 143). A Deep Seabed Authority will be established by the treaty and it may carry out research either directly or through contract and is charged with promoting and encouraging marine research as well as disseminating scientific knowledge.

High Seas

Freedom of scientific research is one of six "freedoms" explicitly listed for the high seas (article 87). High seas are defined as that part of the ocean water column that excludes internal waters, territorial seas, archipelagic waters, and exclusive economic zones. It should be mentioned that freedom of research was not an explicit freedom of the seas in the 1958 Convention on the High Seas.

Other Aspects of UNCLOS III

The treaty introduced a new concept whereby consent is *implied*, and a researching state or competent international organization could start a research program six months after submitting a request, if the coastal state has not denied consent within four months after receiving the request and the information specified in articles 248 and 249. It should be appreciated, however, that the coastal state could just ask for additional information within the four months after receiving the request and effectively postpone a decision by restarting the clock for the four month period. In addition, it is not clear if implied consent is applicable to nonratifiers of the treaty.

Publication of scientific results can be an important issue. Although the treaty in one place encourages publication and the flow of scientific data (article 244, paragraphs 1 and 2), elsewhere (article 249 paragraph 2), it requires "prior agreement for making internationally available the research results of a project of direct significance for the exploration and exploitation of natural resources." If, therefore, a coastal state concludes that the research program for which it already approved is "of direct significance for the exploration and exploitation of natural resources, whether living or non-living" (article 246, paragraph 5a), it can then control or prohibit publication of such results.

The treaty does offer specific mechanisms for the compulsory settlement of disputes, although there are three important exceptions for marine scientific research problems. Dispute settlement, in any case, will be of more importance for lawyers than scientists who generally do not have the will, desire, time or resources to pursue disputes through the courts. In addition, for a project to be successful the goodwill of both the research and foreign state is required. Therefore, pursuing or even initiating a dispute will not auger well for a cooperative scientific venture. The three exceptions to dispute settlement are the right of the coastal state to withhold consent for marine scientific research in the exclusive economic zone, on the continental shelf beyond 200 miles, and to order suspension or cessation of such research. In other words, those parts of the treaty that are most likely to generate disagreement are not subject to compulsory dispute settlement. One might hope, however, that the specter of dispute settlement possibilities could minimize arbitrary or capricious actions by coastal states and that for those instances where there are honest differences of opinion the dispute settlement provisions could eventually provide some interpretative flesh to what are often ambiguously worded articles.

An indirect issue for marine science is military activities in the ocean. A key LOS point for countries with powerful navies was passage through and over international straits and archipelagic waters. Military ships in normal operations often make routine oceanographic measurements. However, it is not clear how such activities will be considered within the treaty. Warships are defined (article 29) as, among other things, being "manned by a crew which is under regular armed forces discipline." Military ships (as well as other ships) may transit territorial seas and archipelagic waters under innocent passage. However, "research and survey activities" are not considered as part of innocent passage (article 19, paragraph 2J). It also appears that warships will be free to collect some oceanographic data from foreign EEZs whereas nonmilitary research vessels (or military vessels with civilians) will require permission.

Implications of the LOS Treaty for Marine Scientists

In my opinion there are two critical negative things that can result from the above-mentioned and other conditions in the treaty. The first concerns the *unpredictability* as to whether permission will actually or eventually be granted. This, of course, will cause problems in ship-scheduling (usually at least one year of lead time is required) and in the consideration and evaluation of grant or requests for funding the program. One mechanism that could reduce this unpredictability is the so-called "implied consent" article (article 252). Its principal point, as previously mentioned, is that if a coastal state does not respond to a permission request within four months, then a research organization may proceed with the work six months after the date that the initial request was made. However, it is dubious that this rule would be officially tested by an institution director (or even a ship captain) who would have to be willing to risk seizure of a research vessel without some very strong assurances and support from his or her government. The treaty also offers a coastal state, if it wishes (either innocently or maliciously), to continuously delay an official response to a permission request, by asking for additional information; in effect, denying the research without actually officially doing so. It should be noted that denial of permission for marine scientific research or delaying the permission process is a relatively painless act, often with little or no political consequences for the foreign country.

The possibility of foreign states denying or delaying scientific permission may be more serious than anticipated since there seems to be increasing nationalistic feelings by foreign countries toward their offshore ocean areas and their real or imagined resources. An indication of this is that several countries have recently implemented restrictions against passage of military vessels in their territorial sea without giving prior notice or getting permission—conditions contrary to the treaty. Whether these nationalistic actions are just posturing due to LOS negotiations or whether they are long-term effects remains to be seen. The second critical negative thing that could affect marine science, concerns the *spontaneity* of the research. Consent requires six months advance notificaton and relatively precise plans concerning the actual program before permission is granted. The opportunity to change the research protocol is thus very limited. This, in turn, could limit a rapid response to a major oceanographic event or opportunity (El Niño, for example) as well as changes at sea based on acquired data. A third issue, concerning publication, has been discussed on previous pages.

On the positive side, having a specific set of marine science articles is probably better than the other principle scenario, which is, each coastal country having specific (and different) rules and regulations in their waters, as many countries presently do. The treaty articles, although difficult, are at least consistent and probably will make it easier for governments and institutions to deal with their counterparts elsewhere. For U.S. scientists or others from countries who have not ratified the treaty it is not clear if they will have the few benefits and protection in the treaty.[10]

Implications of the LOS Treaty for Less Developed States

It is evident that expertise in marine scientific research is available to only a few developed countries. It is an expensive science requiring highly trained scientists, research vessels, support personnel and laboratory facilities. Expertise is generally needed in several fields, including biological oceanography, chemical oceanography, marine geology, marine geophysics, physical oceanography, and ocean engineering. Experienced electronic technicians are required to maintain even elementary equipment. The seagoing operation requires additional skills and experience as well as specifically designed and equipped ships. Many countries have bought equipment and ships well beyond their needs and their ability to maintain them. If marine resource questions are high on a country's priorities the skills of lawyers, economists, and other types of scientists will also be required.

It is often not a simple matter for a developing country to allow scientists from a developed state access to its waters for research, especially if the research can affect its marine resource development. The technological and economic differences between the countries may often cause suspicions even with the best intentions. In addition there are other factors including pride and concern about how the information will or could be used. One of the motivations of UNCLOS III was to reduce the marine differences between states. An earlier agreement, the 1974 UN Charter of Economic Rights and Duties of States, also considered a similar point, i.e., that states should benefit from science and technology regardless of their level of development.[11] Resource development, its study and protection are very common themes in UNCLOS III. The granting of control to the coastal state over the marine resources in its waters should alleviate much of its concern as to being exploited by marine research by a foreign state. In addition the coastal state will have opportunity to fully participate in the research and share the data. These rights, however, can be of limited value if the coastal state does not have sufficient expertise to use these opportunities. Likewise, it is often the developed state that will pose the research questions, and it is not clear as to how much the coastal state may intervene in the research project so as to make the program more in line with its needs and interests.[12]

The question of publication can be a two-sided issue for the coastal state. The wide dissemination of some information, especially concerning resources, might not be in the best interests of a coastal state. Alternatively basic scientific information might not be reported in an adequate manner for use by the coastal state (for example, published in a different language, or not a full assessment or presentation of all data).

General Comments

The marine science articles in the LOS treaty will clearly affect the style and operation of marine scientific research in and by many countries. It will require changes in the approach of scientists, institutions, and funding organizations for work in foreign waters. A considerable amount of additional planning will be necessary prior to the actual development of a program and the request for funding, and this could discourage some researchers. On the other hand, successful planning could make for a much more congenial and scientifically successful program. It is easy to come up with pessimistic viewpoints toward the treaty. However, one might hope, that the numerous requirements in the treaty may, in the long term, just be administrative tasks and the details of the treaty could be very beneficial in reducing misunderstandings.

An additional outcome of the treaty may be an increase in the development of bilateral or multinational programs. The treaty itself (article 243) strongly encourages the development of bilateral or multilateral agreements "to create favorable conditions for the conduct of marine scientific research." Cooperative science and technology agreements between states is not an uncommon practice, however this has not been fully exploited in the marine sciences.

The role of many intergovernmental organizations, at least from a developed country viewpoint, has often been less than successful in marine science ventures. The major marine organization is the Intergovernmental Oceanographic Commission (IOC), which is part of UNESCO. The LOS treaty has a specific article (article 247) concerning international organizations, that describes a new mechanism for obtaining permission for research in foreign waters. Unfortunately, in the case of IOC it has become more political in orientation in recent years than scientific and this trend may well continue. The United States, at the time of this writing, has withdrawn from UNESCO, however, this action does not have to affect participation in IOC. Development of programs within international forums and organizations can be a successful mechanism for scientific research but will require considerable time and involvement.

Future Opportunities

There is an important underlying aspect of the LOS treaty that may help to ultimately overcome many of its potential negative marine science aspects. Simply said, many, if not all, coastal countries are going to be, or already are anxious to ascertain and exploit their marine potential. This, especially with developing countries, will mean that they will turn to developed countries for help in marine science and policy questions. It is in the interest of the developed and developing world, and of marine science in general, to see a rational development of marine science capabilities and resource development. Unfortunately, however, there can be considerable potential for disappointment, especially among developing countries since the distribution of ocean resources and ocean space will be quite unequitable and only a few countries, mostly developed, will receive the major portion of the world's EEZs. Landlocked states (over 30 of them) will not even have an offshore zone. Most marine resources occur either within the EEZ or the continental shelf (legal sense). Essentially upwards of 90 percent of all present fish catch and most, if not all, oil and gas resources will fall in these regions. A "backlash" toward the countries who will receive most of these benefits may result. The manganese nodule "treasure" of the deep sea will never become a major resource.

Nevertheless there clearly is an obvious need to develop good working cooperative marine science efforts between developed and developing countries. The style of how these programs eventually occur will obviously vary within different countries and organizations. Regarding this I will talk mainly from the viewpoint of the United States, where in spite of the apparent need for cooperative efforts there exists no single contact point for foreign interests that can represent the complete spectrum of U.S. marine interests and activities. Various government agencies may have international marine offices, in particular the National Oceanic and Atmospheric Administration, the National Science Foundation, the Department of State and, in addition, several oceanographic institutions have active international operations. However, for a foreign country or scientist their visibility is often limited and these offices generally serve, and correctly so, just the organizations they represent. A foreign country looking for a cooperative program with U.S. scientists could find this array of organizations a labyrinth.

The U.S. marine community has developed extensive expertise in programs that would be especially valuable for developing countries. For example, specific coastal zone management programs have been developed by NOAA's Coastal Zone Management Office; marine resource expertise has been developed through Sea Grant and U.S. industry; and basic scientific and marine policy skills have been produced by academia and others. The question is then, within the United States, are we most sufficiently and successfully making our skills and abilities available for foreign cooperative ventures? My personal feeling is that although the United States has several outstanding programs with individual institutions in foreign countries, we could be doing better and to do better would lead to increased scientific research opportunities and other benefits to the U.S. marine community, the nation in general, and to other countries. In this regard, I propose that the United States establish an Office of International Marine Science Cooperation that could be a focal point for foreign contacts seeking to develop cooperative programs with the U.S. marine scientific community and vice versa. Such an office could be located within the federal government, at an oceanographic institution, or at a neutral site such as the National Academy of Sciences (see reference 12 for further discussion of relative benefits of each possibility). Such a concept could also be adopted on an international scale, for example, by the Scientific Committee on Oceanic Research (SCOR) within the International Council of Unions, IOC or some similar UN body; this concept could also be of interest to other developed countries. For this reason I will elucidate further on this concept.[13] The main objectives of such an office (remember I am using the United States as an example) would be as follows:

—To improve opportunities and efficiencies for those in the U.S. marine community wishing to work with foreign countries (and in foreign waters)
—To improve access for foreign countries and institutions to marine scientific research and training opportunities with U.S. organizations
—To collect and circulate information to the U.S. marine scientific community concerning opportunities, mechanisms and funding sources for foreign programs
—To identify problem countries or areas for the U.S. marine community and advise on mechanisms for dealing with such problems (in particular, from scientific experience in such countries)
—To identify potential U.S. scientists interested in working in specific foreign countries
—To assist in the development of multidisciplinary teams
—To serve as a spokesperson for the U.S. marine scientific interests in working with foreign countries.

One of the rationales for recommending an Office for International Marine Science Cooperation is a 1981 Ocean Policy Committee study, conducted by its marine technical assistance group,[14] that made an assessment of U.S. capabilities to fulfill the needs of developing countries as well as providing recommendations, policies, and mechanisms for future U.S. programs in marine technical assistance and cooperation. A workshop was held in La Jolla, California, involving approximately 60 participants including 20 representatives from developing countries. A key recommendation of that meeting was that an office be established as a central point of contact for U.S. or foreign investigators seeking information on U.S. support for marine-related projects. The meeting also recommended that economists and social scientists be involved in planning, management, and evaluation of marine-related projects to ensure adequate consideration of the socio-political and economic framework of the host country. This is an important point often neglected by developing countries in the establishment of cooperative programs.

In summary the LOS treaty problems facing marine scientists may be even more complex than the research they are trying to perform. It may be no less easy for developing countries. Close cooperation through cooperative programs may offer the opportunity for both to meet their objectives.

NOTES

1. J. A. Knauss, "Marine Technology Drives Marine Policy," *Proceedings OCEANS* (1983), 3:1128–1132—a compelling paper on how the U.S. response to the ocean is influenced by technology rather than by an orderly development of ocean policy.

2. L. M. Alexander, "The Disadvantaged States in the Law of the Sea," *Marine Policy* (1981), 5:196.

3. Third United Nations Conference on the Law of the Sea, Draft Convention on the Law of the Sea (U.N. Document A/Conf. 62/L-78/Rev., August 3, 1981).

4. W. S. Scholz, *Marine Policy* (1980), 4:91; Ocean Policy Committee, *Science* (1977), 197:230.

5. E. Miles, "United States Distant-Water Oceanography in the New Ocean Regime," in P. G. Brewer, ed., *Oceanography: The Present and Future* (Woods Hole, Mass.: Springer, 1983), pp. 283–301.

6. See D. A. Ross and J. A. Knauss, "How the Law of the Sea Treaty Will Affect U.S. Marine Science," *Science* (1982), 217:1003–1008.

7. Much of the following material comes from Ross and Knauss.

8. U.S. Department of State, *Bulletin* 70:389, Washington, D.C.: GPO, 1974.

9. L. Alexander, personal communication.

10. Although the United States has not accepted the LOS treaty, President Reagan, in his March 1983 statement, did acknowledge the right of other countries to exercise jurisdiction over marine research in their EEZs (if exercised reasonably and in a manner consistent with international law). He did

not, at the present time, exercise jurisdiction by the United States over marine scientific research in its own EEZ.

11. Charter of the Economic Rights and Duties of States Adopted by Resolution 3281 (XXIX) of the General Assembly of the United Nations, December 12, 1974.

12. Maria Edwarda Gonsalves, "Science, Technology, and the New Convention of the Law of the Sea," *Impact of Science on Society* (1983), 3(4):344–347.

13. D. A. Ross, "Effective Use of the Sea, Overcoming the Law of the Sea Problems," *Proceedings OCEANS* (1983), 1:1–3.

14. Ocean Policy Committee, *International Cooperation in Marine Technology, Science and Fisheries: The Future U.S. Role in Development.* Proceedings of a Workshop, January 18–22, 1981, Scripps Institution on Oceanography, La Jolla, Calif. (Washington, D.C.: National Academy Press, 1981).

5.
Minerals of the Deep Sea
Myth and Reality

MARNE A. DUBS

ON JULY 9, 1982, the President of the United States announced that the United States would not sign the United Nations treaty on the Law of the Sea that was adopted on April 30 of that year. The President stated that most provisions of the treaty were acceptable to the United States, but those governing the exploration and exploitation of the deep-seabed precluded signing the treaty. This wrote *finis* to a struggle, lasting more than fifteen years, by the United States to negotiate a Law of the Sea treaty with provisions governing the exploitation of the minerals of the deep-seabed that would be satisfactory to the United States and its free enterprise system.

It was early apparent that most of the world, including the Soviet Union and many of the industrialized nations, would sign the treaty. Nevertheless, a treaty without the participation of the United States would be far short of the mark of a realistically universal treaty. It only remained to be seen whether any of the allies of the United States would similarly refuse to sign. In late 1984, the Federal Republic of Germany and the United Kingdom, two of the United States' closest allies, also announced that they would not sign the Law of the Sea Convention. Nevertheless, most of the Western industrialized nations found the treaty satisfactory enough to sign it and to take the next step of trying to develop workable details in the Preparatory Commission.

In contrast, as of late 1984, there were 159 signatories to the convention, including other industrialized nations (France, Japan, Italy, Belgium, and the European Economic Community) and the other superpower, the Soviet Union. The Preparatory Commission created under the treaty agreement had already met several times and was making progress in the same snail-paced fashion experienced during the Law of the Sea negotiations, but this was to be expected with the whole world trying to decide these matters by consensus. As of December 9, 1984 the Law of the Sea Preparatory Commission had also received, in accordance with conditions established in the resolutions adopted simultaneously with the treaty and elaborated by the Commission, applications from pioneer investors in seabed mining from France, India, Japan, and the Soviet Union.

The United States meanwhile had issued a license in accordance with its national legislation to each of the four ocean mining consortia operating from the United States (OMA, OMI, OMCO, and KCON).[1] The Federal Republic of Germany issued a license to OMI for a separate site as did the United Kingdom to KCON for yet another separate site. In addition, a number of the industrialized nations, including the United States, France, Japan, the United Kingdom, and the Federal Republic of Germany, signed a "Provisional Understanding" on August 3, 1984, to avoid mine site conflicts in the issuance of national authorizations to explore and exploit the deep seabed.

By the end of 1983 and prior to the issuance of licenses and the "Provisional Understanding," the conflicts among the entities from the above industrialized countries had been settled under the auspices of a private arbitration agreement. This agreement established the ground rules for settling conflicts and provided for negotiations prior to resort to binding arbitration. This conflict settlement was duly recorded by the arbitrators and is the settlement enshrined by the "Provisional Understanding."

Thus there now exist, *ipso facto*, two legal systems purporting to have authority over the exploration and exploitation of the resources of the deep seabed in the area beyond national jurisdiction. These systems are loosely linked by the "Provisional Understanding," with two parties, namely France and Japan, having a foot in both systems. The system championed by the United States, the United Kingdom, and the Federal Republic of Germany is based on the doctrine of the freedom of the high seas. The other, championed by 159 other nations of the world, is based on what they hope is a "universal" Law of the Sea treaty. These systems have not yet come into open conflict, but could be expected to do so whenever there might arise conflicting claims for exploration and exploitation rights under the two systems that have not already been resolved by the "Provisional Understanding" or if other nations should challenge the right of the United States and its two like-minded allies to operate outside of the treaty. Both of these possibilities appear probable—particularly overlapping claims involving the Soviet Union and one or more participants in the "Provisional Understanding." Thus, the legal aspects of deep-seabed mining could fairly be said to reflect some degree of uncertainty on a global basis. Conflict appears certain to arise, but the present business conditions for the metal mining industry are so poor that real conflict may not arise until some future date when the resources of the deep-seabed are economically viable and are needed by consumers.

Turning from the legal/political to the technical/economic aspects, one similarly finds uncertainty and less than an optimistic outlook for the early exploitation of the resources of the deep seabed. The principal commodities expected to be produced by the exploitation of the manganese nodules, which are the only known potentially exploitable resource of the deep-seabed, are nickel and copper along with by-product cobalt and possibly manganese. It is essential that all nickel and copper be sold at attractive prices if any commercial project is to be economically viable. Attractive prices would, at a minimum, be those which could justify the expansion of capacity of land-based mines for the production of these same metals, prices only likely to be realized when new capacity is in fact needed in the marketplace.

The marketplace today not only does not need any new capacity but in fact is not able to utilize the capacity which exists. The result is that prices are depressed to an historic low for most of the subject metals, production has had to be decreased, and many producers have incurred large operating losses or at best sharply lowered profits. In the United States the situation has been so disastrous that the publication, *Business Week*, published a featured article in its December 17, 1984, edition entitled, "The Death of Mining." One forecaster, quoted in this article, stated that he believed copper prices will likely languish near present levels over the next few years and will be less than $0.90 per pound for the rest of this century. Furthermore he also expected nickel prices to stagnate well into the 1990s. The *Business Week* article also showed that the return on equity for the ten leading independent U.S./ Canadian metals mining companies (which does not include major mining operations such as Kennecott and Anaconda, which are wholly owned subsidiaries of oil companies) has fallen from a positive 18 percent in 1979 to a negative 8 percent, a collective loss of three-fourths of a billion dollars, in 1983. The disillusionment with mining is further emphasized by the action late in 1984 by Arco to sell off Anaconda, taking a large write-off in the process, and the action in early 1985 by Amoco to spin off its mineral businesses to its stockholders in a tax-free transaction. The name of the game in mining is now survival; long-range planning is how to balance cash outflow by selling assets and borrowing. Commercial interest in exploiting seabed resources is close to its nadir.

What then is myth and what then is reality in this world of the deep-seabed minerals? This introduction should have already indicated to the reader a number of areas where there are significant discrepancies between the cold hard facts of reality and the fanciful myths woven by optimistic entrepreneurial innovators, by political and diplomatic protagonists of all persuasions, by those seeking to tap new sources of wealth, and by those fearful of the economic effects of new sources of minerals. Unfortunately it is myth that has largely governed the efforts to develop the Law of the Sea for the exploration and exploitation of the mineral resources of the deep-seabed. This essay will not attempt to provide a comprehensive history, but will, primarily, try to separate myth and reality and point up the major unresolved issues.

This discussion of the principal issues concerning the minerals of the deep-seabed is organized under the following major topics:

Mineral resources
Technology for exploitation
Ocean mining ventures
Law of the Sea treaty
Mine site conflict

None of these topical areas are completely free of myth or distorted reality. The technical/economic area is characterized by many false expectations. The legal/political area is characterized by conflict arising from differences in political and economic ideology and emphasized by false expectations for ocean mining. In this essay, these five topics are taken up in turn, followed by summary conclusions on the outlook for the legal regime for the minerals of the deep-seabed.

Mineral Resources

The only mineral of widely recognized potential economic consequence found in the deep seabed today is the manganese nodule, also called the polymetallic nodule. There has also been much recent discussion of polymetallic sulfide deposits which occur at some ocean floor spreading centers, some of which are within the 200 mile zones of coastal states, but these deposits do not seem likely to be of any great importance in deep-seabed considerations.

Manganese nodules were discovered over a hundred years ago by a British scientific expedition (Challenger Expedition), but it was not until the early 1960s that the nodules attracted the attention of the mineral explorationists in mining companies. This attention was the result of the increased flow of interesting data from an expanding American oceanographic scientific effort and from rapidly expanding technological developments related to offshore petroleum exploration and production. These new data gave greater credence to the existence of mineral deposits of potential interest and to the possibility of economically exploiting them.

Manganese nodules occur on the floors of the deep basins of all the world's oceans, where the water is deep—12,000 to 20,000 feet deep—and the rate of sedimentation is low. They are almost always spread out in a single layer and half-buried in the oozy mud of the seabed. There is a wide range of shapes and sizes for the nodules, but they can be generally thought of as potato-sized. The chemical composition of nodules varies widely, but they will all contain manganese and iron oxides with the incorporation of various quantities of diluent deep-sea clays. The nodules do not contain sulfur and are at best weakly crystalline; this has important consequences for their processing.

The nodules of potential economic interest are rich in nickel, copper, and cobalt as well as manganese. Those of clear, first generation, commercial interest will contain about 30 percent manganese, 1.4 percent nickel, 1.2 percent copper, and 0.25 percent to 0.3 percent cobalt. This combined nickel and copper analysis of 2.6 percent is considered a very attractive metallic content. However, there is a wide variation of metallic content, and deposits are known with almost every conceivable chemical analysis.

A group of experts, assembled under the auspices of the Ocean Economics and Technology Office of the Department of Economic and Social Affairs of the United Nations, attempted to estimate the potential reserves and the resources in nodules.[2] One participant estimated the potential reserves of dry nodules having a combined copper and nickel content of 2.29 percent at 23,000 million tons and estimated the resources having a combined content of 1.5 percent at 175,000 million tons. Potential reserves were defined as being economically mineable if technology then being developed was successfully realized. Resources were defined as deposits that were likely to be economically mineable at some future date. These are very large quantities, indeed, and represent the largest by far untapped mineral resource on the face of the globe.

There have been many other estimates of the size of the nodule deposits of potential commercial interest and almost everyone who has made an estimate is ready to defend his or her estimate and to try to demonstrate that the other estimates are wrong. It is not my intent to enter that argument, because arguing that point is the path to the obfuscations of the past that have caused significant problems in the search for a universally accepted legal regime for the deep seabed. The concerns alternated between extremes: one view being that potential mine sites were so scarce that few could participate in mining and another view being that the resource was so rich and abundant that land-based mining would be displaced. Both views are believed to be far from the truth. The various estimates have most often been expressed in terms of the number of mine sites potentially available to support a mining operation for twenty years at a production rate of 3 million dry tonnes per year of nodules. The range of estimates for the number of mine sites is from over 200 to as low as a half dozen. Actually the argument over the number of mine sites has been mainly political rather than practical. It has been more of an argument about establishing claims to resources, rather than an argument about the size of the resources themselves. By any standard the size of the resource is extremely large absolutely and also in comparison to land-based sources. The real question remains whether deep-seabed minerals can be recovered and processed into minerals at competitive costs. Since this has not been commercially demonstrated and is not likely to be in the near future, the quantity of reserves is theoretically and actually by standard mineral industry practice equal to zero. The quantity of production and the name of the producer and whether resources can be converted into reserves are the uncertain matters, not the size of the resource in-situ.

The most important things to keep in mind about nodule resources and reserves are: (1) the quantities of nodules resting on the seafloors of the world oceans are astronomically large; (2) only a fraction of these nodules are of sufficiently high grade to suggest that they can be economically mined at some future time—but this number is still very large compared with current reserves of the principal metals of interest;

(3) estimates of nodule resources and potential reserves are based on publically available data which is only a small part of actual existing data in private hands. However, the total data, public and private, is not yet even adequate to accurately characterize any single deposit quantitatively. Data to estimate total resources and potential reserves is absolutely and totally inadequate to the task; (4) nodules on the sea floor are not nodules in the hold of a ship. The biggest unknown of all is what portion of the in-situ nodules can be recovered, and estimates of recovery vary more widely than any other factor. Unfortunately, the actual recovery values are not apt to be determined with high confidence until commercial mining is under way and significant progress down the real technological learning curve has been achieved. Furthermore, all estimates of recovery efficiency by potential ocean miners are very conservative because of the concern for obtaining an adequate mine site size, with no estimate being greater than about 30 percent and many being 10 percent or less. It is noted that much higher recovery efficiencies are theoretically possible, but are unlikely to be achieved until considerable operating experience is realized and systems and equipment are modified to reflect that experience.

It might be thought that some indication of the size of potentially mineable nodule areas could be obtained by looking at available data related to pioneer miners. However, the size and number of mine sites sought by miners were dictated by various business strategies and aspirations as well as by the evaluation of the resource itself. The standard unofficially established for a mine site size was the size negotiated for Resolution II, "Governing Preparatory Investment in Pioneer Activities Relating to Polymetallic Nodules," that was adopted by the Law of the Sea Conference. This should not be surprising since the content of Resolution II was largely determined, but not completely, by input of the industrialized countries and their pioneer miners.

Resolution II specifies that a pioneer area shall not exceed 150,000 square kilometers but also requires eventual relinquishment of 50 percent of that area, resulting in a final mine site size of 75,000 sq. kms. In order to provide for a reserved area under the treaty itself, an area twice that size, or 300,000 sq. kms., could be applied for. It is noted that the treaty provides for an exploration area size that is up to twice that for exploitation, which matches the relinquishment of 50 percent for the special rules for the pioneer investor; no size is specified for the mine site itself.

This Resolution II rationale carried over into applications for sites under domestic U.S. law and applicants limited each application to roughly 300,000 sq. kms. However there was no limit to the number of applications that could be filed. The United States has now issued licenses to its four applicants and we can see what is happening in practice. The issued U.S. licenses are all clustered one against the other in the Clarion/Clipperton region of the North Central Pacific Ocean (see figure 5.1). This is not a surprising location from the standpoint of U.S. entities expecting to process nodules in the United States, nor from the standpoint that basic scientific work on nodules by oceanographic institutions was carried out primarily in that area. This is also the area where the National Oceanic and Atmospheric Administration (NOAA) carried out its published basic environmental studies and where Deepsea Ventures early made a public claim of seabed-mining rights. There has thus been an open invitation to prospect in this prime area for at least a decade with constant reinforcement of its desirability. The official announcements of NOAA showed the following licensed area:

Ocean Minerals Company	165,533 sq. kms.
Kennecott Consortium	65,000
Ocean Management, Inc.	136,000
Ocean Mining Associates	156,000
Total	522,533 sq. kms.

The average mine site size is 130,633 sq. kms.

In addition, two of the consortia, Kennecott and Ocean Management, had license applications in the United Kingdom and West Germany believed to be at least as large as the same average area. Finally, it is known that the Japanese entity, DORD, and the French entity, AFERNOD,[3] were participants with the U.S. consortia in an "Agreement to Arbitrate" for settling any mine site application conflicts. The areas and the coordinates for DORD and AFERNOD have not yet been published. However, it is reasonable to assume that conflicts with the U.S. consortia did arise and were settled. This assumption is somewhat substantiated by the blanks in the map published by NOAA and by the geology of the region. It would also be reasonable to assume that any negotiated settlement would have resulted in an area of at least 130,000 sq. kms., and probably closer to 200,000 because of the necessity of providing for a reserved area under the treaty, both for DORD and AFERNOD.

If we assume 175,000 sq. kms. each for DORD and AFERNOD and add in the 260,000 for the second sites of Kennecott and Ocean Mangement, the total area for the six entities would add up to at least 1.15 million sq. kms. This area is clearly considered by these commercial experts as prime, first generation, mine site potential. This does not count the pioneer areas sought by the USSR and India. India's sites are undoubtedly in the Indian Ocean and are clearly in addition to those in the Clarion/Clipperton region. It is not known where the USSR sites are at this time, although it would not be surprising if they were located in the Clarion/Clipperton area along with the other pioneer nodule miners.

What is the implication of this 1.15 million sq. kms.? The evidence is that the six entities believe that this area would provide twelve mine sites (one for each entity and one for a reserved site or a cushion for the future), each capable of supplying 3 million metric tons per year of nodules for twenty or more years. If the average analysis of nickel were 1.26 percent and of copper 1.03 percent, and the average abundance (dry) of nodules on the sea floor were 10 kg per sq. meter, and if the average overall recovery efficiency were twenty percent—as one could expect based on the "UN Experts" discussed above—then we can derive the following concrete picture of the already surveyed nodule resource through the eyes of the essentially known pioneer investors in the Clarion/Clipperton region alone:

In-Situ Quantities	*Metric Tonnes (million)*	
Total tonnage of nodules (dry)	11,500	
Nickel content	145	
Copper content	118	
Recoverable Quantities @ 20% and 40%		
(Recovery efficiency)	(20%)	(40%)
Dry nodules	2,300	4,600
Nickel	29	58
Copper	24	48

These numbers are staggeringly large, particularly when it is realized that they apply to only a part of one region of the world's deep-seabed with nodule potential. To put the number in perspective, the expected total demand in 1985 is only about 1.25 billion pounds, which translates into 0.57 million metric tonnes. The nominal world nickel production capacity is currently about 1.6 billion pounds or 0.73 million metric tonnes. The rate of growth of nickel consumption over the past several years has been nonexistent on the trend line. The old expected growth values of 6 percent per annum are completely discredited and few would expect the growth in the next decade to be at more than 2 to 3 percent per year. At 2.5 percent per year the yearly production capacity increase required would be less than 30 million pounds or 0.014 million metric tonnes. Thus it must be concluded that just the first generation mine sites of the pioneer investors has so much recoverable nickel content that availability of the resource itself at "first generation quality" will not be a factor in the development of exploitation. What will be the prime factor is the economic competitiveness of the resource, particularly in the face of an overbuild in capacity, a slow growth rate and what could only be characterized today as "cutthroat" competition.

What now are the myths and the reality that can be extracted from this resource picture? The myth is that there might not be enough of the nodule resource to permit everyone who wants to and who is able to go into production. The reality is that, even without taking into account the ability of nodule resources to compete with land-based resources, there is more than enough first generation resource available to meet even the most wildly optimistic prediction of production from the seabed. The reality is whether anyone will produce from the seabed in the next three decades based on markets and competitive factors.

The whole matter of practical availability of seabed resources could be easily put to rest by requiring everyone seeking rights to seabed resources to go into full-scale production within five years of receiving the rights; there would be no takers today. No one is prepared to mine the seabed in the near future; the present strategy of those involved is to try to secure rights to seabed resources as a future option, if the cost of doing so is not too high.

This kind of resource problem is easily and directly handled by establishing diligence requirements with red teeth for resource development—namely the requirement to spend very significant money to bring the resource into production and to do so by a date certain, of the order of five to seven years. The result of this is that the seabed game would be quickly over and this important mineral resource would await new mineral economic times and fundamental changes in mineral economics.

The myth is that the nodules are so rich and abundant that land-based mining would be replaced by ocean mining. The reality is that no one has been rushing to put nodules into production because of weak markets and noncompetitive economics. However, the crusading entrepreneurs have most often and unfairly placed the blame for delaying ocean resource exploitation on Law of the Sea issues. The real problem today is economic, and the would-be ocean miner must face a new era of competition in the production of basic commodities. Ocean mining economics and risks will not permit ocean miners to consider entering the competition for many years to come. The land-based producers are quite, quite safe! All of the presently installed nickel and copper capacity will come back into production and a significant number of new mines will be put into production before nodule mining will come into its own. The one possible exception to that prediction is heavily government subsidized operations based on national security considerations rather than economics.

In terse summary—the seabed resource is there in munificent abundance—but there are no miners who will exploit that resource in the next two to three decades. As the facts have developed since the first dreams of the nodule pioneers took shape, the markets have disappeared and the economics have soured along with low prices for metals and severe competition.

Technology for Exploitation

As shown above, the minerals are there in profusion on the floor of the deep ocean, but no one is yet ready to undertake their exploitation. What role does the availability of technology, the costs of developing this new resource, and the projected production costs play in the timing of exploitation of deep-seabed minerals? Is the commencement of commercial production delayed by Law of the Sea questions or is the fundamental delay, as stated above, the result of economic and technical factors? They all play a role, but the real determining factor is projected production costs. Not withstanding the role of economics, the availability of technology and the myths surrounding deep-seabed technology played a critical part in the Law of the Sea negotiations— both in the creation of demands for technology transfer by developing nations that ranged from the trivial to the absurd and in the extreme reaction, of equivalent absurdity, of the industrial states and their industry to those demands.

Where does seabed-mining technology stand and how available is it? At this point it would be possible to deluge the reader with pages of description and analyses of competing technologies and to speculate regarding the availability of these technologies. It is not my intent to so burden the reader, but rather to slough over the details and provide a summary of the real situation.

Perhaps the nature of the technology can best be understood by considering the actions of some of the pioneer nodule mining developers. All four of the U.S.-based consortia, with participants from all the major industrialized free market economy nations, arrived at roughly the same technological approach to mining itself. The major elements of the proposed mining systems consisted of a surface ship or other stable ocean platform, a steel pipeline going from the ship to the seafloor, a pumping system for raising the nodules suspended in seawater through the pipe, with the preferred pump being an air lift, and a bottom mining unit most likely operating on a vacuum cleaner principle to sweep up the nodules from the surface of the seafloor.

The surface ship or platform and its handling equipment is a direct borrowing of offshore oil technology with specific tailoring to fit the nodule requirements. This offshore oil technology is widely available in the industrialized nations and requires no basic further development for application to ocean mining. The only real differences are in the required maneuvering characteristics of the ship because of the necessity of moving the mining unit on the seafloor along specified paths and the somewhat greater weight of the mining system. The control systems for navigation and maneuvering have already been developed for other applications and are available. The pipeline to the bottom of the sea again borrows from offshore oil technology and the deep-sea drilling program of the National Science Foundation. The line itself and the system of joining the individual pieces of it together can be obtained from any number of steel manufacturers and fabricators, no special new alloys or metallurgical systems are required. The pumping systems are somewhat more specialized, but the basic design techniques are available in the technical literature and any lead in this technology has largely been diluted by time. The most specialized of the technologies is the bottom mining unit, but even here the unknowns are more a matter of determining design parameters than of inventing new systems.

In other words, highly competent engineers can draw upon offshore petroleum experience, the deep-sea drilling program, steel manufacturers, and the growing body of related technical information to design and build mining systems that will be basically only marginally distinguishable from those of the major consortia. Furthermore, the generally available knowledge of what has worked in tests carried out by the consortia is a sound guide to rational designs. In addition, a large number of the engineers and technologists employed by the consortia are no longer working for the consortia or for that matter on ocean mining and, pragmatically speaking, constitute a *de facto* dissemination of nodule mining technology. Ten years ago ocean mining was a closed membership club; now it is very near to an open book. It is noted that the technology now in existence should be considered as being dated as 1980 vintage; and therefore is likely to be hopelessly out of date for a probable actual date of exploitation after the year 2000. This means that the engineers designing an ocean mining unit in the twenty-first century will look at what exists today as background only and use the technology of their day.

It is true that many years and considerable expenditures were invested by the pioneers in ocean mining system development, but to a very large extent this effort was required to obtain ocean parameters and to check on the practicality and reliability of designs. Even more importantly, the enormous costs of building a commercial mining facility absolutely necessitated practical tests designed to eliminate problems before considering production scale operations. Research to make new basic technological discoveries was not required to make ocean mining possible.

One might assume from the above that there are no technological problems to be solved to carry out mining on the deep-seabed. This is far from the truth. There are no problems requiring research or basic development and there is a still growing body of good data on which to base designs that would work on paper. There is a pool of technical talent with the ability to design and construct ocean mining equipment. But—there is no sustained operating experience under all conditions with full-scale equipment, experience that is required to eliminate the inevitable "bugs" in any complicated mechanical system and particularly in one which must operate far at sea in all conditions of weather and with long supply lines. Even in the case of mature mechanical technologies used on land, new designs (e.g., a new mine haulage truck) require extensive debugging and testing. Obtaining this experience is extremely costly and is far more time-consuming than anyone has so far acknowledged.

We are talking about the first of the line of a complex equipment system where the actual operating conditions are only imperfectly known and the long-term behavior of the components can only be estimated or, perhaps more accurately, guessed at. An example of this area of unknown is the question of how many days per year a mining unit can actually mine and at what fraction of its full production capacity. This will be determined to a considerable extent by the nature and duration of equipment failures and efficiency losses. The effect of weather on operation is another issue in doubt. An unexpected weather pattern, not predictable from the sparce data available, could result in many days of lost production: for example, it may not be always possible to transfer mined ore from the mining ship to the transport ship because of weather. The economics of ocean mining are very sensitive to the "on-stream" service factors of individual equipment and of the system as a whole. These factors could not only have disastrous effects on economic performance in the first year or two of attempted operations but could adversely affect long-term economics as well.

It should be emphasized that the cost of building and normally operating a rational mining unit can be estimated with quite acceptable accuracy. It is the time and cost of repairs and the actual "on-stream" performance that is up in the air. The reader can examine any number of published cost estimates for ocean mining, for example those prepared at the Massachusetts Institute of Technology which are widely available, and be reasonably well assured that he has good cost information for this stage of commercial development. Accordingly I will not repeat such estimates in this essay. However, I would caution that any published predictions of actual financial business performance must be considered speculation and not taken too seriously. These published costs are all optimistic because they do not and cannot include the lessons yet to be learned in the real world.

The cost of ocean mining, even though reasonable estimates have been published, seems to have been largely ignored or at least not to have been appreciated. Ocean mining is basically an inordinately expensive operation, much more expensive than any viable land-based mining operation today. The cost of delivering a ton of ore from the seabed to an onshore processing plant greatly exceeds the cost of digging a ton of ore from the earth and delivering it to a processing plant. Large-scale mining costs on land are in the neighborhood of $1 per ton of material. Taking into account the necessity of mining waste rock as well as ore, mining costs per ton of ore delivered to processing will be on the order of $3 to $4 per ton. In comparison, the mining costs plus transport to shore for deep-seabed mining will easily exceed $20 per ton on an equivalent basis. In fact, at current copper prices, a copper content in the nodules of 1 percent would only be valued at about $10 per ton—which would do little more than offset the cost of transporting the nodules to shore. The processing cost for nodules will be at the high end of the scale for metallurgical processing and be similar to that for low-grade nickel laterite ores. These approximate relationships are not likely to materially change in the future.

So why has there been any interest at all in nodules? There are two basic reasons: (1) the metal content of the nodules as described in the resource section above is relatively high, which in part compensates for higher costs for nodules; and (2) the metal content of land-based ores has been slowly dropping and is expected to continue to do so. Thus, as the cost of land-based minerals slowly rises as lower grade deposits are brought into production, the time arrives when nodules can compete for a portion of the growing market. It is noted that the height of commercial interest in ocean mining occurred when the general perception was that the world was rapidly running out of resources and people were worrying about where future supplies of metals would come from. The timetable for worry about scarcity has been badly upset by the economic facts of the past ten years and the worry today is what to do with the metal resources on land that are already developed. There is no rapidly growing market and there is no niche today where nodules can compete.

When can nodule mining be seriously considered again? Only when existing installed nickel and copper production capacity is being fully utilized, when remaining known high-grade deposits are brought into production, and when the future growth prospects of nickel and copper are seen to be promising. It is only then that the inherently high costs of ocean mining will be compensated for by the rich metallic content of the polymetallic nodules. When all market and economic factors are taken into account, this magic date is predicted to be sometime in the first quarter of the twenty-first century, probably in the latter part of that quarter.

For the sake of completeness, a few comments should be made about processing technology. The costs of processing were already alluded to above. As far as technology is concerned, it is true that the nodules will require special processing compared to most metallic ores. However, all of the unit processing steps are well known and simply must be tailored to the nodule chemistry and the appropriate choice made of the process flowsheet. This is a highly technical task which must be carried out, of course, by very skilled process metallurgists and engineers. Anyone desiring to construct a processing plant will have to build a large pilot facility first and probably a demonstration scale plant. However, the time, costs, and risks associated with these activities are not the determining factors in an ocean mining project. The factors associated with the proving out of a large scale commercial mining unit are dominant. The nodule processing technology is now rather well known and any patents will have expired before any production begins. In my view the basic technology is now available.

The briefest of comments should suffice to elucidate exploration technology. The tools and technology of seabed exploration are extremely well known. In fact, a specification could be easily written and competitive bids obtained for carrying out all exploration tasks. The geology of the polymetallic nodule deposits is well known and widely published. Data on actual nodule occurrences has also been widely published and even interpreted. In many respects, both nodule geology and exploration technology are far, far simpler than those involved in any other hard mineral or petroleum exploration activity. Exploration technology should be no issue at all. Most of the confusion about availability of this technology arises from the ignorance of nontechnical people and their uninformed speculation.

The time and costs of developing an ocean mining system and metallurgical processing plant have also been much obfuscated. Little can be learned from observation of the behavior of the nodule consortia. For the most part their activities have been determined by the availability of financial resources rather than by conditions dictated by the facts of development. If the consortium concept had not been created, only a fraction of the expenditures which have been made would have been made. Because of this spreading of the financial load and accountabilities, undoubtably much more money was spent on nodule development than ever would have been under conditions of strict project justification, taking into account the real probabilities of early reward. Development activities were stretched out over many years, which incidentally is usually a very wasteful approach, because the managements of companies saw the payouts and risks to be in sufficient doubt that nobody was willing to gamble on a program for rapid development.

Thus the commercial development of the resources of the deep-seabed has not really started yet. What has been happening is an exploration of the potential of what is clearly accepted by almost everyone as a major untapped natural resource. If the markets and production cost competitiveness of the exploitation of nodules were right, even a new entrant, provided he had mine site rights, could spend resources effectively at a rate which could put an operation into production in five to eight years, depending on the difficulty of meeting all environmental requirements for shore-based activities.

Thus, the real strategy, in practice even if not openly avowed, of the management of the nodule entrepreneurs has been to establish rights to the seabed resource, based on the technical evaluations available to them, for future exploitation when conditions permit. It should be noted that the costs of development are quite high because of the necessity of large-scale proving-out of production equipment but they are not all that high in terms of the total investment required for a full-scale operation. However, the risks are high and financial analysis dictates that such large expenditures would have to be made as close as possible to the time of generating revenues. The high risks and distant payouts are the driving force that resulted in nodule development being universally undertaken either by consortia or as a national effort.

Returning now to the theme of myth and reality, several significant technology/economic myths must be dispensed with:

Myth: Commercialization would proceed if Law of the Sea questions were all answered to the complete satisfaction of the industrial nodule entrepreneurs.
Reality: There will be no investment in commercial ocean mining facilities before the latter half of the first quarter of the twenty-first century, even if the LOS questions had been answered years ago.

Myth: Ocean minerals would displace land-based production and high profits would be extracted from ocean mining.
Reality: Estimated production costs are too high to warrant commercialization in the face of perennially weak markets, low metal

prices, excess land-based capacity, and undeveloped, high-grade land-based deposits. High-risk factors for ocean mining dictate the necessity for substantial cost advantage for ocean mining before commercialization can be attempted; these cost advantages do not exist at current land-based ore grades.

Myth: Technology is firmly in hand to proceed immediately with commercialization without further work.
Reality: Extensive and costly large prototype scale operations will be required to reduce currently available technology to commercial practice. Current technology will likely be obsolete by the time commercialization is economically feasible.

Myth: A potential ocean miner must have access to arcane, privately held technology or spend long years developing his technology before he can hope to carry out ocean mining.
Reality: Basic ocean mining technology is openly available and the bulk of it proven-out in other ocean operations. Because of the continuing development of ocean technology and the receding time frame for commercialization, latecomers are not likely to be at a disadvantage to the pioneers and may in fact be at an advantage through acceptance of newer technology. The time for development will be astonishingly collapsed.

Myth: Technology transfer is an important issue with respect to entry of developing world entities into ocean mining and with respect to protecting the competitive advantage of the pioneers.
Reality: The pioneers have little or nothing worth protecting and even any marginal value is rapidly disappearing with the passage of time. One of the most emotional arguments of the Law of the Sea Conference has little foundation in fact, although the diplomats of both sides succeeded on their own in creating problems which did not exist.

Thus, it can be said in summary that the basic technology is widely available and only the difficult and expensive passage along the road to translating that technology into successful operations must be accomplished; technology transfer itself is rather like a tempest in a teapot, being surprisingly more ideological than is apparent at first glance; deep-seabed minerals are an uneconomic resource today and for the next two to three decades; and, as is always the case in the long run, economics is the almost hidden force that is determining when exploitation will occur, not the Law of the Sea nor the frustrated dreams of the explorer/entrepreneur.

Ocean Mining Ventures

No discussion of the minerals of the deep-seabed would be complete without at least listing the major players in the field. This listing is available in a number of references, but there is little published information on the genesis of these ventures and almost no speculation on the strategies and objectives of these players. Finally, it is of some interest to understand the current behavior of the various participants, so that some insight can be obtained regarding future events.

The most complete list of significant players can be obtained from the listings of the pioneer investors in deep-seabed mineral activities in the Resolution II adopted by the Law of the Sea Conference to "grandfather" the major players in deep-seabed mining. This resolution first lists France, Japan, the USSR, and India, covering their state enterprises or entities, which are "closely associated" with these states. By "closely associated" I mean enterprises that are directly controlled by the state or are dependent on the state for funding, thereby effectively making them state enterprises. The resolution then lists the four entities popularly known as the nodule consortia; these will all be described below.

France

The French enterprise is known as AFERNOD. AFERNOD's members are CNEXO, Commissariat a l'energie Atomique, Chantier de France-Dunkerque, and Societe Metellurgique le Nickel. The French government is obviously deeply involved in this effort. The French effort thus includes one of the largest nickel companies in the world, a preeminent ocean research and technology group, and a large equipment manufacturer. With large nickel mines and one of the world's largest nickel resources in French New Caledonia, the driving force for French participation might be considered to be more geopolitical than economic. However, New Caledonia is a long way from France and could at some future time no longer be a secure supply. Thus, participation in deep-seabed minerals could be considered insurance for the future. It also could be considered an evaluation of competitive sources of nickel.

The overall driving force for French participation is probably some combination of all these factors. In the past the AFERNOD program tended to emphasize development of a novel mining system based on a deep ocean version of a "bucket ladder" dredge, a technology generally judged by others to not be in the running. The French exploration activity appears to have been not too dissimilar to what others have done, but was perhaps more scientific in character. The French effort does not appear to have started as early as those in the United States, but has been publicly active for many years. The overall impression today is that the current French strategy is primarily directed toward acquisition of mine site rights rather than toward early development of commercial operations. France has submitted an application to the United Nations under Resolution II as a pioneer investor in seabed mining for a site for exploration and exploitation. It is noted that AFERNOD has comported itself essentially as an industrial organization and participated with other worldwide industry efforts on Law of the Sea and particularly on development of means for settling possible mine site disputes. Thus, potential conflicts over the French mine site have already been resolved under arrangements (to be discussed later) with the U.S. consortia and with DORD, the Japanese entity.

Japan

The Japanese effort, known as DORD, is organized as the Deep Ocean Resources Development Company, under the laws of Japan. DORD is a relatively recent creation, born on September 16, 1982, and is designed to be the focus of deep-seabed mineral activities backed by the Japanese government. DORD is the successor and inheritor of previous Japanese government activities known as the Metal Mining Agency of Japan and the Deep Ocean Minerals Association of Japan (DOMA). It is noted that there is independent Japanese company participation in two of the U.S. consortia, with some obvious resultant problems in keeping government and private activity separate and in order. Along with the formation of DORD a Japanese "national" long-range program to develop deep-seabed resources has been formulated. The predecessor Japanese organizations did carry out exploration work, some metallurgical studies, and some mining studies, but were generally considered behind the efforts of the U.S. consortia. They clearly started late. At the time of formation of the earliest U.S. consortia, it was apparent that even the Japanese giant industrial organizations had not yet given attention to deep-seabed minerals.

The driving force behind the Japanese effort is very clear—obtaining a captive national source of important metals for the Japanese industrial machine. The present effort appears to emphasize obtaining a mine site and the careful planning for the almost certain exploitation of that site in the future. As in the case of France and AFERNOD, an application has also been submitted to the United Nations for a mine site. DORD was also a participant in the agreement for the resolution of mine site conflicts with the Western industrialized country entities. In the case of DORD, and as an exception to earlier statements, exploitation could well occur before the year 2000, since DORD will be heavily subsidized and encouraged by the Japanese government. DORD could well become the first deep-seabed miner.

USSR

Little is known about the deep-seabed mineral activities of the Soviet Union beyond its application to the United Nations for a mine site as a pioneer investor. In the past the only direct evidence of any interest of the Soviet Union in seabed mining was its interest in the LOS negotiations and some reports of Soviet oceanographic work, which included manganese nodules. No direct evidence has surfaced regarding the development of deep-seabed mining technology in the Soviet Union, and offshore oil technology is not highly developed so that it could be a prime technology source.

The driving force for its participation is not entirely clear and might well be primarily geopolitical in nature. The Soviet Union has large internal land-based sources of nickel, copper, manganese, and cobalt, so that the need for resources is not apparent. The location of the Soviet mine site is not known at the time of this writing, but there is indirect evidence that the Soviet site is in the Clarion/Clipperton Zone in the Pacific Ocean. It is generally known that the Japanese and the French sites are in that zone and there is apparently a conflict between the French and/or the Japanese and the Soviets, since otherwise there would be no need for the United Nations conflict settlement procedures, which are now going on. Thus, one could speculate that there is also a conflict with the published sites of the U.S. consortia. It is my prediction that there are serious conflicts regarding mine sites that will surface shortly. At that point the LOS treaty system and the like-minded states system will be in direct conflict.

India

There is also little known about the Indian deep-seabed mineral activities beyond India's application as a pioneer investor for a mine site under Resolution II. The Indian site is beyond doubt in the Indian Ocean and it is believed that there are not any conflicts over that site. There have been a number of non-Indian oceanographic expeditions to the Indian Ocean that have located manganese nodule occurrences and there is data in the public literature. The motivation of India appears to be its need and desire for nationally controlled resources of metals—particularly nickel and copper, since India has domestic manganese resources. It is believed that India will have to obtain needed ocean mining technology from the industrialized states. This should be no great problem. The biggest problem will be the funding of such a large, high risk project as ocean mining.

United States

The activities of the four nodule consortia have been described in detail in many publications over many years, including publications of the United Nations Secretariat. It is not the intent to summarize the existing body of literature, but rather to comment on the present status of and to forecast the future of ocean mining activities. However, it may be helpful to the reader to first describe the makeup of the consortia and to provide a little historical background.

The four consortia include KCON, OMA, OMI, and OMCO. The legal arrangements under which the consortia are managed are not important and differ greatly among them. The nationalities of participants in the consortia include Belgian, Canadian, Italian, Japanese, Dutch, British, and West German, as well as American. The participants involved are primarily natural resource companies, many with both oil and hard mineral interests. However, there is also participation by a few, but important, hardware and system companies. The participants include large and quite large companies; it has not been a game for small players.

The strategies of the four consortia are all based on the business principle of making a profit from the exploitation of the deep-seabed minerals by producing metals and minerals for sale at competitive prices. Although there are some very minor exceptions in the case of some of the non-U.S. participants, the ocean mining activities have all been equity funded by the participants. The result is that the consortia are all forced to react to the real market forces and have done so. Even apparent exceptions to that principle are more a matter of different risk perceptions and different predictions of the future course of markets and economies. Some of the apparent exceptions are also the result of public relations rather than actual internal policies.

KCON was based on the exploration and technological base established by Kennecott Corporation in the 1960s and early 1970s, when the corporation was known as Kennecott Copper. The consortium was formed in January 1974. The original participants were Rio Tinto Zinc and Consolidated Gold Fields from the United Kingdom, Mitsubishi Corporation from Japan, and Noranda Mines from Canada. British Petroleum subsequently joined as well. Interest in the consortium is divided with Kennecott at 40 percent and the others at 12 percent each. Subsequently Kennecott was acquired by the Standard Oil Company (Ohio) and is now a wholly owned subsidiary. The majority stockholder of Standard of Ohio is British Petroleum.

OMA was based on the exploration and technological base established by Deepsea Ventures, which was a child of Newport News Shipbuilding, Newport now being a subsidiary of Tenneco. Newport and its parent Tenneco both finally withdrew from this activity. Deepsea established its consortium in October 1974 with participation through subsidiaries by US Steel, the Sun Company (oil), and Union Miniere, a Dutch mining company. The consortium subsequently added ENI, the Italian national oil company through its subsidiary Samin. Each of the four participants has an equal interest.

OMI was based on the exploration and technological base established by the International Nickel Company. The INCO-founded consortium was formed in May 1975 and included Sedco, Inc., a U.S. ocean oil drilling service company, Deep Ocean Mining Company, a Japanese company with nineteen other Japanese companies as stockholders, and AMR, a West German entity, which includes Salzgitter, Presussag, and Metallgesellschaft. It is noted that Sedco is no longer an independent company, having been only very recently acquired. The four participating entities have an equal interest.

OMCO was based on the technological base established by the Lockheed Corporation by the work of the ocean systems group of Lockheed Missiles and Space Company. Lockheed had been broadly involved in ocean technology and had seen ocean mining as a possible commercial application of its skills. It is noted that Lockheed did work under contract on ocean mining for Kennecott in 1969 and 1970. OMCO participants include Standard Oil of Indiana (Amoco), Royal Dutch Shell through its mining subsidiary, Billiton, and Boskalis, a Dutch company active in dredging. The major interest is held by Lockheed, Amoco, and Shell. It is of interest that Amoco has recently announced the spin-off of its mining interests, but the fate of its ocean mining interests is not known.

Each of the four consortia applied for a license under U.S. domestic legislation in early 1982 and were each granted a license in the latter part of 1984. The coordinates of the licensed areas were given earlier in this essay. It was also noted that a KCON license is expected to issue shortly in the United Kingdom, probably to a Sohio subsidiary established for that purpose. In a similar fashion a license is expected to issue in West Germany for the OMI interests, perhaps in the name of AMR. It is of interest that many conflicts arose with the mine site applications. However, the consortia took a leadership role in estabishing mechanisms for conflict resolution. The system devised was also accepted ultimately by AFERNOD and DORD. As a result, all mine site conflicts involving the four consortia and the French and Japanese national entities were settled. The big unknown is what about the possible—nay probable—conflicts involving the Soviet Union.

During this period of application of license, conflict settlement, and license granting, no further exploration activity and little, and in some cases no other, development activity was carried out by the consortia pending resolution of the license question. The main effort was directed toward obtaining rights to a mine site under domestic legislation. At the beginning of the period there was some continuing shore-side engineering development, but this was rapidly de-escalated in the face of the discouraging business conditions in the mining sector and the continued poor future outlook. Bluntly, there was severe retrenchment of ocean mining development as the facts of life became too obvious to ignore and funds generally became very tight in many of the companies involved. This retrenchment resulted also in release of trained staff in ocean mining, who returned to other corporate positions of greater current value or whose employment was terminated. In essence deep-seabed mineral development was put far back on the shelf and relegated to a low priority status. However, in no case was effort spared in trying to preserve future options for participation in seabed mineral development by seeking to obtain rights to a mine site.

Further understanding of the true status of deep-seabed mining prospects can be obtained from the following quotation from the December 1983 Report to Congress on Deep Seabed Mining by NOAA:

> Activities planned by the consortia for their license phase efforts all involve the continued delineation of the important features of their proposed license sites. All of them already have conducted extensive seafloor studies, as long ago as the early 1960s, as well as at-sea technology testing, so that all license activities are designed to augment what they already know. The activities will deal with: mapping of detailed seafloor topography, including detection of obstacles; assessment of manganese nodule abundance, grade, and variability; learning more about the engineering properties of the seafloor; and the collection of environmental baseline data. Most information will be obtained by remote sensing via acoustic techniques and photography; some will be obtained by sampling.
>
> Further mining tests may be conducted, but probably not early in the license phase.

What this quotation really says is that the work plans submitted by all the consortia are designed to hold on to the rights obtained by doing the minimum creditable amount of work. It must be kept in mind that this is the exploration phase under the license that can continue for ten years. This simply supports the thesis that deep-seabed mining is not commercially feasible today nor in the predictable near future. Only minimum expenditures will be made over the next decade and the chances of concrete steps being taken for bringing these deposits into production during this decade are vanishingly small. In all likelihood any survivors will ask for an extension of the exploration phase.

Obviously we have a mixture of myth and reality in the case of the ocean mining ventures. The biggest myth of all is that private industry was ready to undertake the commercialization of seabed mineral resources as quickly as possible. Almost everyone seemed to believe this at least in part and this belief colored the domestic and foreign political scene. The reality is that there are no concrete plans for commercialization of deep-seabed minerals by private industry and it is unlikely that creditable plans will come into being until some time after the year 2000.

After that length of time most of the early pioneering personnel and champions will have long left the scene of action. Some of the companies involved will have also disappeared and the present consortia alignments will also likely be greatly altered. Ocean mining in the deep-seabed is a project for a future generation of enterpreneurs and technologists; the pioneers are already gone and their first successors are scattered to the winds. Mining may not be as dead as *Business Week* has suggested—but mining of the nodules of the deep-seabed by private enterprise effectively is.

Law of the Sea Treaty

Although this entire book is focused on the Law of the Sea and not on ocean mining per se, this essay has till now barely mentioned the Law of the Sea. This may appear odd because it was the section of the treaty dealing with the seabed in the area beyond national jurisdiction that was the focus of bitter disagreement in the LOS Conference over many years, it was the focus of constant debate and special interest lobbying in the United States, and ultimately was the stated reason for the decision of the United States, the Federal Republic of Germany, and the United Kingdom not to sign the Law of the Sea Treaty and its accompanying resolutions. However, I believe that it would be more useful to look behind the scene at the technical, economic, business, and organizational aspects of ocean mining to provide a better basis for understanding and interpreting the saga of the *search* for a universal Law of the Sea Treaty, than to dwell on the actual treaty itself.

It is tempting to set forth yet another review of the history of the Law of the Sea negotiations and a detailed analysis of the treaty texts to explain where we are and how we got there—all from the viewpoint of the private enterprise deep-seabed miner. Perhaps a little such discussion would be useful, and accordingly will be provided. However, the main themes of this piece will be to examine pragmatically the validity of the complaints of the U.S. government and U.S. industry concerning the treaty and the potential of the existing treaty for becoming a universally acceptable legal system for exploration and exploitation of the resources of the deep-seabed.

Before taking up the two major themes, I will very briefly examine selected aspects of the treaty negotiations and their effect both on the final treaty and the U.S. attitudes thereon. The first and most pernicious aspect is the issue of control of seabed mineral production, an issue which can be seen on the basis of earlier comments in this essay to be founded on mistaken notions of the cost competitiveness of marine minerals and the imminence of their exploitation. These mistaken notions were the fuel for feeding the visions of some developing countries of an easy road to generating wealth for helping them in their own development and as a tool for the transfer of wealth from the developed to the developing world. Simultaneously these notions were the foundation of the almost frenetic search by the land-based mineral producers to build production and other controls of all kinds into the treaty because of their fear that seabed production would displace their own mineral industry. The industrialized states, who should have known better, came to believe that seabed production was ready to commence and would serve essentially as a domestic mineral supply for strategic industrial and security needs. Their strident concerns then tended to feed the fears of the developing nations and the whole vicious circle of control was kept in motion.

The effect of this one misevaluation was further amplified by the completely natural wish of the developing countries to participate directly through what came to be known as the Enterprise in deep-seabed mining. They came to believe that this would ensure that substantial profits would be realized for their benefit. Their desire for direct participation inevitably led to negotiations to ensure that they would have both the technology and the financing necessary to carry out exploitation. The industrial states fought these latter concepts as if their very industrial life depended on it. Again these actions and reactions fed on each other and reinforced differences that were based on a false notion of the availability of technology and what was important and what was unimportant.

Not all believed the general misconceptions, but unfortunately there were also many who used this basic economic struggle for the biggest piece of the pie to further their ideological concepts with regard to the "Common Heritage of Mankind" and the so-called North/South economic issues. The ideological arguments by both developing nations and the industrialized states were often quite strident and to a certain extent masked the basic economic factors derived from these misconceptions. Private industry added to the confusion by its own demand for first-come-first-served systems and its continuous contribution to the overevaluation of the importance of seabed minerals in the near future.

The debates on deep-seabed issues thus all assumed that manganese nodule exploitation was about to commence at very large scale and that large profits would be realized. A more realistic appraisal by all concerned would have permitted them to take a longer view and avoid most of the divisive negotiations. This was not easily possible during the early years and became totally impossible during the last few years of negotiations, given the conviction of the United States that it was both protecting the free market system at the ramparts and securing strategic mineral supplies for its economy and its defense.

Nevertheless, very substantial progress was made with an acceptable treaty almost in hand after the last negotiating session in 1980. At that time the major issues, which clearly had to be improved, were relatively few in number in the judgment of the U.S. negotiators. They included, as a very vital element, the negotiation of "grandfather" rights for pre-treaty seabed investors, improvement of the unworkable terms of the technology transfer provisions, further assurances on award of seabed contracts, amelioration of the production control provisions, and improvements with respect to the review conference and council seat provisions. These were far fewer than the improvements desired by American industry and far from what the incoming administration in Washington considered ideologically and practically satisfactory.

The attitudes of the new administration were from the beginning unlikely to lead to agreement. The always present industry pressures for improving the terms of the treaty as much as possible now began to be taken completely seriously as the bottom-line requirements. Increasingly, the view also began to be taken seriously that no acceptable treaty was apt to be realized based on the fundamentals of control, access, and the parallel system that had become so broadly accepted. Industry, in particular, seemed disposed to lobby against any treaty containing those elements. At this point the misconceptions grew rather than diminished and the end result was almost inevitable. The best way to illustrate the situation is to quote from the 1980 Republican platform:

Multilateral negotiations have thus far insufficiently focused attention on United States long-term security requirements. A pertinent example of this phenomenon is the Law of the Sea Conference, where negotiations have seved to inhibit United States exploration of the seabed for its abundant mineral resources. Too much concern has been lavished on nations unable to carry out seabed mining, with insufficient attention paid to gaining early American access to it. A Republican administration will conduct multilateral negotiations in a manner that reflects America's abilities and long-term interest in access to raw material and energy resources.

The implementation of this political plank was the direct route to the ensuing U.S. review of the treaty and its subsequent rejection of the treaty. Unfortunately, the plank, and even more so the first elaborations in late 1980 after the election, enlarged upon the basic principles to the extent that it is doubtful whether any treaty with the words "common heritage" would have passed muster. Perhaps too extreme a statement, but the flavor is correct.

In addition to the misconceptions noted earlier, a new one has been added, namely national security. It is true that one of the arguments advanced by industry for support of ocean mining was that the seabed would be a source of these minerals that is essentially domestic. However well the economic case might be made, the security case is much more difficult to make. It would be extremely difficult to protect a mining operation very far at sea and relatively little effort could place seabed mining out of service for long time periods. As far as the economic case is concerned, the administration has even been unwilling to provide economic protection for a very sick, established, domestic copper industry, which should be patently desirable from a security viewpoint. Thus, one must conclude that the deep-seabed Law of the Sea issue was related more to political and economic ideology than it was to concrete, provable economic and security issues.

What is wrong with the treaty, as adopted, from the United States government and industry viewpoints? How valid are these defects and are they curable? These latter two questions are the most pertinent for the future, but answering them is made much more difficult since actual seabed exploitation will not occur until very far into the future.

The United States government has been quite clear and consistent as to its reasons for rejecting the treaty. The President's statement of July 9, 1982, announcing that the United States would not sign the LOS treaty, listed the following problems:

a. Provisions would deter future development of deep-seabed mineral resources.
b. The decision-making process would not give the United States or others a role that fairly reflects and protects their interests.

c. Provisions that would allow amendments to enter into force for the United States without its approval.
d. Stipulations relating to mandatory transfer of private technology and the possibility of national liberation movements sharing in benefits.
e. Absence of assured access for future qualified deep-seabed miners to promote the development of these resources.

These are the same reasons given by James L. Malone in his statement at the LOS Conference on April 30, 1982, explaining why the United States voted against adoption of the treaty. These are valid objections to the treaty, but they need to be examined in the context of the treaty implementation, and in particular the establishment of the rules, regulations and procedures by the Preparatory Commission established by the Conference to draft the initial rules and regulations, and in the context of how the treaty could work. The political issues for the United States are probably of greater significance than the actual economic issues related to seabed mining.

It would be expected that American private industry problems with the treaty would be somewhat, but not entirely different from those of the government. However, American industry, as indicated by the policy statements of the American Mining Congress in 1983 and in 1984, stood solidly behind the decision to stay out of the treaty. This included the nodule consortia who would have obtained special rights as pioneer investors. The basic position of the AMC was to continue to argue for a nontreaty arrangement and to establish a reciprocating state regime of ocean mining states by extension of the "Provisional Understanding" signed by the U.S., U.K., France, West Germany, Italy, Belgium, Holland, and Japan in 1984. This agreement basically provided recognition of the private settlement of mine site conflicts involving the four consortia, France (AFERNOD), and Japan (DORD). It is suggested that regardless of the merits or lack thereof of the treaty, U.S. industry will continue to opt for the current first-come-first-served system under domestic legislation with its known tax structure, regulatory scheme, and system of dispute settlement. There is not much of a driving force to do otherwise, since the range of possible disputes over mine site overlaps has been tremendously reduced. The only legal/political problems that can cloud this rosy picture are the possibility of a mine site dispute with the Soviet Union, possible new claims by developing nations, and an international dispute on the right to mine outside the treaty.

In comparison, industry would face some tough problems in operating under the LOS Treaty. One problem of continuing and great concern is dealing with an international bureaucracy rather than the one it knows well. This concern extends to the character of the rules and regulations and their administration.

As even tougher problem is the question of the financial arrangements. This has been a sore point for many years. The treaty financial arrangements have been lavish in imposing significant front-end payments on the miner, payments which would be particularly unwelcome in times such as these. The payments required to be made to the seabed authority after production is initiated are a serious problem as well. If these payments are on top of national taxation, a commercial project would be too heavily burdened. There was no clear sign that payments to the authority would be recognized by domestic taxing authorities. The entire issue of production allotments has been a serious problem for industry from the beginning. This has the potential of removing an important degree of business freedom and could likely be used to control entry into operations.

Although industry raised many questions about technology transfer and a myriad of other treaty provisions, I would be inclined to give them less importance by far than financial implications and freedom of access—and I emphasize freedom of access, not simply nondiscriminatory access. Since the consortia were not prepared to go into production for a long time, some of these questions would appear to have been somewhat academic. On the contrary, the lack of seriousness of purpose in the reasonably near future makes it easily possible to hold to these matters of principle, since there is little or nothing to lose and the whole unwanted treaty might go away before serious plans to go into production are entertained.

If the treaty is so basically unwelcome, how is it that France and Japan have at least gone the next step of signing the treaty and applying for pioneer investor status? The answer is that they are not fundamentally for profit private enterprises, but are organizations designed to look after the interests of states. They do not have the same problems with financial arrangements nor with production requirements. Furthermore, their ability to deal with the international bureaucracy is superior to that of private industry. These two states may have designed for themselves the best of all regimes. Under the treaty they will be treated as pioneer investors with the locked-in ability to be able to produce under the treaty protection just about the time they would like to. Under the "Provisional Understanding" agreement they have protected themselves against the only potential conflict outside of the treaty, namely against the three major industrial nonsigners: the United States, the United Kingdom, and the Federal Republic of Germany. The provisions of the treaty will not really be a problem to them at all. It is doubtful whether any of the provisions that were fought so hard, including technology transfer, financial arrangements, and so on, represent any more than a slight inconvenience here and there. In the meantime, they can take full advantage of the opportunities in the Preparatory Commission to obtain reasonable rules, regulations, and procedures for ocean mining. The Far Eastern industrial rival of the United States, Japan, now joined by France, seems to have done it again by outmaneuvering the United States in the long-range quest for resources in a way that also comes close to making them heroes to the developing world.

As far as the evaluation of the treaty is concerned, we are only now coming to the stage where such evaluation can be made. The treaty appears very complete on the surface, but the real treaty will only be seen when the work of the Preparatory Commission on rules, regulations, and procedures has been completed. At that time the merits of the treaty can be judged much, much more accurately than now. Once drafted, these regulations will be difficult to change and the real regime and machinery will be rather well locked in. The decision as to whether to ratify the treaty and become subject to its terms can then be made after the work of the Commission is completed. There are some rough spots in the treaty texts here and there that may pose some practical problems, e.g., the poor definition of technology that was in fact put forward by the United States and some unworkable aspects of the technology clause, but careful attention to detail should secure a workable system.

It is too early to judge the work of the Preparatory Commission. However, it appears to have done a quite satisfctory job in setting up the pioneer investors procedures and has made a good start on the regulations themselves. The work product from its initial efforts looks quite promising. It is expected that the first extensive progress will be made during the present session of the Commission and the reader should examine that work when it appears as the first real indication of whether the treaty will be workable.

It is my prediction that most of the ills of the treaty, from an open-minded private investor viewpoint, will be sufficiently ameliorated so that it will be a satisfactory vehicle for private investment. Contracts will be granted by the authority, which may be subject to less change and fewer bureaucratic difficulties than operating in many of the developed countries and most individual developing countries. Unfortunately the United States will not be part of that process and has forfeited its opportunity to help forge the real seabed treaty.

It is much more difficult to try and sum up this section in a series of myths and realities. As always, the subject of the treaty becomes very illusive when we try to tie down its exact embodiment in actual operation, particularly when little will happen operationally until a quite distant future. Nevertheless, the biggest myth is that the seabed provisions of the treaty cannot be a satisfactory vehicle for private investment in exploitation of the minerals of the deep-seabed. The reality is that the rules, regulations, and procedures for the exploration and exploitation of the resources of the area can be developed by the Preparatory Commission so that the treaty can be a reasonably satisfactory regime for private investment. The one question the Commission cannot resolve is the taxation levels resulting from a double take by the seabed authority and an individual country, a question that is clearly in the domain of the individual sovereign state.

Mine Site Conflict

Before bringing this essay to a close, a few words need to be said about the settlement of overlapping mine site conflicts. This is an arena where the four consortia have made an extraordinary contribution that has not been fully appreciated by those with an interest in the Law of the Sea. This contribution was the development of a system to facilitate the negotiation of conflicts under the umbrella of compulsory and binding arbitration with clear rules carefully spelled out as to how the merits of the contestants would be judged. The essential core of the approach was to spell out simple but clear criteria before the nature of any conflicts was even known. The result was a fair system and a workable system. The other ingredient in the system was the acceptance by the participants that they had to be able to solve any conflicts themselves in a totally equitable manner that considered the contributions and aspirations of all parties to participate in ocean mining. It was early agreed that direct involvement of governments would be disastrous, but that governments had to generally sanction the process and properly bless the outcome. This they did.

The essential core of the agreement was the five factors to be taken into consideration by the arbitral tribunal in its application of equitable principles in its determination of the awards to be made regarding an area in conflict. These five factors were:

1. the continuity and extent of past activities relevant to each area in conflict and the application area of which it is a part;
2. the date on which each signatory concerned or predecessor in interest or component organization thereof commenced activities at sea in the application area;
3. the financial cost of past activities measured in constant dollars;
4. the time when activities were carried out and quality of activities; and
5. such additional factors as the Tribunal determines to be relevant, but excluding a consideration of the future plans of work of the signatories concerned.

The agreement to arbitrate contained all that was necessary to govern the behavior of the signatories during negotiations and to guide the arbitral tribunal if the conflicts had to come to arbitration. This essay does not permit going into any more detail, but students of this area may be interested in further investigation.

The original agreement was entered into by KCON, OMA, OMI, and OMCO in February 1982. This alone required agreement of about twenty-five industrial companies; such agreement alone is noteworthy. AFERNOD joined the agreement shortly thereafter and participated in all negotiations. These five major parties went through many difficulties in the complex negotiation of the conflicts, but in the end reached a satisfactory resolution. Very late in the negotiations DORD expressed interest in becoming part of the process and this too was eventually worked out. The final settlements then included all six of these pioneer investors.

Figure 5.1 reflects the settlement as far as the U.S. entities are concerned. It is obvious that DORD and AFERNOD are in the same area since there were conflicts that had to be settled. Based on technical understanding of the continuity and nature of nodule deposits, it must

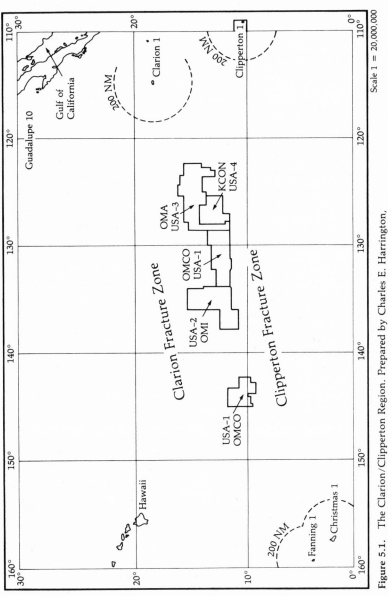

Figure 5.1. The Clarion/Clipperton Region. Prepared by Charles E. Harrington, National Oceanic and Atmospheric Administration.

be concluded that DORD and AFERNOD are located in the vacant areas adjacent to the north and south of the larger area where licenses have been granted and perhaps surrounding the smaller area of licenses. Because of this proximity probability, any conflict with any one of these six pioneer investors is apt to be a conflict with one or more others. Any settlement of merit would also undoubtably cascade among the others.

Only the Soviet Union and India were not included in the private arbitration settlement. India, as expected, has proven not to be in conflict with any of the six and, in fact, not in conflict with the USSR either. However, it is now confirmed that the Soviet Union is in conflict with one of the six—AFERNOD. It is not known what future conflicts may arise, but any AFERNOD/Soviet settlement will quite likely produce conflict with others of the six who settled their claims by private arbitration. This situation is one of the difficult problems likely to surface early between likeminded states and competitors who are only within the treaty. There has already been an exchange of letters between Ocean Mining Associates and the Soviet Union with OMA asserting its claim under customary international law and the Soviet Union rejecting OMA's claim under the treaty. It is not even known whether the OMA and the Soviet areas actually overlap, but the conflict is real and presages the future. It cannot be foreseen how such a conflict might be settled, but it is already late to search out a way.

Some Summary Conclusions

What then is the myth and reality regarding the minerals of the deep-seabed? Is there a thought or two that can sum up the whole situation? This is not easily done and I will be content if only a few hard core facts are retained. The most important of these hard core facts (or perhaps opinions) is that the cost competitiveness of exploitation of minerals of the deep-seabed does not permit such exploitation to compete with land-based sources today nor for the next two to three decades. Any exploitation that does occur during this period will be uneconomic and heavily subsidized by government. The first ocean miner is likely to be Japanese, through the government instrumentality, DORD.

A second hard core fact is that the American technological lead in the development of ocean mineral resources has already largely withered away and will not likely be reestablished by the present parties of interest. Ocean mining in the United States is for all intent and purpose dead, except for the continued attempt through a domestic license to retain a future option at low cost.

With regard to the Law of the Sea treaty, the acid test of achieving minimum acceptability by private enterprise in the industrial nations is now being made by the Preparatory Commission. The possibility exists that many of the concerns generated by worst case analyses will be made to disappear by the Preparatory Commission. Nevertheless, the signs are not promising for a reevaluation by the U.S. government in the next four years, although changes could occur in the attitudes of close allies.

Although deep-seabed minerals sank the treaty for the United States this time around, the subject will return and a universal accommodation will have to be made before extensive exploitation can be considered, because the likelihood of continual conflict is too great. In many respects industry saved the day as far as the "Western" industrialized countries are concerned by having organized broad-based international consortia for ocean mining and by devising a scheme for settlement of mine site application overlaps and making it work by capable and statesmanlike negotiations. The industry idea of cooperation among likeminded states is far from all bad. Nevertheless it suffers by ignoring the aspirations and legitimate rights of the developing countries and by what appears to be the impossibility of bringing Eastern block nations into such an arrangement.

NOTES

1. OMA—Ocean Mining Associates: OMI—Ocean Management, Inc.; OMCO—Ocean Minerals Company; KCON—Kennecott Consortium.

2. UN Ocean Economics and Technology Office, "Manganese Nodules Dimensions and Perspectives" (Boston: Reidel, 1979).

3. AFERNOD—Association Française pour l'Etude et la Recherche des Nodules; DORD—Deep Ocean Resources Development Company.

PART III
Voices of the New Regime

6.
Historical Background of the Evolution of the Exclusive Economic Zone and the Contribution of Africa

FRANK X. NJENGA

THE EVOLUTION OF modern international Law of the Sea has been characterized by efforts of maritime powers to mold the law to accommodate their national interests. Those interests have sometimes conflicted and sometimes have been in harmony. But on the whole they have been at the expense of the weak nonmaritime powers, the countries of Asia, Africa, and Latin America in particular, for whose exploitation in one form or the other, most of these rules were directed. The mighty have always attempted to impose their will on the weak.

Thus even in the Middle Ages we find instances where states imposed their dominance over certain seas by force and levied charges on ships transiting such seas. We find for instance that Venice assumed sovereignty over the whole of the Adriatic while, on the other side of the Italian peninsula, the republic of Genoa advanced a similar claim to the domination of the Ligurian Sea. Denmark and Sweden, and later Poland contended for or shared in the domination of the Baltic. On her part England claimed sovereignty over a considerable part of the waters around her—St. George's Channel, the Bristol Channel, the Irish Sea, and the North Sea.

The most preposterous claim to sovereignty was that made by Spain and Portugal. In the sixteenth century these powers in virtue of the Treaty of Tordeseillas of June 7, 1494, divided the newly discovered world between them by a line of longitude lying 370 leagues west of

The views expressed in this essay are my own and do not necessarily reflect the views of the OAU or those of the Kenya government.

Cape Verde Islands. This was given the papal blessing by bulls of January 24, 1506. Under these arrangements Spain claimed the exclusive right of navigation in the western portion of the Atlantic, in the Gulf of Mexico, and in the Pacific. Portugal on its part arrogated to itself a similar right in the Atlantic south of Morocco and the two powers claimed a monopoly for trade and commerce over the entire continents of the Americas, Africa, and Asia.[1]

In the scramble for new markets and international commerce, such claims could not remain unchallenged by the emerging powers in Europe and this led directly to the new doctrines of the so-called freedoms of the sea, which have dominated the legal theory of the Law of the Sea since the beginning of the seventeenth century. The father of this doctrine was the famous Hugo Grotius, who was an employee of "Great United Company of the East Indies," otherwise known as the Dutch East Indies Company, which had come into conflict with the Portuguese pretension to the monopoly of the whole of the Indian Ocean region. This thesis in support of his employers, set out in *Mare Liberum* (Magoffin translation),[2] was based on the impossibility of occupation of the ocean and its inexhaustible capacity to accommodate all uses. In his own words two conclusions could be drawn:

The first is that that which cannot be occupied cannot be the property of any one, because all property has arisen from occupation. The second is that all that which has been so constituted by nature, that although serving some one person, still suffices for the common use of all other persons, is today and ought in perpetuity to remain in the same condition as when it was first created by nature. . . . All things which can be used without loss to any one else come under this category.

He further expanded his reasoning as follows:

The air belongs to this class of things for two reasons. First it is not susceptible of occupation; and second its common use is destined for all men. For the same reason the sea is common to all, because it is so limitless that it cannot become a possession of anyone, and because it is adapted for the use of all whether we consider it from the point of view of navigation or fisheries. Now the same right which applied to the sea applies also to the things which the sea has carried away from other uses and made its own, such for example as the sands of the sea, of which portion adjoining the land is called the coast or shore.[3]

Though even in his time Grotius' thesis was severely attacked by some other authors,[4] his views on the whole prevailed and the so-called Freedom of the Sea has remained predominant since then. This is however not so much because of the reasons he adduced i.e., the impossibility of effective occupation and its capacity to accommodate all uses, both of which are fallacious today given the modern naval capacities and the frightening degrading possibilities of modern users, but because of the use of the oceans as a means of communication. As one learned author has remarked,

The real reason for the freedom of the open sea is represented in the motive which led to the attack against maritime sovereignty, and the purpose for which such attack was made . . . namely, the freedom of communication, and especially commerce, between the States which are separated by the sea. The sea being an international highway which connects distant lands, it is the common conviction that it should not be under the sway of any State whatsoever. It is in the interest of intercourse between the States, that the principle of freedom of the open seas become universally recognized and will always be upheld.[5]

Before concluding this brief perspective on the historic background on the Law of the Sea it should be pointed out that the untrameled freedom of the sea was qualified by later authors to allow for coastal state domination of a belt of sea along the coast known as the territorial sea. Bynkershoek advocated a territorial sea, or maritime belt adjacent to the coast, which a state could dominate from the coast batteries, and he is thus credited with the "cannon shot" three-mile limit.[6] De Vattel rationalizes the need of such a belt as follows:

A Nation may appropriate such things as would be hurtful to it if open to free and common use; and this is a . . . reason why Powers extend their sovereignty over the seas along their coasts, as far as they can protect their right. It is a matter of concern to their security and their welfare that there should not be a general liberty for others to approach so near their possessions, especially with their ships of war, as to hinder the passage of trading vessels and disturb navigation.. . . These marginal seas, thus subject to a Nation, are part of its territory and may not be navigated without its permission. But access may not lawfully be refused for vessels when their purpose is innocent and they are not under suspicion, since every owner is bound to grant free passage to strangers, even by land, when no harm or danger results from doing so."[7]

The Evolution of the Exclusive Economic Zone Concept

Thus as we have seen the concept of freedom of the sea had become the generally acceptable norm to the then "actors" in the international community by the nineteenth century. This is because it served them in the quest for empires, commerce, and trade. Throughout the eighteenth and nineteenth centuries we find the European powers engaged in ruthless exploitation of both human and material resources of Africa, Asia, and Latin America, and for this, freedom of the sea was absolutely indispensable.

Territorial Sea

As has already been mentioned, however, the territorial sea had become recognized as a derogation from the freedom of the sea concept. During the first half of the nineteenth century the three-mile territorial-sea limit had considerable support in state practice. During the second half of the nineteenth century some states attempted to assert a general jurisdiction beyond the three miles, but all such claims were vigorously resisted. During this period, aside from the Scandinavian states, which claimed a four-mile limit on a historic basis, only Spain claimed more than three miles on basis either of jurisdiction or custom of territorial sea during a substantial period in the nineteenth century.

The position of the three-mile limit of the territorial sea however began to erode in the twentieth century though the majority still supported it at the commencement of the 1958 Geneva Conference. At least forty coastal states of the seventy-three coastal states attending the conference supported three-mile territorial sea. But twenty-seven coastal states claimed a specific breadth of territorial sea broader than three miles, as follows:

6 miles:	Ceylon, Greece, Haiti, India, Iran, Israel, Italy, Libya, Spain, Yugoslavia.
9 miles:	Mexico
10 miles:	Albania
12 miles:	Bulgaria, Colombia, Ethiopia, Guatamala, Indonesia, Rumania, Saudi Arabia, USSR, United Arab Republic, Venezuela

Up to 200 miles: Chile, Ecuador, El Salvador[8]

As is well known the 1958 UN Conference, which was otherwise a codification conference, was unable to fix an agreed limit for the territorial sea. Neither was the 1960 UN Conference, which had been called specifically to deal with the breadth of the territorial sea, and which failed by one vote,[9] to adopt a compromise of a 6-mile territorial sea, plus a further six-mile exclusive jurisdiction over fishing, subject to certain limitations, for a period of ten years, in regard to fishing rights of other states in such Zone.[10]

It should be pointed out that very few African countries particpated in either of the two first UN conferences on the Law of the Sea, since most of them were still under colonial domination.[11] In any case, with the accession to independence of the majority of African states in the early 1960s, which felt no veneration for the cannon-shot rule, the three-mile rule was doomed. Table 6.1 shows the territorial sea claim of Asian-African countries as of 1971.

Continental Shelf

It is not intended here to go into details into the geological/geo-morphological aspects of the continental shelf, the continental slope and rise, or what is referred to as the continental margin. It is only intended to show how the claims to sovereignty and jurisdiction over the continental shelf constituted a further erosion of the so-called freedoms of the sea.

While there had been several claims to exclusive jurisdiction to sedentary fisheries and other resources on the continental shelf,[13] it was the Truman proclamations of September 28, 1945[14] which should be regarded as the origin of modern concept of continental-shelf claims. The proclamation was unabashedly based on the desire of the United States to control oil resources off its coasts. This is clearly brought out in one of the preambles to the proclamation, which states:

WHEREAS it is the view of the United States Government that the exercise of jurisdiction over the natural resources of the subsoil and seabed of the continental shelf by contiguous nation is reasonable and just, since the effectiveness of measures to utilize or conserve these reserves would be contingent upon cooperation and protection from the shore, since the continental shelf may be regarded as an extension of the land mass of the coastal nation and thus naturally appurtenant to it.

The proclamation went on to state simply, and unilaterally, that

Having concern for the urgency of conserving and prudently utilizing its natural resources, the Government of the United States regards the natural resources of the subsoil and the seabed of the continental shelf beneath the high seas but contiguous to the coasts of the United States subject to its jurisdiction and control.

In a White House Press release accompanying the proclamation the United States limited its claim to:

an underwater area 750,000 square miles in extent. Generally submerged land which is contiguous to the continent and which is covered by no more than 100 fathoms (600 feet) of water is considered as continental shelf.[15]

Thus while the United States in its unilateral declaration, mapped its strategy in accordance with its perceived interests, given its geological and geographical situation, there was every reason for other states to take similar calculations in their respective unilateral claims. Some based their claim simply on the continental shelf without defining it; sixteen others with no physical shelf as such based themselves on a distance criteria of 200 nautical miles;[17] others proclaimed sovereign rights to the shelf regardless of depth or extent;[18] while still some others adopted an exploitability test.[19] Still others based their proclamation on the 200 meters isobath[20] (or 100 fathoms contour)[21] while others claimed jurisdiction and control over the seabed and subsoil of the area without bothering about its definition.[22]

Thus the stage was set for full confrontation when the United Nations Conference on the Law of the Sea was held in 1958. While every delegation was in agreement about the concept of the continental shelf, there were disagreements about its definition or criteria. No one doubted the relevance of the geological limit of the continental shelf as the 200 meters isobath. But this was unacceptable as the legal limit of its extent. The Latin American countries, which on the whole are not endowed with a broad continental shelf, had adopted a position that the depth of 200 meters isobath had to be extended to where the depth of the superjacent waters admitted of exploitation of the natural resources of the continental shelf.[23] In the end, the 1958 Law of the Sea Conference, at the recommendation of the International Law Commission, adopted a definition of the continental shelf, which contains both the geological and exploitability criteria. The continental shelf is thus defined in article 1 of the Convention as follows: "For the purpose of these articles, the term 'Continental Shelf' is used as referring (a) to the seabed and subsoil of the submarine areas adjacent to the coast but outside the territorial sea, to a depth of 200 meters or, beyond that limit, to where the depth of the superjacent waters admits the exploitation of the said areas."

Such an elastic definition incorporating the exploitability criteria of course opens the way to indefinite coastal state expansion as technology advances. As one eminent author has observed: "Thus, the concept of exploitability must be constantly reinterpreted in terms of the most advanced standards of technology and economy in the world. Hence, the exploitation of submarine resources must always be reserved to the coastal state, which is empowered to claim the area when the depth of the superjacent waters admits of exploitation. It can be inferred that under this Convention all the submarine areas of the world have been theoretically divided among the coastal states, which are empowered to claim the area when the depth of superjacent waters admits of exploitation."[24]

In the North Sea continental shelf cases the International Court of Justice had the occasion to address itself to the concept of "adjacency" and "natural prolongation" aspects of the 1958 convention on the continental shelf. It stated:

Even if proximity may afford one of the tests to be applied and an important one in the right conditions, it may not necessarily be the only, nor in all the circumstances, the most appropriate one. Hence it would seem that if the notion of adjacency so constantly employed in continental shelf doctrine from the start, only implies proximity in general sense, and does not imply any fundamental or inherent rule, the ultimate effect of which would be to prohibit any state (otherwise than by agreement) from exercising continental shelf rights in respect of areas closer to the coast of another state.[25]

The Court considered the concept of natural prolongation of the land territory as the more appropriate test. It stated:

More fundamental than the notion of proximity appears to be the principle constantly relied upon by all the Parties—of the natural prolongation or continuation of the land territory or domain, or land sovereignty of the coastal state into and under the high seas via the bed of its territorial sea which is under the full sovereignty of that State. There are various ways of formulating this principle, but the underlying idea, namely the extension of something already possessed, is the same, and it is this idea of extension which is in the Courts opinion, determinant, submarine areas do not really appertain to the coastal state because, or not only because—they are near to it. They are near it of course; but this would not suffice to confer title, any more than, according to a well-established principle of law recognized by both sides in the present case, mere proximity confers *per re* title to land territory. What confers the *ipso jure* title, which international law attributes to the coastal state in respect of its continental shelf, is the fact that the submarine areas concerned may be deemed to be actually part of the territory over which the coastal state already has dominion, in the sense that although covered with water, they are a prolongation or continuation of that territory, an extension of it under the sea.

By this interpretation of the 1958 convention the 200-meter criteria became rendundant and the way to indefinite territorial state expansion—at least to cover the continental shelf, continental slope, and the continental margin; i.e., the whole of the continental margin up to the abyssal plains—was opened. Once again due to its geographic and geological position Africa found itself the loser in the quest for the new sea domain, which was beginning in earnest. The continental shelf around Africa is on the whole relatively narrow.

African Reaction in Preparation For UN Third Conference on the Law of the Sea

When the preparation for the third Law of the Sea Conference began in earnest in the Committee on the Peaceful Uses of the Seabed and Ocean Floor Beyond the Limits of National Jurisdiction, the African delegations found themselves with unenviable choices. They were confronted with an existing Law of the Sea, which, as we have seen above, had evolved over the centuries to cater to the interests of maritime powers, a law which had never concerned itself with African interests since Africa had played no role in its formulation. On the contrary most of the principles that had evolved were inimical to Africa. The principle of freedom of the sea had been the channel for the degradation of African resources over the centuries. It was used to further the most barbaric crime against humanity—the slave trade—and also to colonize and subjugate a whole continent to foreign domination. Thus we find that even after the formal abolition of the slave trade, it was prohibited to seize and search ships still engaging in the ignominous trade because of the Freedom of the Sea doctrine. The *Le Louis,* a French vessel which sailed from Martinique on January 30, 1816,[26] destined on a voyage to the coast of Africa and back, was captured ten or twelve leagues south of Cape Mesurada by a British ship and carried to Sierra Leone. There was no doubt about the *Le Louis'* intention—it had been fitted out, manned, and navigated for the purpose of carrying on slave trade, which by then was illegal under French internal law and under a convention between France and Great Britain. It was nevertheless decided by Justice Scott that the seizure of the ship was illegal. According to him: "Under law generally understood and practiced, no nation can exercise a right of visitation and search upon the common and unappropriated parts of the sea, save only in the belligerent claim."

Africa had been watching as the supposedly inexhaustible fishery resources off her coast were being ruthlessly and callously decimated by irresponsible activities of long-distance factory ships, industries of developed countries. It will be recalled that the justification of freedom of navigation and fishing was given as follows:

It is clear that the use of the high seas for the purpose of navigation and fishing is innocent in character and inexhaustible; that is to say, one who sails the high seas or who fishes therein injures no one, and the sea can satisfy the needs of all men. Now, nature does not give men the right to appropriate things the use of which is innocent and the supply inexhaustible and sufficient for all; for since each can obtain from the sea, as common property, what will satisfy his wants, the attempt to make one-self sole master of it and to exclude others would be depriving them unreasonably of the blessing of nature.[27]

This has of course become blatantly false. Not only were fishery resources being systematically depleted, but the seas and the coastlines themselves were becoming dangerously polluted by irresponsible behavior of shipping, particularly by supertankers in the name of freedom of the seas. As is well known, the major supertankers' route from

the Middle East to Europe and the United States, with attendent pollution hazards, goes around the continent of Africa.[28] It was with this
perspective that the Exclusive Economic Zone concept was developed
as a defensive mechanism to safeguard Africa's and developing countries' interests in an increasingly hostile and acquisitive marine
environment.

The Exclusive Economic Zone (EEZ) Proposal

The Exclusive Economic Zone (EEZ) was designed as a mechanism
for harmonizing the legitimate concerns of the international community with those of the coastal state. In other words the proposal was
not a one-sided negotiating position postulated for the purpose of an
envisaged Conference but a serious proposal emanating from a deep-
seated interest in achieving justice and fair play in relations between
nations, in a field characterized by avarice and desire to achieve individual state goals at the expense of the weaker members of the international community. Unlike previous propositions on the Law of the
Sea, the EEZ was not an assertion of a dominant political/economic
force, but a proposition based on justice and equity founded on the
abuse of the previous prevailing notions, which had governed the
international relations on the sea under high-flaunted notions of freedoms, camouflaging nothing but the desire of the strong to justify their
domination of the weaker members of society. As a very perceptive
member of the international scene has stated in connection with the
EEZ, among other proposals which have emanated from the Asian
Africa Legal Consultative Committee:

The new nations have the power of creative suffering. The truth has
to be recognized that spiritual powers speak last in human affairs. The
creative power of suffering has been characterized by the Athenian
poet Aeschylus in which he speculates on the nature and purpose of
Reality seen in the personal forum of a supreme God. St. Paul's description of Christ's act of self-sacrifice in his epistle to the Philippians
is another illustration. Swami Virekanada has asked mankind to serve
mankind as a manifestation of Divinity. This is human culture. Dr.
Toynbee has said that when political nationalism has come to be a
threat to the human race's survival, our paramount royalty must be
transferred from nation to mankind as a whole. The spiritual presence
in the Universe that is greater than Man manifests itself to Man in
more forums than one.[29]

It is against this background that I made the proposal on the establishment of the EEZ as a possible basis for a just and equitable accommodation of competing interests of the developing coastal states and the maritime powers, long-distance fisheries interests, and landlocked states. The proposal was first made during the Colombo session of the Asian African Legal Consultative Committee (AALCC) in 1971.

Representing a developing African country, I was particularly concerned that as the international law had developed, the interest of developing countries had largely gone unheeded in the high-sounding concepts like "freedoms of the sea," which had been used as a license to deplete the developing countries of their resources. I put these feelings in a fairly forthright manner as follows: For a long time our views were unheard and our interests unheeded, when International Law was being formulated by the so-called civilized nations, which by definition excluded both Asian and African Countries. With the grant of independece to these countries, we now have the opportunity of having our views heard and incorporated in the development of International Law."

On behalf of the Kenya delegation I wished to urge the AALCC to take firm action to safeguard the interests of the developing countries in the field of the Law of the Sea. As I pointed out. "This is . . . the last frontier, of this universe, which unless we organize ourselves properly, shall be subjected to even worse colonialism than we have recently been subjected to in our countries."[30]

The delegation of Kenya was opposed to the forthcoming Conference being used as a forum for tackling the issues that had been left unresolved in the 1958 Conventions on the Law of the Sea. I made the following observations in this regard:

Concerning the four Geneva Conventions on the Law of the Sea, . . . most of the States in Africa had not participated in their formulation. . . . These Conventions had codified only those rules of the Law of the Sea which had been evolved by developed countries in their search for empires and that if at all they served the interests of developing countries, it was by coincidence and not by design. Therefore in the light of the above (Kenya) would not accept the proposition that the future Conference on the Law of the Sea should be devoted only to the issues left unresolved in the previous conferences. . . . The Conference must have the competence to reexamine such of those rules which perpetrated inequalities.

One of the key issues to be resolved at the proposed conference . . .

was the question of freedom of fisheries in the area adjoining the territorial waters of a State. Irresponsible interpretation of this freedom . . . had already led to the extinction of many a species of fish; . . . either an appropriate belt of territorial waters should be recognized, or if a 12-mile limit was taken as the limit of the territorial waters, a further area of exclusive fishery and conservation zone beyond 12 miles must be recognized.[31]

This was the origin of the idea of the EEZ. Basically the purpose of such a zone was to safeguard the interests of the coastal state in the waters adjacent to its coast without unduly interfering with the other legitimate uses of the sea by other states. These basic interests of the coastal state include regulation and control of fisheries and other resources, whether living or nonliving, in the adjoining sea and the seabed, and the prevention and control of pollution.

The proposed EEZ was not to be regarded as territorial sea, since some of the freedoms of the high seas, namely the freedom of navigation and overflight, the freedom of laying pipelines and submarine cables would continue to survive. But the EEZ would not be considered as high seas as then currently known since the coastal state would have the exclusive right to explore, exploit, regulate, and control fisheries, take and enforce pollution prevention measures, and exploit the resources of the seabed within the zone. The proposal was that this zone would extend up to 200 nautical miles measured from the baselines from which the territorial sea is measured.

The idea of the EEZ was very well received by the Asian-African Legal Consultative Committee membership with the possible exception of the delegation of Japan, which was then advocating the idea of an undefined preferential area for fisheries beyond 12 miles territorial sea. It was agreed that the AALCC would have further discussion on the EEZ concept at its next meeting, which was to be held in Lagos, Nigeria, in 1972. During the thirteenth session of the AALCC in Lagos in 1972, the basic underlying reasoning behind the concept was further developed and the main elements of the idea were further concretized. The finalization of these discussions was held during the fourteenth session of AALCC held in New Delhi, January 10–18, 1973.

Let me admit at the outset that the idea of a Zone up to 200 nautical miles had previously been expressed. In 1952, Chile, Ecuador, and Peru after a meeting in Santiago in Chile published a proclamation to the effect that their respective governments had decided, in order "to conserve and ensure for their respective people" the natural wealth of those areas of the sea which bathed their coasts, to proclaim a "standard of their international maritime policy" that each possessed "sovereignty and exclusive jurisdiction to a minimum distance of 200 nautical miles, together with the corresponding soil and subsoil."[32] In fact this had been preceded by two decrees by Honduras in 1950 and 1951 claiming control and jurisdiction over an area in the Altantic Ocean "extending 200 marine miles seaward of its coasts."[33] These measures, while based on economic considerations, were an interpretation of the extent of the existing concept of the territorial sea, to accommodate perceived national interests of these countries, an assertion of their jurisdiction over extended areas such as in the Truman declaration on the continental shelf in 1945.

But why propose 200 nautical miles for the breadth of the EEZ? As the father of the modern Law of the Sea had to say in defense of the freedom of the sea: "And what reason operates if the sea can be occupied up to 100 miles, to prevent it being occupied up to 150, then 200 and so on? If water is property up to the 100th mile, why cannot the water which is immediately contiguous to the property. These are the "impasses" to which you must come, once you have departed from the truth."[34]

There are several convincing reasons for the 200-mile criteria. Let me first admit that the existence of 200-mile territorial claims by certain countries did play a part in the establishment of the 200-mile limit. As has already been remarked, the so-called 3-mile territorial sea rule had by this time more or less become obsolete. If a new proposal had to have any chance of success, it had to take into consideration the existing realities. One of these realities was the 200-mile territorial sea claimed by some Latin American countries and later by some African countries, including Somalia and Sierra Leone. To expect that any nation would accept a roll-back from adopted national position, particularly when such position had been enshrined in its constitution, as in the case of Honduras, would be to expect the impossible. It was therefore the view of the proponents of the EEZ, that the 200-mile limit offered the best chance for an acceptable international limit for national jurisdiction.

Besides, The EEZ concept was conceived as a protective zone wherein the state would have fairly enforceable control over its resources both living and nonliving. As for the former, they can be classified as coastal fisheries and highly migratory species.[35] As for the coastal resources, they are to be found mainly within the 200-mile limit and they are of the utmost importance to the developing countries whose fishing industries are not sufficiently developed to mount worldwide fishing expeditions.

It should also be pointed out that at a distance of 200 nautical miles, almost all of the Continental Shelf proper, i.e., 200 meters depth, would have been incorporated within the coastal state national jurisdiction. This would have disposed of the elastic criteria of "exploitability" in the continental shelf convention of 1958, which, as we have discussed above, is inconsistent with an area of common heritage as all the continental shelf is capable of national coastal state appropriation as technology develops. While of course some states, particularly in Africa and Latin America, would have received areas greater in extent than what they had under a 200-meter depth regime, it was felt that equality was equity. In any case a uniform 200-mile limit would have definitely settled the boundary between the national and international jurisdiction. This would have obviated one of the most serious drawbacks of the Law of the Sea Convention, on the definition of the continental-shelf article, which is likely to be a rich source of controversy between the International Seabed Authority and national governments for a long time to come, particularly as new mineral potentials are discovered in the borderlands.

The Lagos meeting of the AALCC in January 1972[36] was followed by a Seminar of African Experts in Yaounde, Cameroun, in June 1972 who deliberated at length on the proposal for the establishment of an EEZ.[37]

During this seminar, extensive discussions were held focusing in particular on the EEZ proposal. The seminar's far-reaching conclusion became the firm basis of the EEZ.[38] The conclusions of the seminar, in which I was privileged to be the rapporteur were in part:

On the territorial sea and on the contiguous Zone and the high seas:

1. The African states have the right to determine the limits of their jurisdiction over the sea adjacent to their coasts in accordance with a reasonable criteria, which particularly take into account geographical, geological, biological, and national security factors.

2. The territorial sea should not extend beyond a limit of 12 nautical miles.

3. The African states have equally the right to establish beyond the territorial sea an Economic Zone over which they will have an ex-

clusive jurisdiction for the purpose of control, regulation and national exploitation of the living resources of the sea and their preservation for the primary benefit of their peoples and their economies, and for the purpose of the prevention and control of pollution.

The establishment of such a Zone shall be without prejudice to the following freedoms: freedom of navigation, freedom of overflight, freedom to lay submarine cables and pipelines.

4. The exploitation of the living resources within the Economic Zone should be open to all African states both landlocked and near-landlocked, provided that the enterprises of these states desiring to exploit these resources are effectively controlled by African capital and personnel.

   To be effective, the rights of landlocked states shall be complemented by the right of transit.

   These rights shall be embodied in multilateral or regional or bilateral agreements.

5. The limits of the economic Zone shall be fixed in nautical miles in accordance with regional considerations taking duly into account the resources of the region and the rights and interests of the landlocked and near-landlocked states, without prejudice to the limits already adopted by some States within the region.

After this seminar, the main elements of the EEZ were already established. One of the questions which is often asked is why the proponents used the word "exclusive" when in fact the zone was not all that exclusive. We have in it the freedom of navigation and overflight and freedom of laying submarine cables and pipelines for all states. The right of exploitation of the living resources in the zone is also recognized for landlocked and other geographically disadvantaged states. Even long-distant fisheries concerns of developed countries may be permitted to fish on basis of specific arrangements and fees. But what is *exclusive* is the jurisdiction of the coastal state with respect to those elements for which the economic zone is established, i.e., the right to make and enforce legislation over the economic exploitation of the resources of the Zone and protect it against pollution and other hazards.

It should be pointed out that during the same period, the Latin American countries were also engaged in the preparations for the forthcoming Conference on the Law of the Sea, and they came out with proposals which were very similar to the conclusions of the Yaounde Seminar.[39] Thus in their proposals, the Latin American countries came up with the idea of "patrimonial sea" within which:

1. The coastal state has sovereign rights over the renewable and non-renewable natural resources, which are found in the waters, in the seabed and in the subsoil of an area adjacent to the territorial sea called the "patrimonial sea."
2. The coastal state has the right to regulate the conduct of scientific research within the patrimonial sea, as well as the right to adopt the necessary measures to prevent marine pollution and to ensure its sovereignty over the resources of the area.
3. The breadth of this Zone should be subject to international agreement, preferably of a wideworld scope. The whole of the area of both the territorial sea and the patrimonial sea, taking into account geographic circumstances, should not exceed a maximum of 200 nautical miles.
4. In this Zone, ships and aircrafts of all states, whether coastal or not, should enjoy the right of freedom of navigation and overflight with no restrictions other than those resulting from the exercise by Coastal State of its right within the area. Subject only to these limitations, there will also be freedom for the laying of submarine cables and pipelines.

The most significant difference however between the Santo Domingo declaration and the conclusions of the Yaounde Seminar is that the Latin American countries envisaged the coexistence of a "patrimonial sea" and a separate continental shelf regime, based on the 1958 convention together with the exploitability criteria, whereas the African proposal was to subsume the continental shelf under the EEZ concept, and thus have definite boundaries between the area under national jurisdiction and the international common heritage area. Also the Santo Domingo declaration contains very little concern for the accommodation of the rights and interests of other states, including the landlocked and geographically disadvantaged states. In the African conception, this is a fundamental provision since no proposal can ignore the rights and interests of such states given their numerical weight. Of the fifty African states, fourteen of them are landlocked states, and many others are facing either closed or semi-closed seas or have very narrow coastlines. See tables 6.2 and 6.3 in the annex.

The EEZ proposal was formally presented to the Seabed Committee in August 1972 by the Kenya delegation.[40] As can be seen from its report, the AALCC gave its blessing to the proposals during the fourteenth session in New Delhi.[41] In introducing the draft articles on EEZ, the views of the representative of Kenya were reflected as follows:

His point of departure had been the premise in Article I, that all States have the right to determine their jurisdiction over the Sea adjacent to their coasts, taking into account such considerations as their own geographical, geological, biological, economic, and national security factors. From that basic premise Article II went on to formulate a premise of vital concern to developing countries, i.e., that they had a right to establish an economic Zone beyond a distance of 12 miles beyond their coasts, over the national resource of which they had sovereignty, and wherein they would excercise exclusive jurisdiction for control, prevention, regulation, and exploitation of both living and nonliving resources, for the primary benefit of their peoples and economies. Jurisdiction would also extend to the prevention and control of pollution.[42]

There were, however, some reservations to the reference to the national security factors in the proposal since such reference would tend to assimilate the new zone to the territorial sea. In time, this reference would fall by the way side though logically the concern of the coastal states with the security of its adjoining sea is not irrational.

The Role of the Organization of African Unity in the Harmonization of the African Position in the Law of the Sea Negotiations

Since the commencement of the negotiations on the Law of the Sea, even before the convening of its Third Conference, the OAU has played a unique and unifying role in the harmonization of African position. With a continent with so many divergencies of interests—between landlocked and coastal states, countries with broad continental shelves and those with hardly any, countries with rich fisheries and those without—it would hardly have been possible to have a coherent African position without the political guidance of the OAU.

Thus it is significant that from 1971 to 1979, the OAU Council of Ministers has passed no less than fourteen resolutions on the question of the Law of the Sea.[43] The African governments were thus able during the entire period of the Conference on the Law of the Sea to provide, through their continental organization, political guidance to their delegation to the Conference.

For the purpose of this paper however it is most pertinent to refer to the OAU Declaration on the Issues of the Law of the Sea, which was adopted by the Council of Ministers in Addis Ababa in May 1973 during its twenty-first Ordinary Session.[44] This session had been preceded by a meeting of African experts charged with forging a common African position on all issues to come before the Third UN Conference on the Law of the Sea. Though the group of experts had accepted the idea of an EEZ beyond a territorial sea of 12 nautical miles, the Council of Ministers and the heads of states were not ready to endorse the concept of a 12-mile territorial sea, given the fact that by then many states in Africa had adopted a broader territorial sea, with two (Sierra Leone and Somalia) claiming up to 200 nautical miles territoral sea.

Thus paragraph 1 provided that pending successful negotiations in the forthcoming Conference, the position adopted in the declaration "prejudices neither the present limits of the Territorial Sea of any State nor the existing rights of States."

It is in part C of the declaration where the EEZ concept including Exclusive Fishery Zone was dealt with. It is therein provided

5. That the African States recognize the right of each coastal State to establish an exclusive economic Zone beyond their Territorial Seas whose limits shall not exceed 200 nautical Miles, measured from the baselines establishing their Territorial Sea;
6. That in such Zones the coastal States shall exercise permanent sovereignty over all the living and mineral resources and shall manage the Zone without undue interference with other legitimate uses of the Sea; namely: freedom of navigation, overflight and laying of cables and pipelines;
7. That the African countries consider that scientific research and control of marine pollution in the economic Zone shall be subject to the jurisdiction of coastal States;
8. That the African countries recognize, in order that the resources of the region may benefit all regions therein, that the landlocked and other disadvantaged countries are entitled to share in the exploitation of the region *on equal basis as nationals* of coastal States on basis

of African solidarity and under such regional or bilateral agreements as may be worked out. (emphasis added)

With this declaration adopted at the highest possible level in the OAU, the African position on the Law of the Sea Conference was tremendously strengthened. During the Conference of the Group of 77 in Nairobi in March 1974, the position adopted by the African states on EEZ received very broad support. There were however some discordant views, which continued to create divisions right through the duration of the Conference, and in the end served to undermine the original vision of the EEZ as a defensive mechanism serving to harmonize the interests of all states whether landlocked or coastal, developing or developed.

One of these was with respect to the continental shelf. As already indicated, the African view was that this should be subsumed under the EEZ and the area beyond 200 miles should be high seas for the water column, and the seabed and subsoil thereof should be part of the common heritage of mankind. This would not only have established firm boundaries between national and international zones, but it would have given the new seabed authority the possibility of acquiring hydrocarbon resources, instead of making it dependent, as it now is on deep-seabed manganese nodules, whose exploitation is at best problematic, and highly dependent on technological know-how of the highly developed states, some of whom are currently determined to sabotage the seabed authority.[45]

The second issue was with respect to the rights and interests of the landlocked and geographically disadvantaged countries. The OAU declaration as we have seen above guaranteed them a share on *equal basis as nationals,* and for the landlocked states this to be made meaningful by endorsement for them of "the right of access to and from the Sea." Some of these landlocked countries' representatives thought they could even get more consensus through the creation of regional exclusive economic zone encompassing *both living and nonliving resources* under joint management.[46] This of course could hardly be acceptable to any coastal state since the continental shelf is considered as part of the land territory. This idea of regional economic zones was concretized in a meeting of developing landlocked countries in Kampala in 1974, which preceded the Group of 77 meeting in Nairobi and prepared the Kampala declaration. This miscalculation, based on the fact of numbers since the group of landlocked and geographically disadvantaged countries, which had jointly a total of 53 states—a possible blocking third in any compromise formula—cost these states dearly as they lost possibility of any further active support for gains achieved in the OAU declaration. In article 69 of the Convention on the right of landlocked states:

Landlocked States shall have the right to participate on an equitable basis, in the exploitation of an appropriate part of the *surplus* of the living resources of the exclusive economic Zones of the coastal States of subregion or region, taking into account the relevant economic and geographic circumstances of concerned. (emphasis added)

When it is taken into consideration that the coastal state has the right to *establish the allowable catch of the living resources* in its exclusive economic zone under article 61 (i) and is further entitled "to determine its capacity to harvest" (and thus the surplus) and give other states access to the right to harvest on such terms as may be agreed (article 62) the so-called right of the landlocked states becomes indeed very precarious.

In fact, paragraph 3 of article 69 enables the coastal state to pass on the "right" of landlocked countries to others. This paragraph provides in part:

When the harvesting capacity of a coastal State approaches a point which would enable it to harvest the entire allowable catch of the living resources in its exclusive economic Zone, *the coastal State and other States concerned shall cooperate in establishment of equitable arrangements on a bilateral, subregional or regional basis to allow for participation of developing landlocked States of the same region in the exploitation of living resources of the exclusive economic Zones of the coastal States of the subregion or region* as may be appropriate in the circumstances and on terms satisfactory to all States. (emphasis added)

In fact article 71 enables a coastal State to exclude landlocked and geographically disadvantaged States from its Exclusive Economic Zone. It provides: "The provisions of articles 69 and 70 shall not apply in the case of a coastal State whose economy is overwhelmingly dependent on the exploitation of the living resources of its exclusive zone."

There are some provisions for the geographically disadvantaged states in article 70. The outcome of this unfortunate result for the landlocked countries should be a salutary lesson to all developing countries in general and African countries in particular. United, we stand some chance in multilateral negotiations; divided we are at best mere pawns in others' power games, some of whose ramifications we may hardly be aware of and we can hope to achieve none of the negotiating positions except incidentally.

Thus after years of negotiations since 1970, the EEZ has become a reality in modern international Law of the Sea. In fact, as reflected in part 5 of the Law of the Sea Convention, the concept has become part of customary international law operative even outside the authority of the Convention. It is the international law of many states today, enacted even before the signing of the Convention. It is neither territorial sea nor high seas, even in respect to the competencies not assigned to either the coastal state over resources or the international community for such freedoms as of navigation and overflight, and laying of submarine cables and pipelines and related uses in article 58 of the Convention. This compromise, worked out after lengthy negotiations between the coastal states and maritime powers in the Castenada Group is now reflected in article 56 (2) dealing with the rights and duties of the coastal state and corresponding article 58 (3) on the rights and duties of other states. Thus the EEZ is a zone *sui generis*. Article 59 provides for resolution of conflicts regarding the attribution of rights and jurisdiction in the EEZ. It provides:

Basis for the resolution of conflicts regarding the attribution of rights and jurisdiction in the exclusive economic zone

In cases where this Convention does not attribute rights or jurisdiction to the coastal State or to other States within the exclusive economic zone, and a conflict arises between the interests of the coastal State and any other State or States, the conflict should be resolved on the basis of equity and in the light of all the relevant circumstances, taking into account the respective importance of the interests involved to the parties as well as to the international community as a whole.

It is unnecessary to go into all the provisions in part 5 of the Convention, but article 56 on the *Rights, jurisdiction and duties of the coastal State in the exclusive economic zone* is so fundamental to the concept that it cannot be abbreviated. It provides:

1. In the exclusive economic zone, the coastal State has:
   a) sovereign rights for the purpose of exploring and exploiting, conserving and managing the natural resources, whether living or non-living, of the seabed and subsoil and the superjacent waters, and with regard to other activities for the economic exploitation and exploration of the Zone, such as the production of energy from water, currents and winds;
   b) jurisdiction as provided for in the relevant provisions of this Convention with regard to
      i) the establishment and use of artificial islands, installation and structures;
      ii) marine research;
      iii) the protection and preservation of marine environment;
   c) Other rights and duties provided for in this Convention.
2. In exercising of its rights and performing its duties under this Convention in the exclusive economic Zone, the coastal State shall have due regard to the rights and duties of other States and shall act in a manner compatible with provisions of this Convention.
3. The rights set out in this Article, with respect to the seabed, and subsoil shall be exercised in accordance with Part VI: Continental Shelf)

Where Do African States Go from Here

It is no exaggeration to say that the African states initiating, nurturing and protecting the concept of the EEZ—of course with the support of other developing countries—is the greatest success they have ever achieved in radically altering international law so as to have their interest recognized and respected. Since Grotius articulated the Law of the Sea under the guise of the so-called "freedoms of the Sea" to cover as a cloak for the interests of the maritime powers there has never been such revolutionary change in the Law of the Sea. Even those states which have so treacherously betrayed the confidence in international negotiations by repudiating the results of over twelve years of intensive negotiations to achieve the concensus *text* now reflected in the Convention of the Law of the Sea, proclaim that the EEZ concept has become customary international law. Thus the last special representative of the United States President has had this to say:

Many countries had expressed some fear that the United States, by removing itself from the Conference process, would reject all jurisdictional claims reflected in the Convention. This fear was unfounded. By establishing an EEZ and clearly setting forth the principles upon which the U.S. national policy will be based, the United States has reassured the International Community and restored U.S. leadership in the development of International Oceans Law. It is a positive demonstration of continued U.S. opposition to certain unacceptable provisions in the Convention but at the same time demonstrates U.S. willingness to conform to *those portions of the treaty that reflect customary International Law.*[47] (emphasis added)

The EEZ concept must be seen as a fundamental part of the new international economic order. In the African context it must be seen as one of the essential aspects for the realization of the goals of the Lagos Plan of Action and the Final Act for the creation of an African Economic Community by the Year A.D. 2000. Yet hardly any African country—for that matter the OAU—is doing anything to realize the immense resources potential of the seas around Africa, which are its economic zone. Apart from the various legislations establishing various national EEZs, there are hardly any regulations at national, regional, or continental level for the exploration, exploitation or conservation of the zone. If anything, the African fish catch today is less than it was in the early '70s. This malaise must be overcome to reverse the trend and realize our potential.

At the OAU level, it is necessary to initiate, in consultation with competent international organizations, the process for formulating model rules and regulations for adoption by the national governments. The EEZs around Africa are all interrelated both in species to be found therein and physical characteristics. As we have seen above the extent of some of these zones are so restricted that it will be suicidal for each coast state to adopt its own unrelated rules and regulations.

In the long run, the member states must still work to realize the aims of the OAU Declaration, which stated in paragraph 11: "That the

African States in order to develop and manage the resources of the region take all possible measures including cooperation in the conservation and management of the living resources and the prevention and control of pollution to conserve the marine environment, establish such regional institutions as may be necessary and settle disputes between them in accordance with regional arrangements."

This now is our most challenging task.

ANNEX
Revised Draft Articles on the Exclusive Economic Zone

(Submitted by Kenya as Member of AALCC)

Article I

All States have a right to determine the limits of their jurisdiction over the seas adjacent to their coasts beyond a territorial sea of 12 miles in accordance with criteria which take into account their own geographical, geological, biological, ecological, economic, and *national security factors.*

Article II

In accordance with the foregoing article, all States have the right to establish an economic zone beyond the territorial sea for the primary benefit of their peoples and their respective economies, in which they shall exercise sovereign rights over natural resources for the purpose of exploration and exploitation. Within the zone they shall have exclusive jurisdiction for the purpose of control, regulation and exploitation of both living and nonliving resources of the zone and their preservation, and for the purpose of prevention and control of pollution.

The coastal State shall exercise jurisdiction over its economic zone and third States or their nationals shall bear responsibility for damage resulting from their activities within the zone.

Article III

The establishment of such a zone shall be without prejudice to the exercise of freedom of navigation, freedom of overflight and freedom to lay submarine cables and pipelines as recognized in internatinal law.

Article IV

The exercise of jurisdiction over the zone shall encompass all the economic resources of the area, living and non-living, either on the water surface or within the water column, or on the soil or sub-soil of the seabed and ocean floor below.

Article V

Without prejudice to the general jurisdictional competence conferred upon the coastal State by Article II above, the state may establish special regulations within its economic zone for—

(a) Exclusive exploration and exploitation of non-renewable marine resources;
(b) Exclusive or preferential exploitation of renewable resources;
(c) Protection and conservation of renewable resources;
(d) Control, prevention and elimination of pollution of marine environment;
(e) Scientific research.

Article VI

The coastal State shall permit the exploitation of the living resources within its economic zone to the neighbouring developing land-locked or near land-locked States and States with a small shelf provided the enterprises of those States desiring to exploit these resources are effectively controlled by their national capital and personnel.

To be effective the rights of land-locked or near-land-locked States shall be complemented by the right of access to the sea and the right of transit. These rights shall be embodied in multilateral, regional or bilateral agreements.

Article VII

The limits of the economic zone shall be fixed in nautical miles in accordance with criteria in each region, which take into consideration the resources of the region and rights and interests of developing land-locked, near-land locked, shelf-locked States, and States with narrow shelves and without prejudice to limits adopted by any State within the region. The economic zone shall not in any case exceed 200 nautical miles, measured from the baselines for determining territorial sea.

Article VIII

The delineation of the economic zone between adjacent and opposite States shall be carried out in accordance with international law. Dispute arising there from shall be settled in conformity with the Charter of the United Nations and any other relevant regional arrangements.

Article IX

Neighbouring developing States shall mutually recognize their existing historic rights. They shall also give reciprocal preferential treatment to one another in the exploitation of the living resources of their respective economic zones.

Article X

Each State shall ensure that any exploration or exploitation activity within its economic zone is carried out exclusively for peaceful purposes and in such a manner as not to interfere unduly with the legitimate interests of other States in the region or those of the international community.

Article XI

No territory under foreign domination and control shall be entitled to establish an economic zone.

Table 6.1.   Breadth of Territorial Sea and Fishing Jurisdiction at Present Claimed by Asian–African States

Country	Territorial Sea	Fishing	Other Claims
Algeria	12 miles	12 miles	
Burma	12 miles	12 miles	
Cambodia	12 miles	12 miles	Continental shelf to 50 meters including sovereignty over superjacent waters
Cameroon	18 miles	18 miles	
Ceylon	6 miles	6 miles	Plus right to establish 100 miles conservation zones
China	3 miles	3 miles	
Congo (Brazzaville)	3 miles	3 miles	
Congo (Kinshasa)	3 miles	3 miles	
Cyprus	12 miles	12 miles	
Dahomey	12 miles	12 miles	
Ethiopia	12 miles	12 miles	
Gabon	12 miles	12 miles	
Gambia	3 miles	3 miles	
Ghana	12 miles	12 miles	Undefined protective areas may be proclaimed seaward of territorial sea, and up to 100 miles seaward of territorial sea may be proclaimed fishing conservation zone
Guinea	130 miles	130 miles	
India	12 miles	12 miles	Plus right to establish 100 miles conservation zones
Indonesia	12 miles	12 miles	Archipelago concept baselines
Iran	12 miles	12 miles	
Iraq	12 miles	12 miles	
Ivory Coast	6 miles	12 miles	
Japan	3 miles	3 miles	
Jordan	12 miles	12 miles	

Table 6.1.   *(Continued)*

Country	Territorial Sea	Fishing	Other Claims
Kenya	12 miles	12 miles	
Korea, Rep. of	Not available	20–200 miles	Continental shelf including sovereignty over superjacent waters
Kuwait	12 miles	12 miles	
Lebanon	Not available	6 miles	
Liberia	12 miles	12 miles	
Libya	12 miles	12 miles	
Malagasy Republic	12 miles	12 miles	
Malaysia	12 miles	12 miles	
Mauritania	12 miles	12 miles	
Mauritius	12 miles	12 miles	
Morocco	3 miles	12 miles	Exception—6 miles for Strait of Gibraltar
Nigeria	12 miles	12 miles	
Pakistan	12 miles	12 miles	Plus right to establish 100 miles conservation zones
Philippines	Archipelago concept baselines; water baselines and limits described in Treaty of Paris, December 10, 1968, U.S.-Spain Treaty of November 7, 1900, and U.S.-U.K. Treaty of January 2, 1930, considered to be the territorial sea		
Saudi Arabia	12 miles	12 miles	
Senegal	12 miles	12 miles	Plus 6 miles contiguous zone
Sierra Leone	12 miles	12 miles	
Singapore	3 miles	3 miles	
Somali Republic	6 miles	6 miles	
Sudan	12 miles	12 miles	
Syria	12 miles	12 miles	Plus 6 miles "necessary supervision zone"
Tanzania	12 miles	12 miles	
Togo	12 miles	12 miles	
Thailand	12 miles	12 miles	
Tunisia	6 miles	12 miles	Territorial sea follows the 50 meters isobath for part of the coast (maximum 65 miles)
Turkey	6 miles	12 miles	
U.A.R.	12 miles	12 miles	
Viet Nam	3 miles	20 miles (10.8 miles)	
Yemen	12 miles	12 miles	

NOTE: The following Asian-African states have no coastline: Burundi, Botswana, Central African Republic, Chad, Lesotho, Malawi, Mali, Niger, Rwanda, Swaziland, Uganda, Upper Volta, Zambia, Zimbabwe.

Table 6.2

Country	Length of Coastline (nautical miles)	Country	Length of Coastline (nautical miles)
Algeria	596	Libya	910
Cameroon	187	Morocco	862
Congo	84	Mauritania	360
Dahomey	65	Mauritius	
Egypt	1,307	Madagascar	2,155
Ethiopia	506	Nigeria	415
Equatorial Guinea		Senegal	241
Gambia	38	Sierra Leone	219
Ghana	285	Sudan	387
Guinea	190	Somalia	1,596
Gabon	399	Tunisia	555
Guinea Bissau		Tanzania	669
Ivory Coast	274	Togo	26
Kenya	247	Zaire	22
Liberia	290		
Albania	155	Malaysia	1,855
Argentina	2,120	Maldive Islands	251
Australia	15,091	Malta	50
Belgium	34	Mexico	4,848
Brazil	3,692	Monaco	3
Bulgaria	134	Muscat and Oman	1,005
Burma	1,230	Netherlands	198
Cambodia	210	New Zealand	2,770
Canada	11,129	Nicaragua	445
Ceylon (Sri Lanka)	650	North Korea	750
Chile	2,882	North Vietnam	382
China	3,492	Norway	1,650
Colombia	1,022	Pakistan	750
Costa Rica	446	Panama	979
Cuba	1,747	Peru	1,258
Cyprus	290	Philippines	6,997
Denmark	686	Poland	241
Dominican Republic	325	Portugal	398
East Germany	191	Romania	113
Ecuador	458	Saudi Arabia	1,316
El Salvador	164	Singapore	28
Finland	735	Spain	1,494
France	1,373	South Korea	712
Greece	1,645	South Vietnam	865
Guatemala	178	Soviet Union	23,098
Guyana	232	Sweden	1,359
Haiti	584	Syria	82
Honduras	374	Taiwan	470
Iceland	1,080	Thailand	1,299
India	2,451	Trinidad & Tobago	254
Indonesia	19,889	Turkey	1,921
Iran	990	Union of South Africa	1,430

Table 6.2   *(Continued)*

Country	Length of Coastline (nautical miles)	Country	Length of Coastline (nautical miles)
Iraq	10	United Kingdom	2,790
Ireland	663	United States	11,650
Israel	124	Uruguay	305
Italy	2,451	Venezuela	1,081
Jamaica	280	Western Samoa	241
Japan	4,842	West Germany	308
Jordan	5	Yemen	244
Kuwait	115	Yugoslavia	426
Lebanon	105		

Table 6.3

68 Disadvantaged States (Coastal)			
France	24	North Vietnam	
Thailand	24	Saudi Arabia	
Honduras	23	Tunisia	
Venezuela	22	Iran	7
Morocco	21	Congo	
China		Singapore	
Senegal		Syria	
Sierra Leone	20	Khmer Republic	6
Ghana		Algeria	5
Pakistan		Yugoslavia	5
Western Samoa		Bulgaria	
Gabon	19	Ethiopia	
Cyprus		Federal Republic of Germany	
Nicaragua	18	Quatar	
Libya	16	Sudan	4
El Salvador		Dahomey	
North Korea		Israel	
Malta	15	Lebanon	
Guyana		Romania	
Trinidad and Tobago		Gambia	3
Turkey		Kuwait	
Tanzania	13	Yemen	
Nigeria		Poland	2
Uruguay		Albania	
Netherlands	12	Bahrain	
Sweden		Bangladesh	
United Arab Emirates	11	Belgium	
Denmark		Cameroon	
Egypt		Finland	
Guatemala		German Democratic Republic	1
Mauritania		Iraq	
Ivory Coast	9	Jordan	
Kenya	8	Togo	
Guinea		Zaire	

Of these 68 states, 54 are developing states, and 14 are industrialized states.

Table 6.3   *(Continued)*

29 Disadvantaged States (Landlocked)	
Afghanistan	Malawi
Austria	Mali
Bhutan	Mongolia
Bolivia	Nepal
Botswana	Niger
Burundi	Paraguay
Byelorussian SSR	Rwanda
Luxembourg	San Marino
Central African Republic	Swaziland
Chad	Switzerland
Czechoslovakia	Uganda
Hungary	Upper Volta
Laos	Vatican City
Lesotho	Zambia
Liechtenstein	Zimbabwe

34 Advantaged States			
New Zealand	435	Iceland	102
Japan	314	Madagascar	90
Indonesia	266	United Kingdom	87
Mauritius	241	Spain	77
Portugal	214	Brazil	
Maldives	211	India	74
Fiji	187	Soviet Union	68
Australia		Sri Lanka	67
Norway	172	South Vietnam	63
United States		Greece	56
Philippines		Oman	54
Chile	164	South Africa	
Tonga	128	Somalia	53
Nauru		Jamaica	52
Mexico	125	Ireland	49
Ecuador	103	Yemen	
Canada		Italy	48

15 States Neither Advantaged Nor Disadvantaged			
Argentina	45	Costa Rica	36
Equatorial Guinea	43	Barbados	
Cuba		Burma	34
Peru	41	Colombia	33
South Korea		Namibia	31
Malaysia	40	Liberia	26
Panama	39	Haiti	25
Dominican Rep.	37		

Of these 15, all are developing states.

NOTE: African states are underlined; index numbers represent percent of theoretical economic zone.

NOTES

1. For historical discussion of these claims see T. W. Fulton, *The Sovereignty of the Sea* (1911; reprint Millwood, N.Y.: Kraus, 1976), pp. 3–6.

2. Grotius, *Mare Liberium* (Oxford: Clarendon Press, reprinted 1916).

3. See *Mare Liberum*, ch. 5.

4. Of principal interest are the works of William Welwood, *Abridgement of All the Sea Laws* (1613), republished in 1972 by Teatrun; Amsterdam and Selden, *Mare Claussum: Of the Dominion or Ownership of the Sea*, translation by Marchamont Medham (London 1635). See also Potter, *The Freedom of the Sea in History, Law, and Politics* (1924), pp. 57–80; and Critchton, "Grotius and Freedom of the Seas" *Juris Review* (1941), 53:226.

5. Oppenheim, *International Law: A Treatise* (8th ed. by H. Lauterpacht 1955), pp. 593–594.

6. Bynhershoek "De Diminio Maria Dessertio" (reprinted by Oxford: Clarendon Press, 1933).

7. De Vattel, *De Droit des Gens* (Carnegie translation, 1916), pp. 106–109.

8. See discussion on the three-mile limit in an article by Bernard G. Heinzen, "The Three-Mile Limit: Preserving the Freedom of Sea" *Stanford Law Review*, 11:597.

9. The proposal, jointly presented by the United States and Canada, failed to be adopted by the plenary, 54 votes being in favor, 28 against, and 5 abstentions, thus not being able to secure the required two-thirds majority.

10. A/Conf. 19/c.1/L 10

11. Only Ethiopia, Ghana, Guinea, Liberia, Morocco, Sudan, Tunisia, and United Arab Republic participated.

12. Asian African Legal Consultative Committee 12th Session, Colombo, *Brief of Documents*, 4:93–95.

13. For instance, Portugal in 1910 prohibited trawling by steam vessels within the limit of the shelf as defined by 100-fathom (200-meter) isobath. The Pearl Fisheries Ordinance of Ceylon of 1925 provided the exclusive control by Ceylon of the adjacent pearl fisheries within a defined area based on 100-fathom isobath. See Cosford, "The Continental Shelf, 1910–1945," *McGill Law Journal* (1958), 4:245.

14. State Dept. *Bulletin* (1945), 13:485.

15. *Ibid.*, pp. 484–485.

16. See, for instance, Brazil by Decree No. 28840 of November 8, 1950, and India Proclamation of August 30, 1955.

17. For instance Chile by Presidential Proclamation of June 23, 1947, and Costa Rica by declaration of July 27, 1948, Decree Law No. 803 of November 2, 1949, and the constitution of November 9, 1949.

18. See Honduras Congressional Decree No. 102 amending the constitution.

19. Proclamation of Israel of August 3, 1952.

20. Presidential proclamation of October 29 by Mexico.

21. Declaration of the Governor General of Pakistan on March 9, 1950.

22. Royal pronouncement of Saudi Arabia of May 28, 1949.

23. See the decision reached at the Inter-American Specialized Conference on "Conservation of Natural Resources: the Continental Shelf and Marine Waters" held at Ciudad Trijillo in 1956.

24. Shigeru Oda, "Proposal on Revision of the Continental Shelf," *Colombia Journal of Transitional Law* (Spring 1968), 9(1):910.

25. (1969) *I.C.J. Reports* 3.

26. 2 Dodson 210, 165 Eng. Repts 1464 (1817).

27. De Vattel, *De Droit des Gens,* ch. 23.

28. See Map No. 2691 prepared by UNITAR, in December 1971, and reproduced by International Petroleum Encyclopedia, 1973.

29. *Twenty Years of Asian–African Legal Cooperation* by A. N. Ray, chief justice of India, contained in the Twentieth Anniversary Commemorative Volume entitled *Essays on International Law,* published by AALCC in 1976.

30. Report of the Twelfth Session of the Asian–African Legal Consultative, p. 37.

31. Report of the Twelfth Session of AALCC, pp. 93–94.

32. *Revista Peruvianade Derecho International* (1952), 12:244–246.

33. Referred to by Goggs, "National Claims in Adjacent Seas," *Geographical Review* (1951), 16:185.

34. Grotius, *Defensio Capitis Quinti Maria Liberi* (Defense of chapter 5 of *Mare Liberum*) (Wright translation), pp. 183–205 (1928).

35. See Annex 1 of the Convention on the Law of the Sea A/CONF. 62/L78.

36. During the Lagos meeting of the Conference, the Kenya delegation submitted draft articles on the Exclusive Economic Zone, which are annexed to this article. See the report of the Fourteenth Session of the AALCC held in Lagos from January 10 to 18, 1973, pp. 61–63.

37. The following countries sent experts to the seminar: Algeria, Cameroon, Central African Republic, Dahomey (Benin), Egypt, Ethiopia, Ghana, Kenya, Nigeria, Morocco, Sierra Leone, Senegal, Tanzania, Togo, Tunisia, and Zaire.

38. Originally issued as a document the Seabed Committee, document A/AC138/79, the Conclusions are now embodied in the *Report of the Committee on the Peaceful Uses of the Seabed and the Ocean Floor beyond the Limits of National Jurisdiction,* Official Records of the Twenty-Seventh Session of the General Assembly, Supplement No. 21 (A/8721).

39. See "Text of the Declaration of Santo Domingo" approved by the Ministers of Specialized Conference of Carribean Countries, Problems of the Sea, held on June 7, 1972, originally issued as a document of the Seabed Committee A/AC138-80 and now contained in the Official Records of Twenty-Seventh Session of the General Assembly, Supplement No. 21 (A/8721), pp. 70–73.

40. Originally issued as document A/A138/SC11/L10 and now contained in Supplement No. 21 (A/8721) above cited, pp. 180–182.

41. See "Report of the Fourteenth Session Held in New Delhi" January, 10–18, 1973, pp. 57–76.

42. See Report of the Fourteenth Session of AALCC, p. 58.

43. The following are the relevant resolutions: CM/Res. 238 (XVI) of June 1971, *Problems of the Seabed;* CM/Res. 289 (XIX) of June 1972, *Resolution on the*

Law of the Sea; CM/Res. 382 (XXIII) of June 1974, *Resolution on the Law of the Sea;* CM/Res. 520 (XXVII) of July 1974, *Admission of Peoples Republic of Angola to the UN Conference on the Law of the Sea;* CM/Res. (XXVII) of July 1976, *International Zone Extending Beyond National Jurisdiction;* CM/Res. 539 (XXVIII) of February 1977, *Resolution on the Law of the Sea;* CM/Res. 570 of July 1977, *Resolution on the Law of the Sea;* CM/Res. 649 (XXXI) of July 1978, *Resolution on the Law of the Sea;* CM/Res. 745 (XXXIII) of July 1979, *Resolution on the Law of the Sea;* CM/Res. 795 (XXXV) of June 1980, *UN Conference on the Law of the Sea;* CM/Res. (XXXVII) of June 1981, *UN Conference on the Law of the Sea;* ECM/Res. 1 (XII) of March 1979, *Resolution Concerning Future Sessions of the Law of the Sea Conference;* ECM/Res. of March 1979, *Resolution on the Law of the Sea.*

44. The document which was originally issued as document A/AC138/89 and subsequently incorporated in the Official Records of the Twenty-Eighth Session of the General Assembly Supplement No. 21 (A/9021), "The Report of the Committee on the Peaceful Uses of the Seabed and Ocean Floor beyond the limit of National Jurisdiction."

45. Of those who signed the Convention in Montego Bay, only France and Japan were included among the major Western powers. Belgium, the Federal Republic of Germany, Italy, the United Kingdom, and the United States refused to sign, an act of unparalleled treachery since these countries had been pivotal in the negotiations of the seabed provisions and had extracted numerous concessions to make the final treaty acceptable to them. See the Official List of *Signatories of the Convention,* pp. 190, of the UN publication, *The Law of the Sea,* United Nations Convention on the Law of the Sea, published in 1983.

46. Proposals presented by Uganda and Zambia in Caracas.

47. See James L. Malone, "Who needs the Sea Treaty?" *Foreign Policy* (Spring 1984), no. 54, p. 61.

7.
Law of the Sea:
The Latin American View

ANDRÉS AGUILAR MAWDSLEY

IN 1945, after the end of World War II, there began a process of revising the international Law of the Sea and bringing it up to date, a process that has culminated, for the time being, with the United Nations Convention on the Law of the Sea which was opened for signature on December 10, 1982 at Montego Bay, Jamaica.

The Latin American states played a very active role in that process and made significant contributions to the elaboration of the new rules of the Law of the Sea.[1] The positions taken and the proposals presented by those countries in unilateral and multilateral claims, in individual and collective policy statements, in regional and subregional forums, and at the three United Nations conferences on the Law of the Sea, unquestionably influenced the changes undergone by that branch of international law during that period of almost forty years. To better understand the position of the Latin American states at the Third United Nations Conference on the Law of the Sea, it is necessary to recall their basic interests and the history of their position on some of the most important subjects and issues pertaining to the Law of the Sea.

The perception of these interests and the position of these states have evolved with time. Several stages can be distinguished in this process: a first stage, from the independence of these countries until the end of World War II in 1945; a second stage, from 1945 until the First United Nations Conference on the Law of the Sea (1958); a third stage, encompassing the First and Second United Nations conferences on the Law of the Sea (1958–1960); a fourth stage, from 1960 until the convening in December 1970 of the Third United Nations Conference on the Law of the Sea, and a fifth and last stage covering the preparatory work for this last Conference (1970–1973) and the Conference itself (1973–1982).

From Independence to 1945

The interest of the countries of Latin America in the Law of the Sea is not a recent development. Since their independence at the beginning of the nineteenth century,[2] they were aware of the importance of the sea for their security and defense, for trade and navigation and as a source of food and raw materials. As far back as 1832 the great Venezuelan writer and jurist, Andrés Bello, who was then in the service of the government of Chile, in his book *Principles of International Law*,[3] gave a clear explanation of the generally accepted doctrine on the legal regime of the sea and the existing practice of states. At the same time, and with great vision, he expounded original ideas on the use of marine resources. Interestingly enough, those ideas became the antecedents of the claims laid many years later by the Latin American countries, and of that new institution, the exclusive economic zone. The following paragraphs from Bello's work are particularly interesting:

As a security measure, it is enough to hold sway over that very small area of the adjacent sea which can never be entirely free, for its joint use would inconvenience us at every step and which we can appropriate without rendering the territory of other peoples insecure and even without disturbing their navigation and trade.

In the last paragraph of his comments on the subject, he states:

However, from another point of view, the sea is like the land. Many marine products are confined only to certain areas, because, just as not all lands yield the same fruits so do the seas not supply the same products. Coral, pearls, amber, whales are only found in limited areas of the ocean, which are being depleted daily and will eventually become extinct. In the past whales were frequently found in the Bay of Biscay; today they must be pursued all the way to the coasts of Greenland and Spitzbergen; and no matter how great nature's fecundity may be in other species, there can be no doubt that participation by too many countries would render fishing the more difficult and less profitable, and could bring about their extinction or drive them away to other seas. Thus, since they are not inexhaustible, it would seem legitimate for a people to appropriate those areas to which no other peoples have laid a claim.[4]

Latin America's interest in the sea was kept alive for the remainder of the nineteenth and into the first decades of the twentieth century, as borne out by the many studies published in various Latin American states on subjects dealing with the Law of the Sea and by the research undertaken in those countries on the geography, geology, biology, and the resources of the marine environment. It may be said, however, that until World War II, the Latin American states followed the rules of the traditional Law of the Sea, based on the doctrine of the freedom of the seas, which had already been generally recognized by the end of the eighteenth century and formed part of positive customary international law.[5] In point of fact, the Latin American countries then had no strong reasons to object to or to seek to change those rules and, given the way the international community was constituted at the time, it is highly likely that any attempt in that direction would have met with considerable difficulties. In this connection, it is useful to recall that at the Seventh Inter-American Conference, held in Montevideo in 1933, under chapter II.6, Problems of International Law: Method for the Progressive Codification of International Law and Consideration of Codification Topics, the agenda included an item on the territorial sea. However, in its Resolution 6, adopted on December 16, 1933, that conference declared that, for the time being, it did not consider it possible to prepare a draft treaty on the subject.

From the End of World War II to the First UN Conference on the Law of the Sea (1958)

As a result of a number of factors the situation began to change in 1945. To begin with, the rapid and sharp increase in the world population and the shortage of land-based resources to meet the growing demand for energy, food and raw materials had stimulated swift scientific and technological advances. These, in turn, made it possible to intensify traditional activities such as navigation, fishing, marine hunting and the exploitation of oil and other resources in the seabed and subsoil at ever greater distances from the coast and at increasing depths. Second, there were radical changes in the composition and organization of the international community after World War II. The establishment of the United Nations Organization, the progressive elimination of colonialism and other forms of dependency, which led to the emergence of many new states in Asia, Africa, and the Caribbean, have all made international relations more democratic, with wider participation, and made possible and encouraged a revision of the rules, which had traditionally governed the Law of the Sea and other subjects.

Without minimizing the importance of the sea even today from the point of view of the security and defense of states and of communications—navigation, overflight and the laying of submarine cables and pipelines—it is obvious that the fundamental basic reason for the changes made in the international Law of the Sea during the last forty years has been the need to draw up new rules in conservation and the rational use and distribution of the resources of the sea. It has been said, and rightly so, that the fundamental objective of the new Law of the Sea has been to establish a generally acceptable regime on resources. Unlike traditional law, which placed the emphasis on communications, the new Law of the Sea is resource-oriented.

At any rate, a careful analysis of the initiatives taken on the subject by the Latin American countries—legislation, declarations, proposals—will clearly show that this question of resources has been in the forefront of their interests and concerns. Moreover, those same interests and concerns were shared by the major maritime powers, as is borne out by the fact that the first claims of sovereignty or of special competence over maritime areas beyond the territorial sea were made by some of those powers.

Indeed, it is interesting to note that the first of such claims, in chronological order, was the treaty concluded between Venezuela and the United Kingdom on the submarine areas of the Gulf of Paria. That treaty, however, had no repercussions, perhaps because its scope was limited. President Truman's proclamations 2667 and 2668 of September 28, 1945, on the other hand, marked the point of departure of a profound and speedy evolution of the international Law of the Sea.

The most important proclamation is number 2667, dealing with U.S. policy with respect to the natural resources of the subsoil and seabed of the continental shelf. According to that proclamation, "The Government of the United States regards the natural resources of the subsoil and sea bed of the continental shelf beneath the high seas but contiguous to the coasts of the United States as appertaining to the United States, subject to its jurisdiction and control." It specifies, further, that "The character as high seas of the waters above the continental shelf and the right to their free and unimpeded navigation are in no way thus affected." That proclamation does not determine the extent of the continental shelf, but in a press communique issued the same day as the proclamation, it was described as "submerged land which is contiguous to the continent and which is covered by no more than 100 fathoms" (equivalent to approximately 200 meters).

It is useful to remember the reasons invoked by the United States to justify that decision:

WHEREAS the Government of the United States of America, aware of the long range worldwide need for new sources of petroleum and other minerals, holds the view that efforts to discover and make available new supplies of these resources should be encouraged; and

WHEREAS its competent experts are of the opinion that such resources underlie many parts of the continental shelf off the coasts of the United States of America, and that with modern technological progress their utilization is already practicable or will become so at an early date; and

WHEREAS recognized jurisdiction over these resources is required in the interest of their conservation and prudent utilization when and as development is undertaken; and

WHEREAS it is the view of the Government of the United States that the exercise of jurisdiction over the natural resources of the subsoil and sea bed of the continental shelf by the contiguous nation is reasonable and just, since the effectiveness of measures to utilize or conserve these resources would be contingent upon cooperation and protection from the shore, since the continental shelf may be regarded as an extension of the land-mass of the coastal nation and thus naturally appurtenant to it, since these resources frequently form a seaward extension of a pool or deposit lying within the territory, and since self-protection compels the coastal nation to keep close watch over activities off its shores which are of the nature necessary for utilization of these resources.

In the other proclamation of the same date, number 2668, the United States set the following policy with respect to coastal fisheries in certain areas of the high seas:

In view of the pressing need for conservation and protection of fishery resources, the Government of the United States regards it as proper to establish conservation zones in those areas of the high seas contiguous to the coasts of the United States wherein fishing activities have been or in the future may be developed and maintained on a substantial scale. Where such activities have been or shall hereafter be developed and maintained by its nationals alone, the United States regards it as proper to establish explicitly bounded conservation zones in which fishing activities shall be subject to the regulation and control of the United States. Where such activities have been or shall hereafter be legitimately developed and maintained jointly by nationals of the United States and nationals of other States, explicitly bounded conservation zones may be established under agreements between the United States and such other States; and all fishing activities in such zones shall be subject to regulation and control as provided in such agreements. The right of any State to establish conservation zones off its shores in accordance with the above principles is conceded, provided that corresponding recognition is given to any fishing interests of nationals of the United States which may exist in such areas. The character as high seas of the areas in which such conservation zones are estabished and the right to their free and unimpeded navigation are in no way thus affected.

This proclamation is preceded by the following considerations:

WHEREAS for some years the Government of the United States of America has viewed with concern the inadequacy of present arrangements for the protection and perpetuation of the fishery resources contiguous to its coasts, and in view of the potentially disturbing effect of this situation, has carefully studied the possibility of improving the jurisdictional basis for conservation measures and international cooperation in this field; and

WHEREAS such fishery resources have a special importance to coastal communities as a source of livelihood and to the nation as a food and industrial resource; and

WHEREAS the progressive development of new methods and techniques contributes to intensified fishing over wide sea areas and in certain cases seriously threatens fisheries with depletion; and

WHEREAS there is an urgent need to protect coastal fishery resources from destructive exploitation, having due regard to conditions peculiar to each region and situation and to the special rights and equities of the coastal State and of any other State which may have established a legitimate interest therein.

The reasons advanced by the United States to justify such measures—basically economic and social—were valid for other states as well. It is not surprising, therefore, that those initiatives triggered a chain reaction. As regards the Latin American countries, President Truman's proclamations prompted most of them to lay their own claims. While in some cases they went further than those of the United States and were based on other considerations, basically their objectives were the same. In fact, those objectives were simply to establish a clear legal title to the marine resources and to take appropriate measures for the conservation and rational use of such resources, without impinging on the freedom of communications. This is clearly borne out by an analysis of their declarations and the constitutional, legal or regulatory norms established by most of the Latin American countries between 1945 and 1958.

Before discussing those Latin American initiatives, however, some explanations are called for. So far, Latin America has been referred to as a whole, and it is indeed a fact that, on some questions, all the states in this group have the same points of view and interests. To begin with, they are all developing countries, members of the Group of 77 (comprising today 126 states), which came into being at the First United Nations Conference on Trade and Development, held in Geneva in 1964. As will be shown later, at the Third United Nations Conference on the Law of the Sea, that Group took a common stand on such important subjects as the legal regime for the seabed and ocean floor beyond the limits of national jurisdiction. Second, what has been called the Inter-American system, which had its beginning at the end of the last century and took on a more finished shape with the establishment of the Organization of American States at the Ninth Inter-American Conference held in Bogota, Colombia, in 1948, allowed for and promoted frequent consultations among those countries, as well as the development of common norms and practices, so much so that one can speak of an "American International Law." Lastly, geographical, historical and, in general, cultural links established since colonial times have contributed to the development of common Latin American institutions and positions.

On the other hand, differences in the geographical location of those states in relation to the sea, and the different characteristics of the areas of the sea close to the coasts of the States of the region have naturally led to divergent positions on some important issues such as the breadth of the territorial sea and the nature and scope of the rights of those states over the resources in the areas of the seas beyond the territorial sea. It has been justly observed that the Law of the Sea is, "par excellence, a Law that takes into account the geographical situation of the State and the possible consequences deriving from that situation."[6] For example, it is obvious that Latin American coastal countries do not have the same interests as the two noncoastal states, Bolivia and Paraguay. Nor among the former is the attitude of those whose coasts face vast, open maritime spaces—Argentina, Uruguay, and Brazil in the South Atlantic, and Chile, Ecuador, El Salvador, and Peru on the South Pacific, the same as the attitude of those whose coasts wholly—or in part—face semi-enclosed seas—Costa Rica, Colombia, Cuba, the Dominican Republic, Haiti, Honduras, Guatemala, Mexico, Nicaragua, Panama, and Venezuela. From other points of view, a distinction can be drawn between the continental and the island states, such as Cuba, the Dominican Republic, Haiti; between states with a broad continental shelf such as Argentina and states with a very narrow continental shelf such as Ecuador, Peru, and Chile. There is a difference between states mainly interested in the living resources of the sea, such as Chile, Ecuador and Peru, and those whose primary interest is oil or mineral resources, i.e., Mexico and Venezuela. Finally, there are states with specific interests in some issues: archipelagic states, like the Bahamas, Cuba and Trinidad and Tobago, and states bordering straits used for international navigation.

This diversity of interests explains the wide variety in the positions of states as can be seen in the unilateral and multilateral claims made by most of the Latin American countries in the period between the publication of the Truman proclamations (September 1945) and the First United Nations Conference on the Law of the Sea (Geneva, 1958). During this period Argentina, Costa Rica, El Salvador, Guatemala, Honduras, Mexico, Nicaragua, and Panama; Chile, Cuba, Dominican Republic, Ecuador, and Peru; Brazil and Venezuela made claims that to a greater or lesser degree differed from those contained in President Truman's proclamations.[7] While almost all claimed rights over the continental shelf, as a general rule they depart from the Truman proclamation on the subject, on such important aspects as the very concept of the continental shelf and its extension and the nature of the rights of the coastal state in this maritime space, and some clearly go further than U.S. claims. Such is the case with Argentina's claim over the epicontinental sea and the claims made by Chile, Peru, Ecuador, and other states, of sovereignty or jurisdiction over areas extending to a distance of two hundred nautical miles from the coast.

During that same period (1945–1958) important agreements were reached on questions relating to the Law of the Sea at a number of specialized conferences and at meetings of organs of the Inter-American system.

Among those agreements, the Santiago Declaration on the Maritime Zone, which was adopted at the First Conference on the Exploitation and Conservation of Marine Resources in the South Pacific, held in Santiago, Chile, in August 1952, is of particular importance. That declaration, which was signed by Chile, Ecuador, and Peru, and later ratified by those states was the first Latin American multilateral instrument to endorse and spell out the claims already made by Chile, Peru, and other states to rights over a two-hundred-mile maritime zone.[8]

The preambular part of that declaration affirms that "Governments are bound to ensure for their people access to necessary food supplies and to furnish them with the means of developing their economy" and that it is therefore "the duty of each government to ensure the conservation and protection of its natural resources and to regulate the use thereof to the greatest possible advantage of its country," and also "to prevent the said resources from being used outside the area of its jurisdiction, so as to endanger their existence, integrity and conservation to the prejudice of peoples so situated geographically that their seas are irreplaceable sources of essential food and economic materials."

For the foregoing reasons, the governments of Chile, Ecuador, and Peru being resolved to preserve for and make available to their respective peoples the natural resources of the areas of the sea adjacent to their coasts, hereby declare as follows: (1) Owing to the geological and biological factors affecting the existence, conservation and development of the maritime fauna and flora of the waters adjacent to the coasts of the declarant countries the former extent of the territorial sea and contiguous zone is insufficient to permit for the conservation, development and use of those resources to which the coastal countries are entitled. (2). The governments of Chile, Ecuador, and Peru therefore proclaim as a principle of their international maritime policy, that each of them possesses sole sovereignty and jurisdiction over the area of the sea adjacent to the coast of its own country, and extending not less than 200 nautical miles from the said coast. (3) The sole jurisdiction and sovereignty over the zone thus described includes sole sovereignty and jurisdiction over the sea floor and subsoil thereof. (4) The zone of 200 nautical miles shall extend in every direction from any island or group of islands forming part of the territory of a declarant country. The maritime zone of any island or group of islands belonging to one declarant country and situated less than 200 nautical miles from the general maritime zone of another declarant country shall be bounded by the parallel of latitude drawn from the point at which the land frontier between the two countries reaches the sea. (5) This declaration shall not be construed as disregarding the necessary restriction on the exercise of sovereignty and jurisdiction imposed by international law in favor of innocent and harmless passage for ships of all nations through the aforesaid zone. (6) The governments of Chile, Ecuador, and Peru express their intention to conclude agreements and conventions for the implementation of the principles set forth in the present declaration. General norms for the regulation and protection of hunting and fishing in their respective maritime zones and for the regulation and coordination of the exploitation and use of all other natural products or natural resources lying in those waters, which may be of common interest, will be established in such agreements or conventions.

Opinions are divided as to the juridical nature of the two hundred mile maritime zone established in that declaration. For some, it would have the status of a genuine territorial sea and in support of that view invoke the terms "exclusive sovereignty and jurisdiction" and "innocent passage," which are characteristic of that legal concept. For others, on the other hand, it would appear to be "more like an 'economic zone,' intended exclusively for the conservation, development and use of the natural resources in the two hundred mile zone they claim these being the only objectives expressly mentioned in the operative part of the Declaration."[9]

Controversy also surrounds the reason (or reasons) for choosing that 200-mile limit. For the Peruvian jurist Aramburu Menchaca,[10] the precedent would be the declaration issued in Panama on September 23, 1939, during the first meeting of consultation of the American states. Although that declaration does not specifically mention the 200-mile distance, it does create a security belt covering all the participating states and arrives at even greater limits. That declaration, according to the same author, had its origin in the decree issued by President Franklin D. Roosevelt, on September 5, 1939, "whereby he ordered that the extensive coasts of his country be patrolled up to a distance of two hundred miles." And he goes on to say that "Apparently, that distance was chosen by Roosevelt because it was the range of the recently discovered radar waves which were being used as a virtual secret weapon when hostilities began."

For others, the 200-mile limit was chosen because of the breadth of the Humboldt current outside the coasts of Chile and Peru. Other arguments have been adduced, among them, the relationship between fishing on the high seas and the guano-producing birds, the relationship between the land and the sea, or the relationship between the continental shelf and the vast expanses of the sea. However, recent research has revealed that this claim had its origin in the arguments presented to the government of Chile by a private Chilean company interested in the whaling industry, which was afraid of competition from the factory ships of countries from other continents once World War II was over. According to those findings, in their search for precedents for the protection requested of the government of Chile, the lawyers consulted by the firm in question came across an article in a magazine commenting on the Panama Declaration of 1939 and including as an annex a map showing that the security zone established in that declaration for the Chilean coasts extended approximately two hundred miles. That was the reason why the 200-mile distance was chosen although actually that security zone varied between 200 and 500 miles and facing Chile it was approximately 300 miles.[11]

Up to this point, we have been dealing with the unilateral and multilateral claims of several Latin American states. It is appropriate now to examine briefly the efforts made by various organs of the Inter-American system during this period (1945–1958) with a view to coordinating and, whenever possible, uniting the positions of the states members of the system. Three of the decisions taken by those organs deserve special mention. The first in order of importance, because it was adopted by what was then the highest ranking organ in the system's hierarchy, is resolution 84, which was approved by the Tenth Inter-American Conference held in Caracas in 1954. The second is resolution 13, approved by the Inter-American Council of Jurists, at its third meeting in Mexico City in 1956, containing the "Mexico Principles on the Legal Regime of the Sea." Third, the resolution adopted by the Inter-American Specialized Conference on "Preservation of Natural Resources: Continental shelf and the Waters of the Sea," held in the capital of the Dominican Republic in 1956.

First and Second United Nations Conference on the Law of the Sea

The United Nations, for its part, took an early interest in the codification and progressive development of the international Law of the Sea. The International Law Commission, established in 1947 by the United Nations General Assembly, included in the agenda of its first session in 1949 a number of items on the Law of the Sea and adopted in 1956 the text of seventy-three articles on that subject. Pursuant to the recommendations of the International Law Commission the General Assembly, in its resolution 1105 (XI) convened the first United Nations Conference on the Law of the Sea, which was held in Geneva from February 24 to April 27, 1958. The Latin American states played an active role at that conference. In general terms, as it is only logical to assume, the Latin American states maintained the positions they had adopted in unilateral and multilateral declarations prior to the conference.

However, the Latin American countries adopted a constructive attitude, and were ready to support moderate positions in connection with some of the more controversial questions. By way of example, twelve Latin American states, i.e., Argentina, Bolivia, Chile, Colombia, Costa Rica, Ecuador, Guatemala, Mexico, Panama, Peru, Uruguay and Venezuela voted in favor of the joint proposal submitted to the Plenary of the Conference by Saudi Arabia, Burma, Colombia, Indonesia, Mexico, Morocco, United Arab Republic, and Venezuela, which established the following:

1. Every State has the right to set the breadth of its territorial sea up to a limit of twelve nautical miles measured from the base line in accordance with articles 4 and 5.
2. In those cases in which the breadth of the territorial sea of a State is less than twelve nautical miles measured as indicated in the foregoing paragraph, that State shall have a fishing zone contiguous

to its territorial sea extending up to a limit of twelve nautical miles from the baseline from where the breadth of the territorial sea is measured, and shall have the same fishing and exploitation rights to the living resources of the sea as in its territorial sea.

That proposal, which was supported by the majority of the Latin American countries, among them Chile, Ecuador, and Peru, which had laid claims to rights to sovereignty and jurisdiction over an area of 200 miles, received 39 votes in favor, 38 against, and 8 abstentions, but failed to obtain the required two-thirds majority.

The participation of the Latin American countries in the discussion of the draft articles on the continental shelf, the high seas and fisheries, and conservation of the living resources of the sea was also highly constructive, as borne out by the fact that those countries were the authors or co-sponsors of a large number of amendments to those draft articles, a considerable number of which were adopted.

To conclude these brief comments on Latin America's contribution to the work of the First United Nations Conference on the Law of the Sea, it is worthwhile recalling that the definition of the continental shelf given in article 1 of the 1958 Geneva convention on the subject, was taken by the International Law Commission from the relevant conclusion of the Inter-American Specialized Conference held in the capital of the Dominican Republic in 1956.

The First United Nations Conference on the Law of the Sea, in which 86 states participated, adopted the following four conventions: the convention on the Territorial Sea and the Contiguous Zone; the convention on the High Seas; the convention on Fisheries and the Conservation of the Living Resources of the High Seas; and the convention on the Continental Shelf. It was unable, however, to resolve questions which were of the utmost importance for the Latin American countries, and for other countries as well, such as the breadth of territorial sea and the nature and scope of the rights of coastal states for purposes of conservation and exploitation of the living resources in areas beyond the territorial sea. It was precisely to solve these questions that a Second Conference, also held in Geneva, was convened from March 17 to April 26, 1960, with the participation of 88 states, but once again, no agreement was reached on those questions. That was no doubt the reason why the 1958 Geneva conventions did not find much support among the Latin American countries. Only four states, i.e., the Dominican

Republic, Haiti, Mexico, and Venezuela ratified the four conventions. Colombia and Guatemala ratified only two.[12] But the vast majority (Argentina, Brazil, Bolivia, Costa Rica, Cuba, Chile, Ecuador, El Salvador, Honduras, Panama, Paraguay, Nicaragua, Peru and Uruguay) ratified none of those conventions.

1960–1970

The fact that no agreement could be reached at those conferences on such important questions as those mentioned in the preceding paragraph no doubt influenced the decision of some states in the region to claim a territorial sea of more than twelve miles. Between 1960 and 1970, Peru (Law 15720 of November 11, 1965 on civil aeronautics and Legislative Decree 17752 of July 24, 1969 on general water law); Ecuador (November 11, 1966); Argentina (Law 17094–M.24 of January 4, 1966); Panama (Act 31 of February 2, 1967); Uruguay (December 3, 1969) and Brazil (Decree-Law 1098 of March 25, 1970) extended their territorial sea up to a distance of 200 miles, but each of these unilateral declarations had its own special features. In some cases, a territorial sea was claimed with all the distinctive characteristics which that concept has in the traditional Law of the Sea (Panama and Brazil), while in other cases, particular areas of the territorial sea were subject to different legal regimes (Uruguay).

In 1969, the United States and the Soviet Union undertook a joint diplomatic demarche aimed at solving, in a new diplomatic conference, the questions left outstanding at the Second United Nations Conference on the Law of the Sea. To that end, they submitted a draft containing three articles on the breadth of the territorial sea, on the regime of passage through straits used for international navigation covered by the territorial sea of the coastal state of such straits, and on the fisheries regime. The United States government added to that draft an alternative text on international straits and a new wording for article 2, paragraph B, which would become a separate article.

Toward the end of the decade of the '60s another movement was initiated to bring the Law of the Sea up to date. In 1967, the Malta delegation requested the inclusion in the agenda of the United Nations General Assembly of the following item: "Declaration and Treaty on the Reservation of the Seabed and Ocean Floor beyond the limits of national jurisdiction for purely peaceful purposes and the use of such resources in the interests of mankind." When the inclusion of that item was approved, the head of the Malta delegation, Ambassador Arvid Pardo, in a speech that has become famous, after a long and detailed description of the legal, economic, and political aspects of that question, proposed that the area formed by the seabed and ocean floor beyond the limits of national jurisdiction and their resources, be declared the common heritage of mankind and an international authority be established to administer that heritage.

To consider that question, which aroused keen interest, the General Assembly, in its resolution 2340 (XXII), set up an ad hoc committee comprising 35 member states, which, pursuant to Resolution 2467 A (XXIII) was replaced by a forty-two-member committee. That committee worked intensely and in 1970, after arduous negotiations, submitted to the General Assembly, at its twenty-fifth session, a draft declaration on the subject, which was adopted by 108 votes in favor, none against and 14 abstentions, in resolution 2749 (XXV). The cardinal principle of that historic document is that which establishes that the area of the seabed and ocean floors beyond the limits of national jurisdiction and its resources are the common heritage of mankind.

These events, together with the imminent convening of a Third United Nations Conference on the Law of the Sea, prompted the Latin American countries to renew their efforts to arrive at a common position. To that end, two important regional meetings were held in 1970. In the first, held in Montevideo, from May 4 to 8, 1970, only those states which had in some way made claims of exclusive sovereignty or jurisdiction up to a distance of two hundred miles from the coast participated; namely, Argentina, Brazil, Chile, Ecuador, El Salvador, Nicaragua, Panama, Peru, and Uruguay. At that meeting, a document was adopted with the title of Montevideo Declaration on the Law of the Sea, which proclaims the following basic principles on the Law of the Sea:

1. The right of coastal States to avail themselves of control over the natural resources of the sea adjacent to their coasts and of the soil and subsoil thereof in order to promote the maximum development of their economies and to raise the levels of living of their peoples;

2. The right to establish the limits of their maritime sovereignty and jurisdiction in accordance with their geographical and geological char-

acteristics and with the factors governing the existence of marine resources and the need for their rational utilization;

3. The right to explore, to conserve the living resources of the sea
adjacent to their territories, and to establish regulations for fishing and
aquatic hunting;

4. The right to explore, conserve and exploit the natural resources
of their continental shelves to where the depth of the superjacent
waters admits of exploitation of said resources;

5. The right to explore, conserve and exploit the natural resources
of the soil and subsoil of the seabed and ocean floor up to the limit
within which the State exercises its jurisdiction over the sea;

6. The right to adopt for the aforementioned purposes, regulatory
measures applicable in areas under their maritime sovereignty and
jurisdiction, without prejudice to freedom of navigation by ships and
overflying by aircraft of any flag;

Furthermore, the signatory States encouraged by the results of this
Meeting, express their intention to coordinate their future action with
a view to defending effectively the principles embodied in this
Declaration.

Two comments may be made on that declaration. The first is that
while the fifth preambular paragraph recalls that "the signatory states
have by reason of conditions peculiar to them, extended their sovereignty or exclusive rights of jurisdiction over the maritime area adjacent
to their coasts, its soil and subsoil, to a distance of 200 nautical miles
from the baseline of the territorial sea," that distance is not mentioned
in any of the basic principles proclaimed in the declaration. The second
comment is that the signatory countries were not united in their view
of the nature of the areas of sovereignty or exclusive jurisdiction which
all those states had claimed. The statements made by the delegations
of the various states which participated in that meeting clearly show
that for some states (Argentina, Chile, and El Salvador) the 200-mile
zone was basically intended to protect economic rights, and the extension of sovereignty or jurisdiction should not "damage respect for the
principle enshrined in international law on free navigation and overflight for ships and airplanes of any flag." On the other hand, for Brazil,
Panama, Peru, Nicaragua, and Ecuador, with some slight differences
in shades of meaning, the 200-mile zone was a territorial sea and,
consequently, in that zone there was only the right of innocent passage.
For that very reason, as regards overflight in that zone, the same norms

should be applied as those which govern that activity over the territorial sea.

In the second, the Latin American meeting on aspects of the Law of the Sea held at Lima between August 4 and 8, 1970, all the Latin American countries were represented, with the exception of Haiti.[13] At that meeting the Declaration of the Latin American States on the Law of the Sea was approved. The common principles proclaimed in this declaration were the following:

1. The inherent right of the coastal state to explore, conserve and exploit the natural resources of the sea adjacent to its coasts and the seabed and subsoil thereof, likewise of the continental shelf and its subsoil, in order to promote the maximum development of economy and to raise the level of living of its people;

2. The right of the coastal states to establish the limits of its own maritime sovereignty or jurisdiction in accordance with reasonable criteria, having regard to its geographical, geological and biological characteristics, and the need to make rational use of its resources;

3. The right of the coastal state to take regulatory measures for the aforementioned purposes applicable in the areas of its maritime sovereignty or jurisdiction, without prejudice to freedom of navigation and flight in transit of ships and aircraft without distinction as to flag;

4. The right of the coastal state to prevent contamination of the waters and other dangerous and harmful effects, that may result from the use, exploration or exploitation of the area adjacent to its coasts;

5. The right of the coastal state to authorize, supervise and participate in all scientific research activities which may be carried out in the maritime zones subject to its sovereignty or jurisdiction, and to be informed of the findings and the results of such research.

Fourteen countries voted in favor of that declaration: Argentina, Brazil, Colombia, Chile, Ecuador, El Salvador, Guatemala, Honduras, Mexico, Nicaragua, Panama, Peru, the Dominican Republic, and Uruguay; against, three countries: Bolivia, Paraguay, and Venezuela; one abstained: Trinidad and Tobago. In spite of the majority vote for the declaration, the explanations of the vote of the eighteen delegations clearly showed the existing differences of opinions among the participating states. Yet the Lima meeting provided an opportunity for a very frank exchange of views on the positions of the different countries of Latin America and the Caribbean on Law of the Sea issues and encouraged a process of consultations among the States of the region with similar interests.

Third United Nations Conference on the Law of the Sea

In that same year, at its twenty-fifth session, the General Assembly, pursuant to its Resolution 2750 C (XXV) decided to convene a further conference on the Law of the Sea, whose mandate was "to establish an equitable international regime—including an international mechanism—for the zone and the resources of the seabed, the ocean floor and the subsoil thereof outside the limits of national jurisdiction; to elaborate a precise definition of the zone; and to deal with a wide range of related questions, in particular those relating to the high seas regime, the continental shelf, the territorial sea (including the question of its breadth and the question of international straits) and the contiguous zone, fisheries and the conservation of the living resources of the sea (including the question of the preferential rights of coastal States), the protection of the marine environment (including, inter alia, the prevention of pollution) and scientific research."

The General Assembly, in that same resolution, reaffirmed the mandate of the Committee on the Peaceful Uses of the Sea Bed and Ocean Floor outside the limits of national jurisdiction, formulated in Resolution 2467 A (XXIII), enlarged its membership and entrusted it with the preparatory work of the Conference. The following Latin American states were members of that expanded committee: Argentina, Bolivia, Brazil, Colombia, Chile, Ecuador, El Salvador, Guatemala, Mexico, Panama, Peru, Uruguay, and Venezuela, as well as three Caribbean countries, i.e., Guyana, Jamaica, and Trinidad and Tobago.

Preparatory Phase (1971–1973)

In 1971, 1972, and 1973, that committee held six meetings. Although it was able to draw up the list of subjects and issues to be discussed at the Conference and to have a general debate on some of those questions, it did not succeed in preparing draft articles for consideration by the Conference.

The first of those meetings held in the spring of 1971, dealt exclusively with procedural and organizational matters, but at the second session, held in the summer of that same year, a substantive discussion was initiated. That discussion was extremely interesting because in it were sketched out possible solutions to the major problems to be considered by the Conference. At that second session, and specifically at the meeting held on August 12, 1971, the Venezuela delegation, after broad consultations with the delegations of the other Latin American and Caribbean countries, presented the bases jfor a possible agreement. In its intervention, Venezuela proposed a territorial sea under the exclusive sovereignty and jurisdiction of the coastal state, the sole limitation being the right of innocent passage, and a reasonable breadth which, in the opinion of Venezuela, should be twelve nautical miles; an economic zone which could be called the "patrimonial sea," the extension of which should not exceed 200 miles measured from the baseline of the territorial sea in which there would be freedom of navigation and overflight, but with the coastal state having exclusive rights to all resources of every kind to be found therein, both in the seabed and subsoil thereof and in the suprajacent waters. Under the system proposed by the delegation of Venezuela in that statement, the concept of continental shelf was to be retained, although in point of fact the "patrimonial sea" would encompass most of those areas over which the various States already exercised rights deriving from the continental shelf. However, since there are States whose continental shelf extends beyond the 200-mile limit, the Delegation of Venezuela proposed that it be established that the portion of the continental shelf, which is not covered by the "patrimonial sea" should extend to that point where the depth of the sea does not exceed 200 meters.

It is interesting to recall that the term "patrimonial sea" was used for the first time by Edmundo Vargas Carreño, a Chilean jurist in a study on the Law of the Sea, which he prepared in 1971 at the request of the Inter-American Committee of Jurists of which he was then a member. However, in Vargas Carreño's work, that term had a different meaning and scope, since it also included the territorial sea and the continental shelf.[14]

The bases for agreement presented by Venezuela in its statement of August 12, 1971, were also submitted to the Informal Consultative Meeting of Foreign Ministers of the Countries of the Caribbean, held in Caracas from November 14 to 26, 1971, on the initiative of Venezuela. At that meeting, which was attended by thirteen countries in the area, namely Barbados, Colombia, Costa Rica, El Salvador, Guatemala, Haiti, Jamaica, Mexico, Nicaragua, Panama, Dominican Republic, Trinidad and Tobago, and Venezuela, questions relating to the sea were the object of special attention, as borne out by the fact that their consideration was entrusted to a general committee composed of heads of delegations. Following a brief substantive discussion, which showed that most delegations held similar views, it was agreed at the meeting "to convene a Specialized Conference of the Caribbean Countries on questions relating to the Sea" to be held in the Dominican Republic in April 1972. It was also agreed that the conference would be preceded by a preparatory meeting to be held in Colombia, in February 1972.

That Specialized Conference of the Caribbean Countries was indeed held in Santo Domingo early in June 1972, with the participation of the following fifteen countries: Barbados, Colombia, Costa Rica, El Salvador, Guatemala, Guyana, Haiti, Honduras, Jamaica, Mexico, Nicaragua, Panama, Dominican Republic, Trinidad and Tobago, and Venezuela. At the end of that meeting at the level of foreign ministers, the Santo Domingo Declaration was adopted on June 9, 1972. That declaration proved to be of the utmost importance for the process of elaboration of a Latin American doctrine on the Law of the Sea, and unquestionably influenced the position of the Latin American countries at the Third United Nations Conference of the Law of the Sea and the work of the Conference itself.

Unlike the aforementioned 1970 Montevideo and Lima declarations, which lack precision on a considerable number of points, as so rightly pointed out by Vargas Carreño,[15] the Santo Domingo Declaration defines with the utmost clarity the common position of the signatory states, namely, Colombia, Costa Rica, Guatemala, Haiti, Honduras, Mexico, Nicaragua, Dominican Republic, Trinidad and Tobago, and Venezuela, on the most important questions relating to the Law of the Sea.

Although the Santo Domingo Declaration is clear and precise, it is desirable to comment briefly on some of the principles proclaimed therein. With respect to the territorial sea, the declaration maintains the traditional concept in almost identical terms as those used in the 1958 Geneva Convention on the subject. As opposed to the 1970 Montevideo and Lima declarations, it establishes that the breadth of the territorial sea and its demarcation shall be the object of an international agreement, preferably universal, and cannot, therefore, be established unilaterally by states. It recognizes, in the meantime, the right of every state to set the breadth of its territorial sea up to a limit of twelve nautical miles.

Reflecting an increasingly generalized opinion, and to take into account, as far as possible, the positions and legitimate interests of the

Latin American countries which had claimed sovereignty or jurisdiction up to a 200-mile distance, the declaration advocates the creation of a new zone, adjacent to the territorial sea, called the "patrimonial sea," the breadth of which should likewise be the object of international agreement but which, added to the breadth of the territorial sea, should not exceed 200 nautical miles. In other words, in the hypothetical case that geographic circumstances should enable a State to adopt the maximum breadth of those spaces proposed in the declaration, that state could set the breadth of its territorial sea at twelve nautical miles and of its "patrimonial sea" at 188 nautical miles so that the sum of those two spaces should not exceed 200 miles. The "patrimonial sea," according to the declaration, would not be part of the territorial sea or of the high seas. Inspired by the regime established in the 1958 Geneva Convention on the continental shelf, the declaration establishes that the coastal states exercise sovereign rights over all the resources of every kind to be found in the waters, the seabed and subsoil of the "patrimonial sea." In other words, the coastal state would have functional, but not spatial sovereignty over that area. It would also have special competences in the field of scientific research and protection of the marine environment. None of the foregoing would affect the right of freedom of navigation or overflight, the laying of submarine cables and pipelines, which rights would be maintained in the "patrimonial sea" with no restrictions other than those which might result from the exercise, by the coastal state, of its own rights in that zone.

With respect to the continental shelf, the declaration maintains the concept and definition of the 1958 Geneva Convention on the subject. However, the signatory states of the declaration being aware of the need to establish precise limits for that maritime space, recommended that a study be undertaken on that question. The declaration shows that those states were inclined to favor a definition based on geomorphological criteria, for it expressed the idea that such a definition should take into account the outer limit of the continental rise. In this connection, the solution offered by the Santo Domingo Declaration to the question concerning the regime applicable to that part of the continental shelf that is covered by the "patrimonial sea" is most interesting. In fact, on that point, the declaration states that the juridical regime of the "patrimonial sea" would apply to that part of the continental shelf, and that the regime established by international law for the continental shelf would apply only to that part of the continental shelf that lies beyond the "patrimonial sea." It is therefore clear that the creation of the new "patrimonial sea" zone would not imply the elimination of the continental shelf concept, and that it can extend beyond the 200-mile limit established for the "patrimonial sea." Thus, the interests of a number of Latin American States whose continental shelf extends beyond that limit, were taken into account.

The Santo Domingo Declaration then proceeds to deal with the international seabed and, in that connection, begins by stating the principle that the seabed and its resources, beyond the patrimonial sea and the continental shelf not covered by the latter, should be declared the common heritage of mankind, pursuant to the declaration adopted by the United Nations General Assembly in its resolution 2749 (xxv) of December 17, 1970. It goes on to state a very clear position on the regime to be established for that area, adding that the regime shall create an international authority empowered to carry out all activities in the area, specifically, the exploration, exploitation, protection of the marine environment and scientific research, either by itself or through third parties in the manner and conditions to be established by common agreement. Accordingly, the declaration advocates the creation of a strong international authority, with wide powers and capable of undertaking all the necessary activities in the area, without prejudice to its carrying them out through third parties, if it deems fit.

That part of the declaration which deals with the high seas calls for two comments. First of all, it makes quite clear that the "patrimonial sea" is not part of the high seas. Second, it is to be noted the assertion made in the second sentence to the effect that the freedom to fish should not be unlimited or exercised in a discriminatory manner and should be the object of appropriate international regulation, preferably universal and generally accepted.

The declaration's provision concerning the protection of the marine environment are equally important. On the one hand, the duty of every state to refrain from acts which may pollute the seas and the seabed both within and outside its respective jurisdiction is established, and the international responsibility of physical or juridical persons harming the marine environment is recognized. On this last point, the declaration states that it is desirable to conclude an international, preferably universal, agreement. Finally, the declaration established regional cooperation norms which are self-explanatory.

We should add, however, that although no other regional or subregional meeting has been held subsequent to the Santo Domingo Conference, to deal specifically with the Law of the Sea, informal meetings between all the Latin American and Caribbean countries with a view to establishing a common position were held in 1972 and 1973. While those and other efforts did not lead to a solution acceptable to all, nevertheless a propitious climate for dialogue and cooperation was created. In any event, those meetings served to explain the various positions in greater detail and to dispel doubts about the true motives and objectives of the different groups.

In fact, as became clear in those meetings, the Latin American countries were basically pursuing the same goals, though proposing different means and formulas to attain them. Some felt that the answer was the one they had already adopted: namely, the establishment of zones of sovereignty or exclusive jurisdiction over the waters, seabed and marine subsoil adjacent to their coasts, out to a distance of 200 miles, under the name of the territorial sea, or any other denomination (national sea, adjacent sea). These countries, which were dubbed the 'territorialists," did not of course have, as we have seen, any joint position concerning the legal regime for this zone, since some of them were claiming a purely territorial sea, while others had departed from the norms traditionally applied to this maritime space, permitting freedom of communications. Others felt that the shared goal of exercising effective control over the resources in the marine areas out to a distance of 200 miles could be achieved, without altering the concept and the legal regime of the territorial sea, or extending it to that distance, through the creation of the new zone of the patrimonial sea, or exclusive economic zone, as proposed in the Declaration of Santo Domingo. For that reason the states in this group came to be known as "patrimonialists." As is well known, the latter position was the one which finally prevailed.

During the work prior to the Conference another interest group was formed which was to have considerable influence: the group of coastal states, in which Latin American countries, both territorialists and patrimonialists, were to play an active role.

At the meeting of the Seabed Committee held in Geneva in the summer of 1972, the Santo Domingo Declaration was distributed as an official working document at the request of the Venezuelan delegation. Besides, the delegations of Venezuela, Mexico, and Colombia on that occasion made detailed statements on the principles contained in this declaration. At the meeting held in New York in the spring of 1973 and in order to formalize their position, the delegations of these three countries submitted draft treaty articles on the territorial sea, patrimonial sea and continental shelf.[16]

This draft follows very closely the Santo Domingo Declaration but presents the principles established therein in the form of articles of a treaty and in some aspects develops ideas or concepts merely outlined in the Declaration. Article 2 states that the breadth of the territorial sea shall not exceed twelve nautical miles to be measured from the applicable baselines, and article 3 makes express reference to the right of innocent passage through the territorial sea. This draft also presents an outline of the part pertaining to the territorial sea which would have three sections: the first, "General Provisions," which is the only section that is fully developed, and other sections dealing with limits (applicable baselines and delimitation between states) and with the right of innocent passage.

The part dealing with the patrimonial sea contains nine articles reflecting and stating in precise terms the principles of the Santo Domingo Declaration on the subject. Of particular interest are the provisions contained in article 11, paragraph 2 of the draft and in article 12, tending to reconcile the rights of the coastal state with the freedoms and rights of other states of the zone.

As regards the continental shelf, the draft articles clearly adopt the geomorphological criteria by stating in article 13 that "The term 'continental shelf' means: a) The seabed and subsoil of the submarine areas adjacent to the coast, but outside the area of the territorial sea, to the outer limits of the continental rise bordering on the ocean basin or abyssal floor; b) the seabed and subsoil of analogous submarine regions adjacent to the coasts of islands."

For tactical reasons the draft avoids the then very controversial issue of whether or not the patrimonial sea should be considered as part of the high seas, despite the fact that the three states sponsoring this draft held the thesis that this zone was different both from the territorial sea and the high seas.

It is also worthwhile noting the provisions of article 18 of this draft pursuant to which "No provision of this Treaty shall be interpreted as preventing or restricting the right of any State to conclude regional or subregional agreements to regulate exploitation or distribution of the living resources of the sea, preservation of the marine environment or scientific research, or as affecting the legal validity of existing agreements."

Uruguay, Brazil, Argentina, Bolivia, and other states, as well as Jamaica, and, together, Ecuador, Panama, and Peru also submitted draft treaty articles at the 1973 session of the Seabed Committee.

It follows that in this preparatory stage of the Conference the Latin American states paid special attention to the subjects pertaining to the areas under national jurisdiction, particularly to the territorial sea and to the new concept of the patrimonial sea or the exclusive economic zone.

In this phase, however, they did not neglect the subject of the international regime of the seabed and ocean floor zone and its subsoil beyond the limits of the national jurisdiction.

Over and above the contributions of the various States of the region to the bodies established by the General Assembly of the United Nations to examine this subject from 1967 onward, special mention deserves the working paper submitted by Colombia, Chile, Ecuador, El Salvador, Guatemala, Guyana, Jamaica, Mexico, Panama, Peru, Trinidad and Tobago, Uruguay, and Venezuela to the 1971 summer session of the Seabed Committee. This draft, co-sponsored by practically all of the Latin American and Caribbean states members of the Committee, is one of the most comprehensive and original drafts of this initial stage of the Conference.

The draft has five chapters. The first deals with the "Fundamental Principles," the second with "The Authority"—membership, functions and mandate, the third with "Structure and Organs of the Authority," the fourth with "Settlement of Disputes," and the fifth with "Final Provisions."

Chapter 1 embodies and reiterates the fundamental principles in the declaration adopted in this connection by the General Assembly in resolution 2749 (xxv)of December 17, 1970. It contains some important clarifications, however, such as those in article 3, whereby "Exclusive jurisdiction over the area and administration of its resources shall be exercised on behalf of mankind by the Authority established under this Convention"; in article 5, which stipulates that "Exploitation of the resources of the area shall be carried out in a rational manner so as to ensure their conservation and to minimize any fluctuation in the prices of minerals and raw materials from terrestrial sources that may result from such exploitation and adversely affect the exports of the developing countries"; and in article 8, the final article in chapter 1, whereby "In the activities carried out in the area, the rights and legitimate interests of coastal states shall be respected. Consultations shall be maintained with the coastal states concerned with respect to activities relating to the exploration of the area and the exploitation of resources with a view to avoiding infringement of such rights and interests. Coastal states shall have the right to adopt such measures as may be necessary to prevent, mitigate or eliminate grave danger to their coasts or related interests that may result from pollution, the threat of pollution or from any other hazardous occurrences resulting from or caused by such activities."

Chapter 2 proposes a strong Seabed Authority, with broad powers, capable of itself undertaking exploration and exploitation activities in the area, or of availing itself for this purpose of the services of persons, natural or juridical, public or private, national or international, by a system of contracts or by the establishment of joint ventures. It may undertake scientific research activities directly, or authorize and supervise such research by other persons. Article 16 of this draft is of particular interest: it contains a set of measures to ensure the participation of developing countries on terms of equality with developed countries in all aspects of the activities carried out by the Authority in the area.

Chapter 3 stipulates that the principal organs of the Authority shall be the Assembly, the Council, the International Seabed Enterprise (hereinafter referred to as the Enterprise), and the Secretariat. The Assembly would be the supreme organ of the Authority, would consist of all states members, and would have broad powers laid down in article 24 of the draft. The Council, comprising 35 members elected by the Assembly, with due regard to the principle of equitable geographical distribution, would be the principal executive organ of the Authority, with the powers and duties set forth in article 32 of the draft. However, the most original aspect of this draft is the creation of the Enterprise, which would be the Authority's operating arm. More specifically, article 33 of the draft states that "The Enterprise is the organ of the Authority empowered to undertake all technical, industrial, or commercial activities relating to the exploration of the area and exploitation of its resources, by itself or in joint ventures, with juridical persons duly sponsored by States." In proposing the creation of the Enterprise, the Latin American countries cosponsoring the draft were consistent with their position on the role to be played by the Authority. In fact, the best way to ensure or facilitate direct exercise of the powers attributed to the Authority or its direct participation in joint ventures is through an organ such as the Enterprise. Furthermore, this organizational structure was based on experience which had already proven useful in several of the proposing countries, producers of oil or other mineral resources, which had set up national enterprises, under a variety of legal formats, for the total or partial exploitation of such wealth, directly or via service contracts. Such was the case with Venezuela, for example, which in 1960, while the system of concessions was still in force, set up a state enterprise, the Corporación Venezolana del Petróleo, as the instrument for the implementation of the Venezuelan government's policy of active and direct participation in this fundamental sector of the national economy.

The draft presented by the Latin American countries advocates the so-called unitary system, very different, as can be seen, from the concessions system originally proposed by the United States and other Western industrialized countries, since they felt that the concessions system was incompatible with the fundamental principle that the area and its resources are the common heritage of mankind, and would preclude full and active participation by the developing countries in the administration of the common heritage.

Chapters 4 and 5 of the draft, on settlement of disputes and final provisions, are a simple listing of matters requiring subsequent elaboration.

The Conference (1973–1982)

By the summer of 1973, after six sessions, the Seabed Committee had only partially discharged the mandate it had received from the General Assembly in Resolution 2750C (xxv) of December 23, 1970. The Committee had prepared the full list of subjects and issues to be considered by the Conference, but had not managed to adopt draft articles for the treaty. Nevertheless, the General Assembly, in resolution 3067 (xxviii) of November 16, 1973, decided to adhere to the programme of work originally laid down in its aforementioned resolution 2750C, and to convene the first session of the Conference for later in 1973, to deal solely with the organization of work and the adoption of Rules of Procedure. At that first session, held in New York from December 3 to 15, 1973, this mandate was partly fulfilled: agreement was reached on the organization of the Conference, and the members of the bureau and the three main committees were elected, as well as the chairman of the drafting committee and the rapporteur general. Owing to lack of time, however, it was not possible to complete the discussion and adoption of the Rules of Procedure.

The second session, held in Caracas, Venezuela, between June 20 and August 29, 1974, marked a very important stage in the history of the Conference. This session saw the adoption of the Conference's Rules of Procedure, drawn up according to the principle enunciated in the "Gentleman's Agreement," approved by the United Nations General Assembly at its 2169th meeting, on November 16, 1973, whereby "The Conference should make every effort to reach agreement on substantive matters by way of consensus, and there should be no voting on such matters until all efforts at consensus have been exhausted"; this principle, reiterated in the declaration by the president of the Conference, received the support of the Conference at its nineteenth meeting, on June 27, 1974. The principle was scrupulously applied, so much so that the only substantive decision voted upon throughout the entire Conference related to the adoption of the Draft Convention as a whole, on April 30, 1982. This session also saw the commencement of the substantive work of the Conference, and although no decisions were actually reached on matters of substance, discussion in plenary meetings and in the three main committees made it possible to appreciate the various positions more clearly, and to assess the degree of support for the possible compromise solutions.

Special mention should be made of the work performed by the Second Committee, charged with studying the following items and issues from the list approved by the Seabed Committee: Territorial Sea (item 2); Contiguous Zone (item 3); Straits Used for International Navigation (item 4); Continental Shelf (item 5); Exclusive Economic Zone Beyond the Territorial Sea (item 6); Coastal State Preferential Rights or Other Nonexclusive Jurisdiction over Resources Beyond the Territorial Sea (item 7); High Seas (item 8); Land-Locked Countries (item 9); Rights and Interests of Shelf-Locked States and States with Narrow Shelves or Short coastlines (item 10); Rights and Interests of States with Broad Shelves (item 11); Archipelagos (item 16); Enclosed and Semi-Enclosed Seas (item 17); Artificial Islands and Installations (item 19), and Transmission from the High Seas (item 20).

The work performed on these items during the preparatory phase of the Conference had been insufficient, lagging behind that entrusted to the two other main committees. For that reason, and in view of the importance of these items, the work of the Second Committee provided the principal focus of interest during the second session of the Conference.

After general debate and separate discussion on each and every one of the items earmarked for the committee, in which nearly all delegations took part, and in the light of statements made during that debate, as well as in plenary meetings of the Conference, the bureau of the Second Committee was duly authorized to draw up a document, entitled "Main Trends." This represented the first attempt to deal in an orderly and systematic way with the numerous proposals put forward in the preparatory phase of the committee, as well as in this session, and to reduce possible solutions to single formulas or to a maximum of two or three variants. The committee's work was thus considerably advanced, and this led to the Conference's decision at its following session to entrust the chairmen of the three main committees with the preparation of informal negotiating texts. No article of the treaty was definitively approved, but discussion in the Second Committee made clear the close relationship existing between the various items entrusted to it, as well as the general lines of a possible compromise solution. Indeed, at the closing meeting of the committee for that session (forty-sixth meeting, August 28, 1974), I, in my capacity as Second Committee chairman, could state the following:

Generally speaking, up to now each state has stood by the positions which ideally cater to the range of interests it has in the seas and oceans. Having established these positions, we now have the possibility of a negotiation based on an objective and realistic appraisal of the relative strength of the various schools of thought. I am not proposing, in this statement, to present a complete description of the situation as I see it. I can, however, offer some assessments and commentaries of a general nature. The way things stand now, the 12-mile territorial sea, and an exclusive economic zone running from beyond the territorial sea up to a maximum of 200 miles, constitute the core of the compromise solution favored by the majority of states participating in the Conference. This has emerged from the general debate in plenary, and from the debates in our own Committee. Acceptance of such an argument does, of course, depend upon the satisfactory solution of other issues, and in particular the question of passage through straits used for international navigation, the outer limit of the continental shelf, as well as the very maintenance of such a concept, and last—though by no means least—the aspiration of landlocked countries and others which, for one reason or another, consider themselves to be geographically disadvantaged. There are, moreover, other problems which have to be studied and resolved in connection with this argument, such as those relating to archipelagos, and to the regime of islands in general. It is also necessary to go fully into the question of the nature and characteristics of the concept of an exclusive economic zone, a subject on which there are still major differences of opinion. Noticeable progress has been made on all of these issues, however, and the foundations thus laid for negotiations during the intersessional period and in the next session of the Conference.

During that session consideration of the major issue of dispute settlement was begun in a working group under the co-chairmanship of Ambassadors Galindo Pohl and Harris, the heads of the delegations of El Salvador and Australia, respectively.

Starting with the third session, held in Geneva from March 17 to May 9, 1975, the Conference entered a period of intense negotiations, generally carried out in informal meetings of the plenary, the main committees, and various subsidiary bodies, as well as in groups set up outside the formal conference structure in order to provide for greater flexibility in the negotiating process—to wit, the Evensen group, led by the head of the Norwegian delegation, Minister of State Jens Evensen, and subsequently the Castañeda group, led by Ambassador Jorge Castañeda, the head of the Mexican delegation. The result of those discussions is to be found in the successive informal negotiating texts prepared by the chairmen of the three main committees, and later by the president of the Conference in connection with the items allocated to plenary. Thanks to long and laborious work revising and consolidating these papers, the official text of the Draft Convention was finally arrived at during the tenth session (New York-Geneva 1981), and was presented for consideration by the Conference during the first part of its eleventh and last session, held in New York in the spring of 1982. There it was adopted, after some amendments made during this final stage, on April 30, 1982, by 130 votes in favor, 4 against, with 17 abstentions. Thus, while it was not finally possible to adopt the Convention by consensus, the result of the vote shows that the efforts made in all those years of intense negotiations had not been in vain. It is clear that, as far as the great majority of states participating in the

Conference were concerned, the text as adopted represents an acceptable compromise. This was certainly the view of nearly all the countries of Latin America and the Caribbean,[17] even though some of the states which voted for the text did not sign the Convention when it was opened for signature on December 10, 1982, in Montego Bay, Jamaica.[18]

This attitude is very understandable. Even though, as we have seen, the Convention was the result of a collective effort over many years, to the elaboration of which many states contributed in greater or lesser degree, there can be no doubt that the contribution by the states of Latin America and the Caribbean was very important, particularly with respect to the juridical regime of the territorial sea, the exclusive economic zone, and the continental shelf. It is not possible, of course, to follow the position of these countries step by step throughout this lengthy and complicated negotiating process, nor to set forth in detail the contribution they made to the well-nigh impossible task of reconciling the different, and at times opposing, interests of so many states, and of drafting, with a view to adoption by consensus, a convention consisting of seventeen parts, with 320 articles and nine annexes. Accordingly, we shall confine ourselves to stating, in general terms, what their attitude was on the items of greatest interest to these states, and to determining the extent to which the solutions adopted by the Convention are in keeping with their fundamental aspirations and objectives.

As we have already seen more than once, the shared, priority objective of the Latin American coastal states was to secure the recognition of rights to sovereignty or exclusive jurisdiction over the renewable and nonrenewable resources of the waters, seabed, and subsoil in the maritime spaces closely linked to their continental or inland territories by reason of geography, biology, or geology, even though they may have differed as to suitable legal titles with which to attain their objective. This is borne out by the numerous initiatives, mentioned and commented upon in this work, which were taken by these countries prior to and during the Conference. It was logical, therefore, that their attention focused upon items 2 through 10 of the Convention, relating to the Territorial Sea and Contiguous Zone, Straits Used for International Navigation, Archipelagic States, the Exclusive Economic Zone, the Continental Shelf, the High Seas, the Regime of Islands, Enclosed and Semi-Enclosed Seas, and the Right of Access of Land-Locked States to and from the Sea and Freedom of Transit, respectively. When all is said and done, the compromise solutions accepted in the Convention under these items correspond in essence to the arguments maintained by the majority of the countries of Latin America and the Caribbean.

Where the territorial sea and the exclusive economic zone are concerned, the solution adopted in the Convention is, of course, fully satisfactory to the states' signatories to the Declaration of Santo Domingo, and to those other Latin American and Caribbean states which espoused the principles contained in that declaration. The same cannot be said with respect to the so-called "territorialist" countries: their arguments that, within reasonable limits, and subject to various criteria, each coastal state should be permitted to determine the breadth of its own territorial or national sea, or be authorized to extend it to a distance of 200 miles, even under a system involving a plurality of regimes, were not accepted. These countries realized very quickly, however, that their arguments enjoyed very limited support. Indeed, as was said before, it became apparent at the second session of the Conference that the solution favored by the majority of countries participating in the Conference was the one to be ultimately adopted in the Convention. In this connection, it is interesting to note that the fundamental elements of that solution emerged as early as the single informal negotiating text, published at the end of the third session of the Conference, and were retained in the successive revisions of that text. Bearing this in mind, the "territorialist" countries very wisely adopted the strategy of working actively for a strong exclusive economic zone, without thereby formally abandoning their positions. In this undertaking "territorialists" and "patrimonialists" were in agreement. Both groups in fact vigorously opposed the proposal by certain powers that the exclusive economic zone should be categorized as part of the high seas, with all of the consequences that this would have entailed with respect to the so-called residual powers, and generally fought all attempts to restrict or weaken the rights of coastal states in this zone. Ultimately, the prevailing opinion was that expressed by the chairman of the Second Committee in his words of introduction to the first revision of the single informal negotiating text, published at the end of the fourth session of the Conference (New York 1976): namely, that the exclusive economic zone was a *sui generis* maritime space, subject to a specific legal regime, and therefore unlike either the territorial sea or the high seas. It similarly became quite clear that all the residual powers with respect to economic activities in the zone fall within the purview of the coastal state, and article 59 of the Convention sets forth the formula proposed by Ambassador Castañeda, Head of the Mexican delegation, as the basis for the resolution of conflicts regarding the attribution of rights and jurisdiction in the exclusive economic zone. To conclude these brief comments, it is evident that the Latin American positions influenced the decision, adopted in the Convention, setting the maximum width of the zone at 200 miles.

Regarding the rights of landlocked states and states with special geographical characteristics with respect to the living resources of the exclusive economic zone, the formulas adopted by the Convention in articles 69, 70, 71 and 72 were the result of a prolonged and very difficult negotiation, in which several Latin American countries took an active part. It has been said that these formulas are scarcely generous, but it should be remembered that participation by third states in the exploitation of the living resources in the exclusive economic zone presented major difficulties for those states, in Latin America and other regions, which had claimed sovereignty or exclusive jurisdiction over all resources, of whatever kind, in marine areas constituting part of the zone. At all events, the solutions adopted by the Convention on this issue were the only ones which could be adopted by consensus in the working group specifically constituted to study the matter, as well as in the Conference itself.

The provisions in part 3 of the Convention relating to straits used for international navigation did not present difficulties for the countries of Latin America and the Caribbean; they supported the solution proposed in the first informal negotiating text, which was not subject to major alterations in the successive treatments of the draft which was to be finally adopted. Nevertheless, they were always prepared to consider the amendments proposed by certain states bordering such straits, and to support those amendments which were intended to protect the security and defense interests of such states without detriment to the general interest of ensuring unimpeded transit through such straits by the ships and aircraft of all states.

The same can be said of part 4 of the Convention, dealing with archipelagic states. Although few Latin American and Caribbean states are beneficiaries under the special regime established in this part of the Convention (Bahamas, Cuba, Trinidad and Tobago), all of them from the outset supported the aspirations of the archipelagic states. It is worth adding that a number of states from different regions, including Ecuador, repeatedly argued that this regime should apply to all archipelagos, including those forming part of the territory of a continental state, but this position at no time enjoyed widespread support.

The Convention's provisions on the continental shelf, contained in part 7 of the Convention, are also satisfactory to the majority of countries in the region. Indeed, on this matter the Convention incorporates the views and opinions of nearly all the coastal states in Latin America and the Caribbean. It retains the legal concept of a continental shelf, and sets its limit at the outer edge of the continental margin, as proposed by many of these states. Unlike the 1958 convention on the matter, the new Convention defines the continental shelf principally in terms of its geomorphological characteristics, setting a precise outer limit, and indicating the methods to be applied in determining this limit whenever the margin extends beyond 200 nautical miles. Furthermore, it provides for the creation of a new commission on the Limits of the Continental Shelf, the composition and attributes of which are detailed in annex 2 of the Convention. These solutions favor countries with a broad continental shelf, of course, but the latter found themselves obliged, as part of the compromise reached on this matter, to agree in article 82 of the Convention, to make payments and contributions with respect to the exploitation of that part of the continental shelf which extends beyond 200 miles. The negotiation on all these points was not easy. In particular, the groups of landlocked and geographically disadvantaged countries, and the group of Arab states, argued until near the end of the Conference that the creation of the exclusive economic zone made the concept of the continental shelf unnecessary. Other states, while in favor of retaining this concept, argued that a precise limit to this space should be set, based on criteria of distance from the coast or depth. There can be no doubt that the very firm and united stand which the Latin American group, with very few exceptions, maintained out of solidarity with those countries in the region which were particularly concerned by this issue, had a considerable bearing on the difficult negotiations on these questions, as well as on the solutions which were finally adopted.

Very little needs to be said about part 7, dealing with the high seas. The provisions contained in this part, many of which repeat the norms of the 1958 convention on the matter, present no difficulties for the states of Latin American and the Caribbean. It is, however, necessary to emphasize their concern to have it clearly established that, as article

86 of the Convention states quite unequivocally, the exclusive economic zone is not part of the high seas, as well as the contribution they made to the study and elaboration of the norms in section 2 of this part, relating to the conservation and management of the living resources of the high seas.

With respect to the regime of islands, set out in part 8 of the Convention, it should be pointed out that Venezuela, as well as states from other regions, objected to the provision in paragraph 3 of article 121, the only article in this part, whereby rocks which cannot sustain human habitation or economic life of their own shall have no exclusive economic zone or continental shelf. As these countries' delegations stated, this norm presents numerous difficulties of interpretation. However, this position did not find sufficient support, and this norm is retained in the text of the Convention as finally adopted.

As finally drafted, part 9, dealing with closed and semi-enclosed seas, does not present difficulties for those countries in the region which are concerned by this issue, namely those bordering the Caribbean, since it confines itself to the promotion of cooperation among states bordering such seas on matters of common interest, an issue previously proposed by the Latin American and Caribbean states in policy statements adopted at regional and subregional meetings, among which special mention may be made of the Declaration of Santo Domingo.

The coastal states of Latin America had no difficulty in supporting the provisions on the right of access of landlocked states to and from the sea and freedom of transit, set forth in part 10 of the Convention, which are more advantageous for these countries than those contained in earlier international instruments on that matter. The fact is, this problem does not have the same characteristics in Latin America as in other parts of the world. There are only two landlocked countries in the region, Bolivia and Paraguay. Bolivia lost its marine coast as a result of the War of the Pacific (1879–1884), but it is still seeking an outlet to the sea, and this aspiration enjoys considerable sympathy among the Latin American community. It is possible, therefore, that through the negotiations it has been conducting over recent years it may achieve this goal. Paraguay, on the other hand, has been landlocked ever since its independence, but it has always had easy access to the sea via the river network comprising the Paraguay, Parana, and La Plata rivers. Neither case, therefore, is typical of the situation of landlocked countries in other continents, although this does not mean, of course, that

Bolivia and Paraguay were not concerned by the issue. In fact, both played a very active role in the group of landlocked and geographically disadvantaged countries, participating constructively in the negotiations which culminated in the adoption of the norms in this part of the Convention.

While the first priority for the Latin American states was the items dealt with in these parts of the Convention, they did not thereby neglect the legal regime governing the seabed and ocean floor beyond the limits of national jurisdiction, set out in item 11 of the Convention and in several annexes thereto. In this they were motivated not merely by the interest which these countries attach to the general problem of the distribution and exploitation of the resources in the marine environment, but also, and above all, because of the major questions of principle this raises in connection with the establishment of a new international economic order.

As has already been said, the delegations of the Latin American and Caribbean states played a very active role in the elaboration of the general lines of the unitary system proposed by the developing countries. It is useful to recall, in this regard, the draft—in some respects a pioneering one—presented on this item by nearly all the states from the region, sitting as members of the Seabed Commission, during its 1971 summer session. Later on, when the convergence of opinion of the developing countries led them to channel their efforts through the Group of 77, the countries of Latin America and the Caribbean, individually and collectively, figured prominently in this group, and in the difficult negotiations with the industrialized countries which concluded only a few hours before the adoption of the Convention, on April 30, 1982. It should be said, however, that this interest was dictated more by the possibility of all states participating and cooperating in the activities of the zone, pursuant to the fundamental principle that this zone and its resources are the common heritage of mankind, than by the possible profits these countries might receive from the exploitation of such resources. The fact is, the countries of Latin America and the Caribbean, like other developing countries, were not carried away by wishful thinking as to possible short- or medium-term income to be derived from a share in such profits. What these countries sought from the outset was a democratic and participatory system for administering this common heritage. Accordingly, they proposed the aforementioned unitary system, which, as has been said, presupposes a strong international authority, empowered to engage in exploration, exploitation, transport, and marketing activities on its own, though with the option of having them performed by third parties, through service contracts or some form of association

As is well known, this system ran into tenacious opposition from the industrialized countries. To get out of the deadlock in the negotiations on this item, the so-called parallel regime was put forward as a compromise solution, which the countries in the Group of 77 accepted, subject to certain conditions, including the possibility of revising the arrangement at the end of a given period of time.

The text as finally adopted is not the one advocated by the Latin American and Caribbean countries and the other members of the Group of 77, particularly after the many major concessions made by the group, especially in the last session of the Conference, in order to reach an agreement. Nevertheless, where this item is concerned, the provisions in the Convention and its annexes are generally acceptable as a compromise solution, and, of course, as an integral part of the so-called "package deal," consisting of an adequate regime with respect to freedom of communications and to security and defense facilities, in exchange for an equitable regime for the international seabed zone and its resources.

Parts 12, 13, and 14, relating to protection and preservation of the marine environment, marine scientific research, and the development and transfer of marine technology respectively, all carefully crafted, are the result of a genuine consensus and therefore do not present difficulties for the countries in the region.

In the preparation of part 15, entrusted to the plenary of the Conference and covering settlement of disputes, the participation and contribution by the states of Latin America and the Caribbean was very constructive. Undoubtedly, the most controversial question under this heading related to the advisability of establishing obligatory procedures leading to decisions binding in all cases. On this point the countries in the region were not of one mind, since some were in favor of applying these procedures in all cases, whereas others considered that while this solution could be accepted as a general rule, it was necessary to establish certain limitations and exceptions. The Convention ultimately endorsed the second approach. This solution appears to be generally acceptable, even though in the view of certain delegations the location of some of the norms is not ideal, and the drafting of certain provisions, particularly those in section 3 of this part of the Convention, is not always sufficiently clear and precise.

Part 16, relating to general provisions, requires no commentary. On the other hand, with reference to part 17, the last part of the Convention, containing the final provisions, it should be said that article 309, according to which no reservations or exceptions may be made to the Convention unless expressly permitted by other articles of the Convention, did give rise to controversy. This article was drafted on the assumption that the Convention would be approved by consensus, and since this was not the case two amendments were put forward, one by the delegation of Venezuela, intended to permit reservations concerning the delimitation of maritime spaces, and the other by Turkey, which proposed the outright deletion of article 309. Venezuela withdrew its proposal in favor of the Turkish one, which was the sole amendment to the draft convention to be put to a vote. The result of the roll-call vote on this amendment was as follows: 18 votes in favor, 100 against, with 26 abstentions. Accordingly, it was rejected. It is interesting to note that Bolivia, Ecuador, El Salvador, Guatemala, and Venezuela voted in favor of the proposal, while Argentina, Brazil, Dominican Republic, Panama, Paraguay, Peru, and Uruguay abstained.

After this brief analysis of the various parts of the Convention, it is possible to conclude that the interests of the majority of countries in Latin America and the Caribbean are sufficiently protected in this new international instrument, as is shown by the fact that twelve out of the twenty states in Latin America,[19] and ten of the thirteen Caribbean states,[20] have signed the Convention, and some of them have already ratified it.[21] Nevertheless, the Convention does present serious difficulties to some countries in Latin America. Whereas some of the countries in the territorialist group, such as Brazil, Panama, and Uruguay, voted for the adoption of the Convention and signed the instrument, other states in that group, such as Ecuador, El Salvador, and Peru, are faced by a problem which is not easy to resolve. This is due not merely to the fact that acceptance of the Convention implies the alteration of norms in domestic law, some of constitutional rank, but also due to the fact that the claim made by these countries to a 200-mile territorial sea is a matter of deep concern to public opinion, and is considered a true manifestation of sovereignty.

Other countries, though they do not have problems of this kind, have refrained from signing the Convention due to problems confined to only a few of the provisions in this international convention. This is the case with Venezuela, which did not sign the Convention, and probably will not do so in the near future, owing to its objection to the norms relating to the delimitation of maritime spaces.

It is not possible to say with certainly when the number of ratifications required for the Convention to come into force will be reached. The unwillingness of the United States and other Western industrialized countries to sign the Convention is a factor which undoubtedly has to be borne in mind in assessing the prospects of its coming into force in the near future. It is to be hoped, however, that a realistic appraisal of the advantages and disadvantages in the Convention will lead these and other countries to the conclusion that this constitutes the best possible solution to the problems of the Law of the Sea.

At all events, some parts of the Convention may already be regarded as norms of positive international law. By way of example, through norms of domestic law many countries, including several from Latin America, have established exclusive economic zones which are generally compatible with the relevant provisions in the Convention.

NOTES

1. Before going any further, it should be explained that whenever Latin America is mentioned in this paper, we mean states to which the term traditionally applies: that is to say, Spanish, Portuguese or French-speaking countries in North, Central, and South America and the Antilles. They are, in alphabetical order: Argentina, Bolivia, Brazil, Chile, Colombia, Costa Rica, Cuba, Dominican Republic, Ecuador, El Salvador, Guatemala, Haiti, Honduras, Mexico, Nicaragua, Panama, Paraguay, Peru, Uruguay, and Venezuela. Therefore, the reference does not encompass the newly independent states in the Caribbean (Antigua and Barbuda, Bahamas, Barbados, Belice, Dominica, Grenada, Guyana, Jamaica, St. Kitts and Nevis, St. Lucia, St. Vincent and the Grenadines, Suriname, and Trinidad and Tobago). Nevertheless, inasmuch as the latter have joined the United Nations Latin American group and played a very active role in the Third United Nations Conference on the Law of the Sea, mention will be made from time to time of their interests and points of view, which, in some respects are identical with, or similar to, those of the Latin American countries as such.

2. The Latin American states became independent during the first quarter of the nineteenth century, Cuba, the sole exception, becoming a sovereign state in 1901.

3. The first edition of this work was published in Santiago, Chile, in 1832 with the title of *Principios de Derecho de Jentes* (Principles of the law of Nations). In 1844 a new edition, updated and enlarged, was published with the more modern title of *Principios de Derecho Internacional* (Principles of International Law). A third and last edition of this work, with some corrections and many new additions was published in 1864, a year before Bello's death. Numerous reprints of all of these editions were published in Latin America and in Europe.

4. These quotations are taken from part 1, ch. 2, section 4, of the third edition reproduced in volume 10 of the *Complete Works of Bello*, Venezuelan edition (Caracas, 1954). It must be noted, however, that these observations were already contained in the first edition, although with some minor differences of language.

5. The traditional Law of the Sea, as Truyol y Serra affirmed, "Was not affected during the XIX century, either by its extension to the American continent nor by the East having joined international life, because in both cases Western standards were transposed." "L'Expansion de la Societe International au XIXe. et au XXe. siecles," Recueil des Cours, Academy of International Law, 1965, p. 158.

6. René-Jean Dupuy, "Droit de la mer ou Droit sur la Mer," *Revue Iranniene des Relations Internationales* (1975, 1976), p. 31.

7. See UN Legislative Series, Laws and Regulations on the Regime of the High Seas, ST/LEG/Ser. B/1 New York: United Nations, 1951. UN Legislative Series, ST/LEG/Ser. B/6 New York: United Nations, 1957. UN Legislative Series , National Legislation and Treaties Relating to the Territorial Sea, the Contiguous Zone, the Continental Shelf, the High Seas, and the Fishing and Conservation of the Living Resources of the Sea, ST/LEG/Ser. B/15 New York: United Nations, 1970.

8. The Santiago Declaration of 1952 was ratified by Chile by Decree No. 432 of September 23, 1954; by Ecuador by Decree No. 275 of February 7, 1955; and by Peru by Legislative Resolution No. 12.305 of May 6, 1955.

9. E. Vargas Carreño, "América Latina y el Dorocho del Mar," *Fondo de Cultura Economica* (Mexico, 1973), pp. 26 ff.

10. Andrés Aramburu Menchaca, "History of the 200-Mile Territorial Sea," University of Piura (Peru), 1973.

11. On this point see Ann L. Hollick, "The Origins of 200 Miles Offshore Zones," *American Journal of International Law* (July 1977), 71(3):494 ff.; María Pilar Armanet Armanet, "Economic Reasons for President Gabriel González Videla's Declaration of June 1947 in *International Studies*: The Exclusive Economic Zone—A Latin American Perspective." Edited under Francisco Orrego Vicuña's direction by the Institute of International Studies of Chile, Santiago de Chile, 1982.

12. Venezuela entered reservations on article 12 and on paragraphs 2 and 3 of article 24 of the Convention on the Territorial Sea and the Contiguous Zone and on article 6 of the Convention on the Continental Shelf.

Colombia ratified the Convention on Fisheries and the Conservation of the Living Resources of the High Seas and the Convention on the Continental

Shelf; Guatemala ratified the Convention on the High Seas and the Continental Shelf.

13. Costa Rica was represented by an observer.

14. On the origin of the term "patrimonial sea," see Edmundo Vargas Carreño, "América Latina y el Dorocho del Mar," p. 74, n. 21.

15. *Ibid.*, page 49.

16. Originally issued as document A/AC. 138/SC.II/L.21, April 3, 1973.

17. The following Latin American states voted in favor of the draft: Argentina, Bolivia, Brazil, Colombia, Costa Rica, Chile, Cuba, Dominican Republic, El Salvador, Guatemala, Haiti, Honduras, Mexico, Nicaragua, Panama, Paraguay, Peru and Uruguay. Venezuela voted against, owing to its disagreement with the provisions in the text relating to the delimitation of maritime spaces, and Ecuador did not take part in the vote, due to its difficulties in accepting the provision setting the maximum breadth of the territorial sea at twelve nautical miles. With respect to the countries of the Caribbean, Bahamas, Barbados, Grenada, Guyana, Jamaica, St. Lucia, St. Vincent and the Grenadines, Suriname, and Trinidad and Tobago also voted for the text. Antigua and Barbuda, Belize and Dominica were not present during the vote.

18. Such was the case with Argentina, Bolivia, El Salvador, Guatemala, Nicaragua, and Peru, though this does not necessarily mean that they all have difficulties in accepting the Convention.

19. Brazil, Colombia, Costa Rica, Cuba, Chile, Dominican Republic, Haiti, Honduras, Mexico, Panama, Paraguay and Uruguay.

20. Bahamas, Barbados, Belize, Grenada, Guyana, Jamaica, St. Lucia, St. Vincent and the Grenadines, Suriname and Trinidad and Tobago.

21. Jamaica, Mexico, Bahamas, Belize, St. Lucia, and Cuba.

8.
A Southeast Asian Perspective

HASJIM DJALAL

In 1967, Arvid Pardo, the distinguished Ambassador of Malta to the United Nations, made his famous speech describing the enormous wealth on the floors of the deep oceans and raised the legal status of the resources. As everyone knew, the 1958 Geneva convention on the continental shelf limited the sovereign rights of coastal states over the resources of the continental shelf up to the 200-meter depth of water or to where exploitation of the resources were still possible. In view of the development of science and technology, a much more precise definition of the continental shelf was felt necessary. This statement led to the establishment of an ad hoc UN committee, later developed and became known as the United Nations Seabed Committee, to study the problems.

In 1967 also, the world witnessed the tragedy of the *Torry Canyon*, in a giant super-tanker accident in the Dover Strait that caused enormous pollution to the coast of France. The era of giant tankers as a result of the Arab-Israeli war in 1967 had brought considerable problems to the protection and preservation of the marine environment as well as the problems of safety of navigation, especially through narrow, shallow, and "sensitive" straits. Although most of these problems were discussed by IMCO (now IMO) the attention of the world community to the problems of pollution and protection of the marine environment was strongly aroused. This was also one of the reasons that had motivated the convening of the Law of the Sea Conference.

At about the same time, President Nixon announced the so-called Guam Doctrine, which in essence stipulated that as of that time, in view of the U.S. difficulties in Vietnam, the United States would be concentrating on "offshore strategy," thus reducing its land involvement in Asia. As a corollary to this doctrine, the United States would more than ever require a freer movement of its naval forces through the world waterways. It seemed that the development of the law of territorial sea which unmistakably went in the direction of the recognition of the twelve-mile limit, posed problems to this doctrine. The recognition of the twelve-mile territorial sea by the world community would, in the mind of the Americans, make hundreds or so vital straits part of territorial sea; thus, in accordance with article 16, paragraph 4, of the Geneva convention of 1958 on territorial sea, made the regime of nonsuspendable innocent passage applicable to those straits. This was a nightmare for United States defense strategists.

At about the same time also the Soviet Union, which in the early 1960s decided to develop its naval power to be one of a world force (thus changing the centuries-old Russian image as a basically continental power into a sea power as well) had begun to be a global maritime power. Toward the end of the 1960s the Soviet Union had become a major world naval power. The Soviet Union required a much freer movement for its naval force, especially through the warm waters in the southern seas, than it did in the 1950s. A strange historical incident had placed the United States and the Soviet Union in the same camp requiring the freedom of naval forces through narrow waterways of other countries. Many years to come would see the close cooperation, if not coordination, between the United States and the Soviet Union on navigational issues during the Law of the Sea Conference.

There were two other Law of the Sea issues at that time that are worth mentioning and that motivated the United States and the Soviet Union. First, there was the fisheries issue. It became obvious by mid 1960s that the fisheries regime under the Geneva convention of 1958 was no longer sufficient to handle fishery matters. The United States, which in the previous decade acted as a far-distant fishing nation frequently in confrontation against the developing countries in Central and Latin America, by now was aware of the danger to the fishery resources along its coasts as the result of encroachment from other far-distant fishing nations such as Japan. Moreover, the Soviet Union had also been developing far-distant fishing capabilities which more and more began to encroach upon the coasts of the United States. This situation made it necessary for the United States to seek an acceptable regime on fisheries protecting its far-distant fishing interest as well as the interest of its coastal fishermen vis-á-vis other far-distant fishing nations.

The other issue at that time which motivated the United States to look for a solution was the increasing technological possibilities to exploit natural resources in the continental shelf. As stated earlier, the technological development had made it possible to exploit those resources further and further toward the ocean and deeper and deeper under the seabed. The existing rules under the Geneva convention of 1958 on the continental shelf did not answer clearly and precisely the outer limit of the continental shelf over which the coastal states had sovereign rights over the resources. The so-called "exploitability criteria" under the convention had become more and more ambiguous. A clearer definition of the outer limit of the continental shelf was felt necessary in order to avoid conflicts between states, thus hopefully advancing the development of those resources. Both the need to define a clearer regime on fisheries and the outer limit of the continental shelf were shared by the Soviet Union which at the same time had also become a significant maritime power.

As the result of all those situations, we saw toward the end of the 1960s the United States and the Soviet Union were sending delegation after delegation around the world proposing the holding of a Law of the Sea Conference having an agenda primarily to deal with the three issues: the limit of territorial seas and the corollary issues of navigation through straits used for international navigation, fisheries, and the continental shelf.

It was easy to perceive that those three issues did not represent the interest of all states in the world. In fact, as Ambassador Pardo had outlined, the issues of resources on and under the deep oceans were equally important. Many other countries, especially the developing countries, saw their interest differently in the proposed Law of the Sea Conference. Consequently, they would like the proposed conference to tackle their problems as well.

Indonesia

To cite a few examples, Indonesia saw its major interest in developing a Law of the Sea that would protect its national unity, political stability, economic and social development, and national security and defense.

As it turned out later all its positions on the Law of the Sea were motivated by the fact that it was a country consisting of thousands of islands with hundreds of ethnic groups having different and varied sociocultural heritage. These situations made it paramount for Indonesia to seek a Law of the Sea regime that would promote its national unity, political stability, economic and social development, as well as its national defense and security. Moreover, its experience as a colony for more than three hundred years had made it aware that its geographical structure, its population composition and its natural resources had made Indonesia a victim rather than a beneficiary of the Law of the Sea in the past. In fact it felt that the principle of the freedom of the sea enunciated 350 years ago by a Dutch jurist, Grotius, and now to be propagated again by the United States and the Soviet Union, had been motivated by the Dutch desire to conquer the East Indies, now Indonesia. In fact, as late as 1957 Indonesia was still faced with problems of provincial rebellions aggravated by foreign powers using Indonesian waters and straits to assist the rebellions, arguing that those waters are high seas, thus free for all to use as they see fit.

It was therefore not difficult to understand why the Indonesians were suspicious and opposed the wishes of the United States and the Soviet Union to have the regime of freedom of navigation through straits used for international navigation be recognized as a part of international law. A simple glance at geography would indicate that that kind of navigation regime would endanger Indonesian national unity and stability which it had fought for decades to establish. In fact Indonesia felt that the regime of navigation sought by the United States and the Soviet Union was primarily intended to make it easier for them to pass through the Indonesian archipelago which straddles two major oceans, the Indian and the Pacific, and two major continents, Asia and Australia.

In view of this situation, it was the Indonesian view that any conference dealing with Law of the Sea matters must discuss and recognize the uniqueness of the situation faced by archipelagic countries like Indonesia. Any Law of the Sea Conference must recognize the need for, and ensure the achievements of, national unity, political stability, economic and social development, as well as the safeguard of national defense and security of an archipelagic state like Indonesia. Any Law of the Sea Conference must recognize the function of the waters between the islands of an archipelagic state as a unifying factor for the state, and no longer as a dividing factor as in the past.

Singapore

On the other hand, a country like Singapore had a completely different perception from Indonesia on Law of the Sea matters. Geographically, Singapore considered itself to be most unfortunate since it was a small island country tucked in between Indonesia and Malaysia. Singapore was an important seaport and trading center in Southeast Asia but had no possibility of extending its maritime jurisdiction to the sea. It therefore considered that its major interest in the Law of the Sea was the continued uninterrupted flow of navigation to and from its port and the recognition of its position as a geographically disadvantaged state. Therefore, when Indonesia and Malaysia concluded a treaty delimiting their respective territorial seas in the Strait of Malacca and later on asked Singapore to cooperate in the promotion of safety of navigation in the straits in 1971, Singapore could only take note of the Indonesian and Malaysian legal position on the status of the Strait of Malacca while it agreed to cooperate on the promotion of the safety of navigation in the Strait. Singapore agreed that the legal status of the Strait of Malacca could only be decided by an internationally agreed convention.

It was also Singapore's major interest to maintain and promote its access to the resources of the seas of its neighbors. It was therefore easy to understand why Singapore at times was sympathetic to the position of the maritime powers on navigational issues and to the position of landlocked countries on resources issues. On many occasions the different perception between Indonesia and Singapore due to many factors as outlined above had made it difficult for Indonesia and Singapore, good and friendly neighbors though they were, to streamline their position in the Law of the Sea Conference.

Thailand

Other countries in the ASEAN region had also their own perception. Thailand, a country located in the semi-enclosed seas, the South China Sea, and the Andaman Sea and whose sea-communications from one coastline in the west to another in the east required passing through the waters of Indonesia, Malaysia, and Singapore in the Strait of Malacca and Singapore, was also preoccupied with its needs to have an access to and from the oceans. Being located in semi-enclosed seas,

Thailand also visualized herself to be "enclosed" by the Indonesian and Philippine archipelagoes. Thailand, which had developed sub-stanial far-distant fishing capabilities toward the end of the 1960s, would also like to have access as much as possible to the resources of the seas of its neighbors. Although Thailand is a much larger country and has the possibility of extending its maritime jurisdiction, due to its geographical location, however, she seemed to have had similar perception with Singapore on navigational and resources issues.

Malaysia

Malaysia, on the other hand, was seriously concerned with the prob-lems of navigation in the Strait of Malacca and Singapore and with the problems of its national unity, being a country consisting of West Malaysia (Malay Peninsula) and East Malaysia (Sarawak and Sabah in Borneo) and divided by a wide South China Sea dotted with Indonesian islands and archipelagic waters in the middle. Therefore on naviga-tional issues in the Strait of Malacca and Singapore, Malaysia main-tained a very close association and similar outlook with Indonesia. Indonesia had declared a 12-mile territorial sea in 1957 and enacted it into law in 1960. In 1969, Malaysia had also declared a 12-mile territorial sea, thus making the Strait of Malacca of less than 24 miles as territorial seas of Malaysia and Indonesia. Both Malaysia and Indonesia, espe-cially after they signed a treaty delimiting their respective territorial seas in the Strait of Malacca in 1969, were committed to defend their territorial sovereignty over the portion of the Strait of Malacca delimited in the treaty.

On the national unity issue, however, Malaysia sought several guar-antees from Indonesia that the application of the Indonesian archipe-lagic principles in South China Sea would not adversely affect the national unity and political stability of Malaysia. This guarantee was to be formulated in the internationally accepted Law of the Sea Con-vention and later to be confirmed and regulated in detail in a separate treaty between the two countries.

On resources issues, Malaysia maintained a less vocal position, per-haps because its interests in the resources of the South China Sea would be guaranteed anyway, one way or another.

Philippines

The Philippines, having similar geographical features with Indonesia, maintained a similar position with Indonesia on navigational issues. In fact, it maintained a much stronger and inflexible position compared to Indonesia primarily because of its more compact geographical setup. The Philippines claimed that its national and territorial unity had historically been a fact recognized by the United States since the end of the Spanish American War in 1898. Its territorial claim therefore was based on the Spanish American Treaty of 1898, resulting in uneven extent of its claimed territorial sea from a few miles from the coast to more than 200 miles in some parts. Only in 1961 did the Philippines determine its baselines connecting the outermost points of its outermost islands. Based on this historical antecedent, in addition to promoting the idea of archipelagic states like Indonesia, the Philippines had also fought for the recognition of its "historic right" which, from time to time, had brought it into difficulties with some of its neighbors. On the other hand, like Indonesia, the Philippines had no difficulty with the resources aspects of the emerging Law of the Sea since it bordered with an open Pacific Ocean and the sufficiently wide South China Sea and the Celebes Sea.

It was therefore clear that even among member countries of ASEAN their perceptions on the Law of the Sea were not the same. In fact, Indonesia and the Philippines later attempted to coordinate the views of ASEAN countries on Law of the Sea issues, but this attempt did not go anywhere. The first and only meeting of experts of ASEAN countries was held in Manila in 1971 but it was very clear that Singapore and Thailand were not interested in making the Law of the Sea issues the regional concerns of ASEAN. In view of this, it was then felt that the Law of the Sea issues existing in Southeast Asia should be resolved through principles internationally agreed upon in the Law of the Sea Convention. The Law of the Sea Conference therefore gained prominence in the minds of Southeast Asian countries through which they will negotiate and resolve their regional issues.

In view of the various perceptions and interests as outlined above, the proposals of the United States and the Soviet Union to hold a Law of the Sea Conference dealing with the three issues that concerned them met with mixed reactions from other countries, including those from Southeast Asia. They supported the idea and the need to hold a Law of the Sea Conference but they wanted to have the agenda of that Conference include all matters that concerned every state in the world, not only matters that concerned the two superpowers. After lengthy consultations, the United Nations finally agreed in 1970 to hold a Third United Nations Conference on the Law of the Sea to discuss in a "comprehensive" manner all matters that were submitted by all states. The United Nations also entrusted the United Nations seabed committee to prepare for the Conference.

In understanding the process of negotiation that followed, it was therefore essential to remember that the solution to the Law of the Sea problems must be a "comprehensive" one covering all subjects under discussion. Any piecemeal approach or partial solution to the problems was contrary to the basic understanding agreed upon since 1970. This "package deal" approach should be respected and had been the guideline for delegations during the years of negotiation that followed. On the basis of this resolution the United Nations seabed committee, acting as Preparatory Commission for the Law of the Sea Conference, took more than two years to agree on "subjects and issues" to be dealt with by the Law of the Sea Conference. The list of subjects and issues included numerous items covering all matters of the Law of the Sea from internal waters to deep-seabed mining, from scientific research and pollution control to peaceful settlement of disputes, and so on. Nine years of negotiations in the Conference, plus five years of negotiations in the United Nations seabed committee, resulted in various compromises either on each specific subject and issue or among the various subjects and issues.

During the first years of negotiation the major and dominant issues were those related to navigation. The United States and its allies on this matter, primarily the Soviet Union, constantly threatened the Conference that, for them, the navigational issues were matters that would "make or break" the Conference. If the navigational issues were not solved to their satisfaction it would "break" the Conference. During all those years they argued and maneuvered in such a way as to alienate the coastal states bordering the straits used for international navigation, the so-called "straits states" as if the straits states were against mankind and humanity. The United States and the Soviet Union projected themselves as the defenders of world communication, which was essential for international trade and cooperation, while in fact they were simply defending the freest possible maneuverability of their own naval forces. The majority of the developing countries, who were originally supportive of the position of the straits states, later became aloof, perhaps because most of them did not have the straits to reckon with or because the major maritime powers and their allies in the East and the West were able to persuade those developing countries to stay away from the conflicting positions—by indicating *quid pro quo* in other issues. In the meantime, the major maritime powers began to make deals with some individual coastal states, thus breaking up the unity of the strait states. The text in the Law of the Sea Convention dealing with navigational issues could be classified as a victory for the maritime naval powers, leaving the straits states hoping for a *quid pro quo* in some other provisions of the Convention, especially in the resources provisions. The navigational issues through archipelagic states met with a somewhat similar solution as in straits used for international navigation.

After the maritime powers, especially the United States, won their "make or break" issue on navigation, they began to fight on another "make or break" issue, namely on the resources issue. Because they were coastal countries, their adversaries on these issues were the landlocked and the geographically disadvantaged states. The maritime powers, however, continued to have problems with the developing coastal countries with regard to the status of the Exclusive Economic Zone (EEZ). Fearing the effects of the EEZ concept on the freedom of navigation, the major maritime powers strongly insisted that the EEZ should continue to have the legal status as high seas. On the other hand, the developing coastal countries, fearing that the notion of freedom of navigation might have adverse effects on the exploitation and preservation of the EEZ, fought very hard to reject the status of the EEZ as high seas.

There were very few differences between the maritime powers and the developing coastal states with regard to the resources aspects of the EEZ and the continental shelf. In fact, both camps stood together in opposing the landlocked and the geographically disadvantaged states with regard to the control over the resources. The developing coastal states and the major maritime powers would like to nationalize those resources while the landlocked and the geographically disadvantaged states would like to internationalize them, or at least to "regionalize" them. While some compromises were worked out later especially with regard to the living resources of the EEZ, there were fewer such compromises with regard to the extent and the resources of the continental shelf. Broadly speaking, the battle over the resources along the coast was won by the coastal countries, primarily by the major maritime powers. Again on the resources issues the major maritime powers, especially the United States and the Soviet Union, had won their "make or break" issues.

After gaining victories on the two fronts, the United States and its allies began concentrating on new "make or break" issues, thus continuing what many delegates began to call a "salami tactic," namely to carve out victories slice by slice. Now the issue was scientific research. The United States scientific community wanted to have free hands in conducting what they called scientific research on far-distant waters. Many developing countries, however, were suspicious of the possible relationship between the scientific research and its military implication as well as its resources exploitation. The maritime powers, for a while, attempted to make the scientific research issues another "make or break" issue of the Conference. For better or for worse, the issue was solved rather quickly after the solutions of the navigational and resources issues were reached.

There were many other issues in the Conference between various neighboring states, such as the delimitation of maritime zones between states, right of transit of landlocked states, enclosed and semi-enclosed seas, etc. These issues were not classified as "make or break" issues primarily because they did not deal with the interests of the major maritime powers.

One of the most important "make or break" issues was certainly the seabed mining problems. From the very beginning, even before the opening of the Conference, the world community of nations had declared through a United Nations resolution that the seabed area and all its resources beyond the limits of national jurisdiction were the "common heritage of mankind." The United Nations resolution also stated that those resources shall only be exploited under a legal regime to be established. Pending the establishment of such a regime, another

United Nations resolution called for moratorium on the exploration and exploitation of the resources.

Since the beginning of the Conference the developing countries, faithful to those United Nations resolutions, believing that they were reflecting the opinions of mankind, demanded that the seabed resources be exploited only by an international authority through its commercial arms, the Enterprise. The developing countries believed that this "unitary system" would be a correct translation of the principle of common heritage.

The industrial countries, however, thought differently. They were seeking assurances for their companies to be able to exploit those resources as free and as independent as possible from the supervision or regulation of the international community. In fact they were looking to apply the principle of free enterprise in exploiting the resources which did not belong to them and which had been declared as the "common heritage of mankind." They looked at the proposed unitary system as unworkable and as a move toward "socialism" in exploiting the resources of the seabed.

After years of negotiation and as proposed by the United States itself a compromise was struck and the "parallel system" was adopted. Under the parallel system the international authority through the Enterprise would have equal access to the seabed resources as the private entities. Negotiations to translate the principles of the parallel system into detailed treaty provisions took years of negotiations resulting in the end that the developing countries little by little gave in to the industrial countries, especially to the United States.

The provisions in the Law of the Sea Conference dealing with the organizational setup of the authority and all its organs, the decision-making process in all those organs, the provisions dealing with financial arrangements, transfer of technology, protection of land-based producers, production policies, and so on, were primarily victories for the industrial countries. The developing countries were reluctantly prepared to give in, hoping that such compromises would keep the industrial countries in the Convention and hoping that by so doing the international authority and all its organs, including the Enterprise, would be realizable and workable. The developing countries even went so far in their desire to lure the industrial countries by agreeing to recognize the principle of "pioneer investors," giving those private investors the privilege and the priority in claiming mining sites on the seabed area. Unfortunately, the readiness of the developing countries to recognize the priority status of the pioneer investors still had not been sufficient to satisfy the insatiable appetite of the new American administration on the Law of the Sea matters.

It was therefore ironic that the United States, after winning the navigational issues, the resources issues, the scientific research, the seabed mining, etc., was now to reject the Convention and seemed to have worked hard to convince its allies to stay out of the Convention also. The United States was even working against the Convention by trying to conclude a competing regime through reciprocal arrangements with its allies to exploit the resources of the international seabed area outside the context of the Law of the Sea Convention. This was the height of high-handedness.

After rejecting the Law of the Sea Convention, which the United States had participated in negotiating through successive administrations, both Democratic and Republican, and which the rest of the world had participated in in good faith, the United States now exercised the wisdom, or more appropriately the "non-wisdom," of "choose and pick." It chose the provisions of the Convention that suited its interest and rejected those that did not. It considered that the regime of navigation in the Convention applied to it even though it had rejected the Convention, arguing that the provisions dealing with navigation had become part of the customary international law.

I for one disagreed. In my opinion the existing customary rules of international law dealing with navigation through straits used for international navigation was the regime of nonsuspendable innocent passage as codified in the Geneva convention of 1958. The regime of transit passage and for that matter the regime of "archipelagic sealane passage," were new rules formulated on the basis of compromises in a comprehensive package. It should therefore only be applicable to those who accepted the package.

As article 311(1) of the 1982 Law of the Sea Convention stated, the provisions in the Convention shall prevail over the 1958 Geneva convention only "as between states parties." At least, the strait or archipelagic states would have the right to deny the application of those rules to nonparties of the Convention. Here, in this context, the United

States had simply placed its friends around the world in a difficult position since most of those straits and archipelagic states were friendly to the United States. They were now facing a situation of having to recognize the right of archipelagic sealane passage and the right of transit passage through straits used for international navigation to the Soviet Union and its allies who had signed the Convention and had to reject or at least to doubt the validity of those rights or regimes of navigation to the United States and other friendly nonsignatory states. It was more discomforting to remember that the new regime of navigation was primarily negotiated with the United States with the understanding that the United States would be a party to the Convention in a grand package. There was therefore a tremendous sense of disappointment and desperation among those straits and archipelagic states friendly to the United States to witness that after all those compromises to lure the United States to stay in the Convention, the United States simply decided not only to stay out of the Convention but to vehemently oppose it.

The United States also claimed and applied the regime of EEZ and continental shelf for itself without being a signatory to the Convention, arguing that the regime on those items had also become part of customary international law. Here the wisdom of "choose and pick" had also been opposed and criticized by the developing countries and the rest of the world. It should be further noted that the United States had not been strict in applying the regime of EEZ and continental shelf because it only applied those provisions which it considered beneficial to it and disregarded the provisions in the EEZ and continental shelf that it considered not good for it. The U.S., for instance, refused to adhere to the rules on highly migratory species and to the rule on revenue sharing for the exploitation of the continental shelf beyond 200 miles from the baselines.

The most glaring example of U.S. defiance against the community of nations was its rejection of the provisions relating to seabed mining. After years of negotiation and concession after concession by the developing countries the text as adopted on seabed mining was rejected by the United States on various grounds. Basically, what the United States wanted was to apply the principles of free enterprise to seabed mining. This was certainly not acceptable to the community of nations who regarded the seabed resources as the "common heritage of mankind." The unfettered application of the free enterprise system to the seabed resources would in the end result in the exploitation of the seabed resources by private companies that have the technology, the financial capabilities, and all the other resources to exploit them. That in the end would result in the new colonization of the seabed resources. The United States seemed determined to impose its philosophical approach to the seabed mining issues on the rest of the world.

On the basis of these basic philosophical differences the United States later raised numerous difficulties with regard to the seabed mining articles. First it said that seabed mining was a complex and difficult endeavor that would require the investment of enormous amounts of capital before it could produce any benefits. Therefore the United States was fighting for an extremely lenient production policy and financial arrangements. It said that the resources were not as enormous as had been thought. It also said that seabed mining was far-off in the future and therefore the world community of nations should not expect too much. But what the United States could not explain was why then the seabed mining issues, if they were not feasible now and would not be competitive in the foreseeable future, were regarded as so important by the United States to the degree that it was ready to scuttle the Convention or to place in doubt all the benefits of the Convention that it would or could reap from the regime of navigation, EEZ, and continental shelf. In fact, why then was the United States ready to defy the whole world for such an "insignificant" issue? There was a sense of insincerity in the United States argument.

Then the United States also objected to the provision dealing with the transfer of technology although the provisions as appeared in the Convention had been extremely watered down to make it practically meaningless. All this was done to placate the United States to stay in the Convention. In fact the developing countries initially considered the provisions on transfer of technology as some of the most important provisions if the Enterprise was going to work. Otherwise how would an international Enterprise with no knowledge of seabed mining, with no capital to work with, and with no experience in business management, be able to operate without some kind of technology transfer from those companies that had gathered some experience? The reluctance or the objection of the United States to agree to some kind of transfer of technology could only be interpreted as its opposition to the concept of the Enterprise, thus its willingness to see the community of nations take some benefit from the resources of the "common heritage of mankind." The United States seemed to be prepared to give the international community only what it was willing to share in term of profits—which would be insubstantial. The U.S. was not prepared to recognize what the international community deserved.

There were many other objections raised by the United States to the provisions relating to seabed mining. In my mind, important though they were, they were not sufficiently important to scuttle the achievement of the Conference as a whole, especially if one took into account the fact that the leaders of the United States, including President Reagan himself, had stated that most of the provisions of the Convention were acceptable to the United States. The provisions relating to seabed mining were therefore only a small portion of the Convention as a whole.

What now would happen to the Convention without the United States? It would be an ideal situation if one day the United States would rejoin the world community of nations and sign the Convention. Such a likelihood, however, is remote under the Reagan administration. The participation of the United States, important though it might be, is not a precondition for the entry into force of a convention or for effectiveness of the Convention. The U.S. contribution to the establishment of rules of law in the world is important, but that does not mean that there are not rules of law without the United States. In my mind the world community of nations, including those in the Pacific region, should continue to be guided by the provisions of the Convention, whether or not the United States becomes party to it. As far as we are concerned, we are going to apply the Law of the Sea provisions nationally, regionally, and internationally, at least as between the parties.

Nationally, I believe the countries of the world will continue to prepare for the ratification of the Convention and will continue to take benefit from its provisions. In southern Asia, the Philippines has already ratified it while Indonesia is making preparations to ratify it. Other ASEAN countries are expected to take similar action.

Regionally, the states will continue to seek and formulate various regional cooperation and arrangements stipulated in the Convention. Bordering states or states in front of others will continue to delimit their respective maritime zones by agreement, taking into account the various maritime zones recognized in the Convention. The world community of nations, through the Preparatory Commission, will continue to implement the decisions of the Conference regarding the establishment of the international authority and all its organs. In fact, the Preparatory Commission, to establish international authority for seabed mining, continues to make progress during its last session. I myself feel and hope that the United States in due course, will come around to respect the Convention.

First there was a strong opinion in the United States itself in support of the Convention. I could not believe that the American people, who had a very strong tradition in favor of law and order, would continue to let their government pursue an egoistic policy disregarding world opinion, international law, and international order. I believed that in the end this highly valued American tradition in favor of law and order will prevail. Second, the United States will realize in due course that the protection of its interest in seabed mining will be far more secure under a generally internationally agreed regime as formulated and negotiated rather than under a unilaterally formulated national legislation or any kind of minitreaty outside the context of the Law of the Sea Convention. It was my opinion that the seabed mining regime under the Convention was far more workable and secure than an opposing seabed mining regime under unilateral legislation or minitreaty. Perhaps the time had not come to test this hypothesis because the reality of seabed mining was still somewhat far in the future.

One of the problems in the United States at present is of course the decreasing attention given by the American public and academia to the Law of the Sea matters, especially to the Law of the Sea Convention. This might work in favor of the present administration because slowly the Law of the Sea matters are being delegated into an increasingly less significant issue in the American mind. Although the effect of this situation in the short run would be negative to the Law of the Sea Convention, in the long run however the American public would realize that in the global strategic setup, the isolation of the United States would be felt more detrimental to the United States than to adopt the Convention.

For us in the Pacific region, especially in ASEAN countries, the United States position on the Law of the Sea has been extremely disappointing. As friends of the United States and as countries mutually bordering on the Pacific region we expected that the United States would be prepared to work together and cooperate in the establishment of law and order in the Pacific basin. We thought that this would be in the United States' interest as well. Indonesia, for example, had tried very hard at all levels, even the highest level, to press the United States to come into the Convention but so far it has been to no avail. The Law of the Sea Convention was extremely important to the Pacific region especially because major seabed mining operations would take place in the Pacific Ocean and major navigational issues would develop in the Pacific region. It is not an exaggeration to say that the Pacific Ocean is the ocean of the future and that the Pacific region countries would play a much more important role in the future world strategic setup. It is in this region that major world powers such as the United States, the Soviet Union, Japan and China converged. Unless the maritime interest of these powers as well as the interests of the states in the region were properly regulated through an internationally and generally agreed regime, the Pacific Ocean would become a new center of conflagration. This is not in our interest and we believe that it is not in the interest of the Pacific rim countries. I believe that the Law of the Sea Convention provides a framework, the only framework, for cooperation in maritime affairs in the region. Any other framework, such as the unilateral legislation or minitreaty, will not provide such a framework for peaceful cooperation; in fact it will only provide seeds for conflict and conflagration.

It is therefore clear that we must continue to defend the Law of the Sea Convention and pursue the objectives provided therein. We would have liked to see the United States participate but we will not abandon the Convention simply because the United States opposes it. In my mind the nonparticipation of the United States is regrettable and will perhaps cause some difficulties in realizing seabed mining within the time frame that we expect; but seabed mining is only one of the many issues tackled and regulated. In this context, the Convention remains the most useful framework for cooperation.

The nonparticipation of the United States has been extremely enigmatic. It seems to us that it has been motivated simply by narrowly conceived national interests. In view of the U.S. claim to be the leader of the "free world," it is difficult for us to understand why the world should follow the leadership of the United States who is mindful only of its own interests. In our area, the notion of a leader that we respect and follow is someone who would place the interest of the community above his own personal interest. The United States position on the Law of the Sea seems to suggest that it places its narrowly conceived national interest above the interest of the world community of nations. This is not the kind of leadership that we can respect or follow.

PART IV
Unfinished Business

9.
The United States and the Law of the Sea Conference

THOMAS A. CLINGAN, JR.

THE ROLE OF the United States, indeed of any country, in the Law of the Sea negotiations, has a chameleon-like quality that causes it to defy descriptive characterization. As the Conference moved and evolved, U.S. policy and strategies necessarily were reshaped and recast to meet new conditions. A full evaluation of these shifts, their causes and effects, would not be possible in this brief overview and, in the ultimate course of events, might not prove particularly revealing or useful. Instead, I shall attempt to sketch out my own perceptions of the objectives of the U.S. government in the light of shifting needs. Since the Conference lasted for many years, it should not be surprising that U.S. evaluation of its national interests should, from time to time, have been modified or recast in the light of shifting political alignments within the U.S. government itself, and in the light of significant events that occurred during that long period of time.

In an extremely simplistic and general sense, the United States perceived its role throughout the Conference as an expediter in the pursuit of a broadly accepted global agreement on the Law of the Sea that would accommodate, to a satisfactory degree, U.S. interests, whether these be cast narrowly in terms of national security, resource allocation, and the like, or more broadly in terms of global foreign policy, i.e., a treaty that would contribute to world public order and the advancement of new cooperative mechanisms for the evolution of international law.

In a real sense, the Law of the Sea Conference was convened in response not only to significant gaps in the law as it then existed, but also as a major effort to come to grips with the fact that customary law, long a substantial foundation for the evolution of international law, was proving inadequate for keeping pace with the rapidly changing face of international relations. As noted by Lissitzyn in 1965,

The sense of a "crisis" in international law experienced by many observers today is a product of the acceleration of the processes of change in the international community that is characteristic of our era. The factors that have caused this acceleration are well known. They include rapid technological progress; the rise of new ideologies and systems of public order . . . ; the appearance of many new states of widely different cultural backgrounds and levels of development; rising demands for social reform; the fear of war and the growing reluctance of the more advanced states to protect their interests by coercive means; and the increase in the number and functions of international organizations.

This statement was made roughly at the time preliminary overtures were being made that led, eventually, to the convening of the Third United Nations Law of the Sea Conference. The United States, as a large and sophisticated developed country, could not have been immune to these signs of rapid change. Indeed, it was its particular manifestations on the sea that prompted the acceptance of a global conference. Since the failure, in 1960, to achieve an acceptable accommodation between navigation interests and the resource interests of coastal states, coastal state claims to extended jurisdiction off its shores had been increasing at an alarming rate. In addition, UN General Assembly debates were beginning to reflect the influence of a growing number of newly emerged developing states that had radically different views on the subject of global allocation of resources. It was against such a background that the United States decided to participate in the exercise that would eventually result in a new Law of the Sea convention. This route was seen as the most effective, and least risky, means of containing the expansionist trends that posed a threat to certain U.S. interests, particularly those relating to navigation, while at the same time protecting U.S. resource interests, than the chance evolution of customary international law.

The initial efforts of the United States, as is well understood, were directed at seeking to solve a problem that was not resolved by the 1960 Conference. This issue was how to accommodate coastal state demands for control over the natural resources of the seas adjacent to its coasts without interfering with traditional freedoms of navigation and overflight, and related uses.

To address the problem, the United States first suggested a limited agreement, one that would establish an agreed limit to the territorial sea, would guarantee unimpeded transit through straits used for international navigation and, in addition, address the question of coastal state control over fisheries. It was soon clear, however, that the discussions could not be so limited. In 1968, the General Assembly of the United Nations established an ad hoc committee on the seabeds, which eventually led to a formal committee and preparatory sessions, for an eventual Law of the Sea conference, that extended from 1971 to 1973. The establishment of this committee provided the forum for a wide-ranging discussion of all issues related to ocean usage. These meetings reflected the widely held view that any agreement that might emerge must cover a broad range of subjects, including the management of resources beyond the limits of national jurisdiction. Any discussion of that issue, of course, would mandate a consideration of the precise boundary between national and international areas, and, in particular, the limits of the continental shelf. There was, during the meetings of the seabed committee, and during the early stages of the Conference, convened in 1973, a view among a number of participants that the major U.S. objective was the protection of navigation and, in particular, the incorporation of an adequate straits regime, and that the United States was less interested in resource matters.

History does not support this view. On resource issues, the U.S. position is reflected in its actions, although these actions were taken in such a low profile that one would have to examine the record carefully to divine the strategy that lay behind them. Some of the more important steps taken include the tabling of the "species approach" to coastal state fisheries management in 1971. While this may have been perceived by some as a concession to gain support for navigation rights, the United States stood to gain immensely from jurisdiction over fisheries adjacent to its own extensive coastlines.

Another example of U.S. efforts to advance its resource interests is seen in the 1970 "trusteeship" proposal. On its face, this proposal had a distinctly international flavor. It declared the seabed beyond the depth of 200 meters to be an international area where no state could assert sovereignty or claim sovereign rights. But two elements of this proposal are significant. First, by creating an international trusteeship zone, extending from the 200-meter isobath to beyond the base of the continental slope, over which the coastal state would have complete resource control, the coastal state would garnish the major advantages of a broad continental shelf that contained virtually all of the oil and gas resources. Second, the waters above the international seabed area, including the trusteeship zone, would have retained their legal character as high seas.

Reading these together, it can be seen that the United States was at that early stage as interested as any state in protecting its access to fish, oil, and gas in broad zones adjacent to its coasts, while protecting to the maximum the freedoms associated with navigation and overflight.

As somewhat of an aside, it is interesting to note that the U.S. proposal contained substantial revenue-sharing requirements, both with respect to the trusteeship portion of the international area, and beyond. Despite that fact, the proposal did not receive sufficient international support. There were at least two difficulties encountered. First, while the proposal made reference to the continental margin, it did so within the overall context of the international seabed area. This was not popularly received by the states having the broadest continental margins because it tended to undercut the basic principle of jurisdiction based upon the natural prolongation theory. Next, the proposal was not well received by those states, numerous and influential, that were pressing for resource jurisdiction to an outer limit not greater than 200 nautical miles.

The prominence of U.S. interest in resources is also reflected in its approval of the institutional structure of the seabed committee and the Conference itself. I do not believe that it was by mere chance that the deep-seabed resource question was institutionally split from other resource issues and assigned to the jurisdiction of the first committee. The willingness of the United States to accept this structure can only be seen as evidence of an assignment of a lower priority to the mining of manganese nodules as compared with the infinitely more valuable primary resources represented by fish, oil, and gas. Since questions bearing upon these resources were assigned to the second committee, i.e., those relating to the continental shelf and what was to become the Exclusive Economic Zone (EEZ), it was possible to deal with them in a more objective way outside of the highly political atmosphere that surrounded the subject of deep-seabed mining. Within the U.S. government, the departments of State, Commerce, Interior, and Defense, having substantial interests in resources and navigation, were the primary beneficiaries of this organizational structure.

In such a scenario, it was no accident that the United States was quick to accede to the general principle of the 200-mile exclusive economic zone, nor was it an accident that it associated itself with the group of broad margin states (the Margineers). Perhaps, it was no accident that the United States was perceived in Caracas as contributing to the politicizing of the deep-seabed mining question in the first committee while quietly pursuing its more important objectives in the second committee.

Rhetoric aside, there was a high degree of concordance of interest between U.S. resource interests and those of other coastal states participating in the Conference. For that reason, the nub of the negotiations concerning the exclusive economic zone was focused on the protection of navigation related rights within the overall context of broad coastal state resource jurisdiction. This was not an easy task. Initially, those states falling within the group characterized as "territorialists" sought an understanding that the economic zone was to be a zone of national jurisdiction. Particularly vocal in this effort were several influential Latin American states.

The United States, on the other hand, viewed the waters beyond the territorial sea as having the legal status of high seas as that term was understood in the 1958 convention, except for coastal state powers regarding resources and resource related activities. When one examines the treaty, it can be seen that neither of these polar positions found their way into the texts in so many words. The ultimate compromise reflects a balance wherein the zone might be considered national for some purposes, but high seas for others.

At stake for the United States was not merely freedom of navigation and overflight in the EEZ, which were readily conceded by the coastal states, but the protection of certain other uses of the zone and associated with the movement of ships and aircraft. This concession was yielded to the United States in the contact group formed and chaired by Ambassador Castaneda of Mexico and, by mid-Conference, a stable economic zone regime was agreed upon. How stable that regime remains is yet to be seen.

There is a great deal of flexibility in the regime for how a coastal state is to manage its zone. This flexibility is necessary and desirable from a managerial point of view, but it also invites excesses which, if practiced, would lead to a further territorialization of the zone. This concept, usually referred to as "creeping jurisdiction" represents a real danger for the future. However, that danger existed prior to the Conference, and the new treaty, despite its potential weaknesses, at least serves to provide an additional restraint upon temptations to enlarge coastal jurisdictions. Perhaps that is all that could have been expected in any event.

Through the economic zone, the United States gained control over fisheries adjacent to its coasts. This control now can be said to be accepted even though the United States is not a signatory to the treaty, and without sacrifice to its navigation interests. The United States also made substantial gains in other areas under the purview of the second committee. It obtained agreement to a set of articles on international straits far superior to the straits regime contained in the 1958 conventions, converting innocent passage for which there was no right of overflight or submerged transit, to transit passage, where such rights were guaranteed. The Margineers succeeded in capturing all of the significant continental shelf for themselves in exchange for a revenue-sharing formula applicable to the outer margin that is of questionable value and low cost.

The United States also fought off, along with its maritime allies, all attempts to create any meaningful provisions regarding enclosed and semi-enclosed seas, and it was virtually assured that there would be no formula for the delimitation of maritime boundaries that would prejudice its national interests, although the final formula would not be adopted until the final stage of the Conference. These were accomplishments of considerable magnitude, although with these latter gains it remains to be seen how they will be applied with respect to the United States as a nonsignatory.

During the first part of the Conference, the United States continued to occupy the time of the first committee by pressing its version of the free market approach to deep-seabed mining. This had the result of drawing delegates interested in advancing the objectives of the New International Economic Order away from the second committee and the important issues being discussed in that forum. Once those issues were well in hand, however, it became necessary to consolidate those gains by seeking an acceptable solution to the mining question.

Hence, in 1975, in a speech given in Montreal, Secretary of State Henry Kissinger broached what was to become known as the "parallel system of access," a proposal advanced earlier by Canada and Australia, but which had not until that time gained a great deal of support. The Kissinger proposal was aimed at breaking the log-jam and permitting the negotiation of specific implementing texts to begin.

In the following months, the United States insisted that part and parcel of this deal would have to be a guarantee of nondiscriminatory access to deep-seabed resources, and an international seabed authority that could not be dominated by the developing countries. When the bargaining began, the Group of 77 countered with a number of proposals of their own, including a demand that there be a system of protection for the exports of land-based producers of metals that would be extracted from the oceans through deep-seabed mining. In principle, the idea of limiting production from the oceans was not opposed by the United States because, at the time, it was perceived that a formula could be developed using nickel as the base metal for computation that would protect developing country copper producers against unlikely contingencies without seriously impeding the development of nickel within the parameters of world nickel consumption.

When the version of the text known as the Revised Single Negotiating Text (RSNT) appeared, it contained such a formula. Canada, however, as a major land-based nickel producer, immediately recognized that the formula protected copper producers, but did little to protect nations in their situation. Satisfaction of Canadian interests only served, in the long run, to produce a formula cited as one of the reasons for the U.S. rejection of the treaty.

The pendulum was to swing several times on such seabed issues before coming to rest. In 1976, the United States conceived and set in motion a plan whereby a small group of interested countries would be convened to work on specific draft articles that, after broader discussion, would be fed to the chairman of the first committee who would then produce the compromises in his committee as his own proposals. For this plan to be successful, it was necessary that there be no public acknowledgment of the group's existence, therefore meetings were held quietly in the mission of Brazil. It was the intention of the group that its work product be considered as that of the chairman.

As is often the case in international negotiations, the existence of the group was privately known to a number of delegations which chose to let the process continue to see what might emerge, with the knowledge that at any point the process could be stopped by public denunciation of the "secret" negotiations. In the end, that is precisely what happened. The group's existence and work were publicly disclosed by one country that had been excluded from the group, and felt that it was being prejudiced thereby. While the work of the group did in fact find its way in substantial part into the RSNT, the public disclosure of the mode of negotiation changed the atmosphere in the Conference and made it impossible to say that the final compromise had been struck.

A number of factors prevented acceptance of the texts at that time. Canada was unhappy about the production limitation provisions. Mexico, which had participated in the work of the Brazil group, became uneasy about the possibility that its participation might impinge upon its growing reputation as a leader in the third world. And India was offended at not having been included in the small group. Such attitudes made it impossible for the Group of 77 to reach a consensus on the texts, although they did not reject them.

After the spring of 1976, the United States returned to the negotiations with a new list of desired changes. It was feared by some in the United States that this strategy might prompt the Group of 77 to reverse course, and thus U.S. strategy shifted to one of stonewalling the negotiations while it considered further its options. When Secretary Kissinger visited the Conference, he offered further suggestions to meet some of the concerns voiced by developing countries. He responded to the concern of India that the Enterprise, the mining arm of the Seabed Authority under the parallel system, would never be competitive with the private enterprise side by offering first-generation funding of the Enterprise, a review conference on the system of exploitation after fifteen years, and a promise to "see to" the transfer of mining technology to the Enterprise. These were viewed by developing countries as positive steps, although they were not greeted with equal enthusiasm by other industrial countries interested in deep-seabed mining.

Upon the election of President Carter, the United States was presented with the opportunity to review its positions. A change in administration is expected to produce some shifts. It could, on the one hand, revert to a harder line to set the stage for obtaining further concessions, or, on the other hand, it could move ahead on the existing course on the theory that any significant pull-back might jeopardize the success of the Conference. The decision was to move ahead.

In the winter of 1977, Jens Evensen of Norway convened, with apparent U.S. support, an informal meeting to discuss seabed questions and to seek possible solutions. Chairman Paul Engo did not appreciate what he perceived as interference with his role as chairman of the first committee. In the Evensen group, new texts were prepared, but when they were presented to Engo for discussion in the first committee, he rejected them in favor of a new draft of his own. This new text, which appeared in the Integrated Composite Negotiating Text (ICNT), was pronounced "fundamentally unacceptable" to the United States, which took the view that the text could not even be used as a basis for further negotiations. While this created an initial crisis in the Conference, it had the beneficial result of causing the adoption of new Conference procedures that would preclude any single person or group of persons from introducing any new provisions into the texts without the blessing of the plenary of the Conference, and without demonstrating the probability of moving toward a consensus. With this change, the negotiations went forward.

During the Carter administration, there was a general U.S perception that the treaty was not far from being completed. Momentum picked up substantially, and delegations, sensing the end of a long process, stepped up their efforts to make the final compromises. During 1978, a revised production control formula was produced that was acceptable to Canada. The United States had accepted a provision dealing with the transfer of technology.

This rapid movement began to worry U.S. mining representatives attached to the U.S. delegation. These representatives, by and large, were the managers of offices responsible to their corporate boards for the development of seabed mining programs, and not the chief executive officers of their companies. It was their desire to achieve treaty provisions which protected the private mining side of the parallel system to the maximum degree in order to enhance their bargaining position with the Seabed Authority when contract negotiation might begin. They did not view the direction being taken in the Conference as achieving that result. Without sufficient iron-clad guarantees in the treaty, they would be in a weaker position to persuade their corporate backers to invest still larger funds in mining development.

Accordingly, they began to concentrate their efforts on the U.S. Congress. They had two objectives. First they wished to increase opposition within certain influential segments of the Congress to the treaty itself and, as a second related tactic, they sought the enactment of legislation to protect U.S. mining plans on a unilateral or small multilateral scale.

The motivation of these individuals is not entirely clear. Surely some sincerely opposed the treaty, and would not have been satisfied no matter what changes could be achieved. Others, however, seemed to be following this strategy as a means of mounting pressure on the U.S. Law of the Sea delegation to achieve adequate concessions from the other side. What is clear, however, is that they were being extremely successful in their efforts. The prospect of U.S. seabed mining legislation created new concerns within the Conference as to the real intentions of the United States with respect to the emerging treaty.

At this stage, the attitude of the U.S. delegation was best reflected in the views of its leader, Ambassador Elliot Richardson. He believed that if a treaty were to be successfully concluded, the U.S. objective should be the minimization of risks to the mining industry, but not their total elimination. This included risks of a political nature. He thought that if this objective could be achieved, the risks of conducting a mining operation could be contained within insurable limits. This perception, coupled with the substantial gains in the second committee, led him to the conclusion that the treaty that was slowly emerging was better than no treaty at all, but this was a perception that only further fueled the concerns of U.S. mining representatives.

Nonetheless, U.S. efforts were then directed at achieving the last minute "tuning" that might improve the general structure of the seabed mining chapter. A decision was also taken to defer some of the detail of the mining regime to rules and regulations to be worked out by a preparatory commission to be created after the treaty was concluded. It was thought that this would have two benefits. First, since it would take several years before a treaty could achieve the advice and consent of the U.S. Senate necessary to ratification there would be ample time to work out satisfactory rules and procedures in the preparatory commission. And this could be done in a more neutral forum in which the political elements present during the Conference itself would be minimized. Second, this strategy would hasten the conclusion of the Conference, freezing the compromises of the second committee, which would no longer be subject to retaliatory attacks.

With some of this detail thus deferred, the Conference was freed to devote itself to the more fundamental problems still remaining. One of these issues was the question of how the Council of the Seabed Authority would take its decisions. This, as Secretary Kissinger had earlier indicated, was of fundamental importance to the United States. Since the council was to be the body empowered to implement specific policies of the authority and, in particular, the power to approve changes to the mining provisions of the convention, it was important to the industrialized countries that they have the ability to block decisions that affected their ability to mine, and thus their ability to finance the operations.

In the summer of 1981, after extremely difficult negotiations, a compromise was reached. This became possible mostly because of the widespread and growing feeling within the conference that if the industrialized nations could be satisfied on this point, the treaty would be successfully concluded. In this almost raging spirit of final compromise, the so-called three-tiered voting system emerged. Under this system, decisions of great importance to the industrial countries could only be taken by consensus, while those of lesser importance could be taken by lesser majorities within the council. When this emerged many, including the president of the Conference, were of the view that the negotiations were essentially over, and all that remained was final consideration of such matters, albeit important ones, such as the protection of investment during the period between the conclusion of the Conference and the entry into force of the treaty, and when the Seabed Authority would be organized.

As must be clear, this Conference, like any other dynamic institution, was subject to the impact of the occurrence of sudden events. Such an event, of major proportions, occurred with the election of Ronald Reagan to the presidency of the United States. With his election came the realization that there had been a major shift in the U.S. political spectrum on the national level. That shift made it necessary for the U.S. government to conduct a complete and thorough review of the treaty to ascertain the degree to which it did, or did not, align with the new political conservatism of the country. The President announced, in January following his inauguration, that such a review would be undertaken.

Given the fact, as was subsequently to become clear, that the administration had as an agenda item the deregulation of certain segments of the U.S. economy, it was not surprising that its view of the treaty, and specifically, the deep-seabed mining provisions, would be significantly at variance with previous administrations. This change of attitude was to produce a new order of priorities for the United States with respect to the oceans. New significance, heavier than ever before, was attached to provisions concerning seabed mining than ever before.

The provisions were seen to be overly burdensome and restrictive, and as creating a massive international bureaucracy which, in concept, ran against the administration's stated objective of reduction of governmental interference domestically.

Perhaps one of the more significant shifts of emphasis within the U.S. government occurred in the Defense Department. As has been explained, the initial Defense emphasis in the Conference was on issues related to navigation. The mining industry, seizing upon the introduction of the new, more conservative administration, took advantage of the opportunity to strengthen its opposition to the treaty by arguing, successfully, to the new appointees within the department that, while naval mobility was indeed an important consideration, an even more important element in our national defense strategy in the long run was guaranteed access to strategic metals, particularly those the oceans could provide. The thrust of these arguments was directed particularly toward the transfer of technology, limits on production, and the decision-making elements of the treaty, that were seen to inhibit this objective. Accordingly, the Defense Department took an increased interest in the mining provisions. The shift, however, was one of emphasis, and not of a major change of course.

Upon completion of the treaty review process, the President, on January 29, 1982, announced that while most provisions of the treaty were acceptable, many of those concerning deep-seabed mining were not. He instructed his delegation to return to the negotiations to seek changes in that regime that would satisfy six basic objectives. These related to the assurance of access to mineral resources and the encouragement of their development, the decision-making procedures in the council, the prevention of amendments coming into force without U.S. ratification, and the ability to achieve the approval of the United States Senate. In addition, President Reagan attached particular emphasis on achieving a treaty that would "not set other undesirable precedents for international organizations." The "undesirable precedent" he had in mind was undoubtedly the principle of the "common heritage of mankind."

With this new mandate, the delegation returned to the bargaining table. It was, however, a substantially different delegation. Its leader was now James Malone, the new Assistant Secretary of State for ocean matters. In addition, several of the previous members of the team had been replaced by new negotiators more in tune with the President's philosophy. The role of the delegation was also modified. Previously, the delegation played a strong role in generating policy as well as in deciding questions of Conference strategy and tactics designed to achieve that policy. Now, the delegation was more restricted to the latter considerations. Under this new team, emphasis shifted from an effort to achieve a final "clean-up" of the treaty to renewed attention to basic principles.

One of these principles was, of course, the principle of the "common heritage of mankind." When the United States accepted the UN General Assembly's Declaration of Principles, which included the common heritage, it made clear that its acceptance was conditioned on the negotiation of an agreement that would give the principle acceptable content. Throughout the Conference, the U.S. delegation was of the view that the principle's substantive content was to be that defined by the terms of the treaty itself. In other words, absent the treaty, the term had no specific substantive content of its own. The United States, therefore, set about negotiating the specific provisions in the treaty that would define, limit, and clarify the precise meaning of the "common heritage of mankind" within the context of the treaty itself.

The developing countries, however, viewed the principle as having inherent substantive content, i.e., a principle of common ownership of the seabeds beyond national jurisdiction that transcended the treaty itself. Apparently, in their view, this concept emanated from the Declaration of Principles itself. Such an interpretation could not have gained approval of the United States at any stage of the negotiations, and this was even more so in the present U.S. administration. Because of this situation, the principle of the common heritage became a central target for the Reagan team.

During 1982, the delegation sought to achieve the changes the administration wanted. But the negotiating atmosphere had decidedly changed. In the first place, there was widespread disappointment, even discouragement, at the prospect of further extended negotiations when the end had seemed so close at hand. Second, over the last few years of the Conference, power had shifted slowly within the Group of 77 away from Latin dominance and toward the Africans, who were much less patient with the United States and much more suspicious of its motives. The Africans were much more vocal in the pursuit of the common heritage principle. Accordingly, the 77 announced that they would consider no changes that affected the basic principles or structure of the treaty. In this atmosphere, the Conference became increasingly polarized between the moderate influences who desired to "pull" the United States back into the fold, on the one hand, and those who had become increasingly resentful of manipulation by a system that did not respect their interests, and who were tired of the process, on the other.

This atmosphere was further darkened by what may have been an elaborate breakdown in communications. Under the belief that the leadership of the 77 was demanding that the United States produce its "bottom line" position that would set forth in some detail specific language changes that were desired, the U.S. delegation produced its now infamous "green book" of proposed amendments to the seabed mining provisions, a list that was so complete and comprehensive that it shocked the Conference.

The book was prepared to show every change desired by the U.S. in order to achieve a maximally acceptable treaty. It was viewed by the developing nations, however, as an ultimatum and, as a result, many developing delegations become convinced that U.S. demands could never be met and that the United States had abandoned the treaty. It subsequently appeared that the 77 had in fact taken no formal decision to make the request that produced the "green book," but by that time the damage had been done. Time was now running short. President Koh had made clear his insistence that this be the last negotiating session of the Conference. In the brief time remaining, a group of small industrialized countries, known as the "Group of 11" or the "Good Samaritans" prepared a much reduced list of proposed amendments in the hope that the negotiations could be saved. Because that initiative did not include a consideration of improvements in the structure and voting in the council, a major U.S. concern, the draft was rejected by it, and the initiative died.

In spite of all of this, significant gains were still made of benefit to the industrialized countries. The PIP resolution, concluded in the final days of the Conference, was seen as a major last-ditch concession to the United States and its industrialized allies. This resolution had the effect of permitting a limited number of identified miners to commence prospecting during the period before the treaty would go into effect, and to give them a priority of treatment when the treaty regime became effective. In essence, it handed to the existing mining consortia and national mining companies a virtual monopoly over first-generation mining. The United States was skeptical of this resolution, while its western allies were less so. The tempting elements of this offer served to undermine the unity of the industrialized countries, and thus reduced their bargaining power. This division was to become more obvious when Japan and France later signed the Convention, and the FRG and the UK announced that they would await the results of the work of the Preparatory Commission before taking a decision. As history records, on the final working day of the Conference, the United States demanded a vote on the treaty as a whole, and it voted no. Shortly thereafter, the President of the United States announced that his stated objectives had not been met, and that the treaty as a whole was fundamentally flawed, particularly with reference to the mining provisions. This break with the treaty seemed irrevocable and final, although subsequent events have shown that the United States is indeed seeking, through a variety of ways, to preserve all of the non-seabeds portions of the treaty.

In retrospect, it can be seen that the United States played not one role during the Conference, but rather a series of roles as conditions changed. At the outset, with seabed mining a low United States priority, it sought to solidify its resource interests in the economic zone and on the continental shelf, while at the same time protecting its navigation rights. Through these means, it sought to place a lid on and, in some cases, to roll back expanding coastal state claims to territorial jurisdiction. Mining was not then perceived of major economic or strategic value.

The seabeds question was used, and sometimes with great skill, to draw political attention away from the more fundamental questions in the second committee, enabling that committee to resist the occasional feeble attempts to inject the principle of the common heritage of mankind into second committee debates. The second committee was heavily dominated by coastal state interests and, as a result, over 35 percent of the oceans were eliminated from the area of common heritage. Interestingly, a number of coastal states in the first committee were staunch defenders of the principle, but in the economic zone the shoe was clearly on the other foot. Thus the committee structure in the Conference played an exceedingly important role in permitting the coastal states to protect their national resource jurisdiction.

This procedural tactic was very nearly successful. It was not because of two major factors. First, the United States did not, and perhaps could not in the early stages, have anticipated the political importance that was to become attached to the common heritage principle and the depth of commitment that would be generated on its behalf. Second, it could not have been anticipated by the Group of 77 that there would be such a fundamental shift in the attitudes of the American people. Or if this was not a shift, it was an emergence of a latent attitude that was rekindled by the Reagan campaign. But the change had its impact upon the U.S. Law of the Sea delegation. Essentially, the delegation abandoned its major emphasis on second committee matters, including resource issues, and shifted its strategy to do battle over the fundamental principles contained in the mining texts, while at the same time preserving beneficial texts in other areas.

Conferences of the complexity of this one, of course, do not tolerate well, nor well react to sudden changes of this magnitude and, indeed, this one did not. Perhaps they are structurally unable to do so. The time was too short at the end, and the confusion too permeating for the Conference to adjust and continue. The Conference, having been rapidly pressed to the brink of decision, was unwilling and perhaps unable to turn back.

In the two years that have expired since the conclusion of the Conference, much criticism has been leveled at the President's decision not to sign, particularly from the academic community in the United States, as well as from some former members of the U.S. negotiating team. In particular, the United States is criticized for its unwillingness to continue, if the opportunity should arise, with the negotiating process. It has demonstrated this unwillingness graphically by boycotting the Preparatory Committee meetings, although it is entitled to attend as an observer.

These criticisms are based mostly upon legal analysis which purports to show, first, that the mining provisions are not as bad as they appear. This analysis is supported by a close reading of all of the provisions and not the language of one or the other taken in isolation. Second, it is argued, if there are unacceptable provisions, it would still be possible to correct the deficiencies. And, last, it is argued that the President, in placing emphasis upon provisions relating to an activity that is neither likely to occur for a long time in the future, nor is as economically important as other resource activities, threw the baby out with the bathwater.

This last argument is based upon the view that there is a real risk that the United States will not be able to preserve for itself the benefits of the non-seabed provisions of the treaty without signing the Convention, or that the cost of doing so will be high and continually escalating. The argument reflects the fear that without universal acceptance of the treaty the temptation to further territorial encroachments will be strong, and that the treaty holds the only real promise of inhibiting this undesirable tendency on the part of many important coastal states, the United States included.

If one looks at this treaty not from a legal perspective, but from a political one in the United States, it could have been anticipated that the rejection of the treaty was inevitable for the foreseeable future. If one assumes that the President of the United States was responding to a perceived mandate from the public to move his government to a distinctly more conservative mode, then he could hardly have failed to note and disapprove of a regime that was so highly regulatory of industry. Second, I think we often lose sight of the fact that the Senate of the United States has long been largely conservative on issues affecting American industry, and this has been true despite the particular political majority in power at any given time. The President, therefore, may well have been accurate in his assessment that it would require a great deal of his personal political capital to persuade the Senate to accept the treaty in its present form, particularly in view of the history of criticism of the mining provisions in the treaty appearing in the public debates of the Congress.

One may question whether the President's perspective of his political mandate was accurate. Only time will tell, but the most preliminary indications tend to show that he was. U.S. organized ocean industry groups, be they suppliers of technology, miners or fishermen, almost uniformly have applauded his decision. In addition, the mood of the general populace in the United States seems behind him. Of course, the average person knows little, and perhaps cares less about the Law of the Sea treaty or the U.S. stake in the oceans, but there is substantial evidence of a resurgence of patriotism and national pride in the United States as the natural pendular reaction to a widespread feeling of national depression or guilt following Vietnam. The President is widely perceived as the personification of this patriotic upsurge. Thus there has been general support for a President who "courageously" rejected a treaty sponsored by the United Nations and viewed it as an instrument protective of the interests of the Third World to the detriment of this neo-nationalistic upwelling.

In this light, the rejection of the treaty might reflect the growing wave of neo-isolationism apparent in the United States today. This trend, I believe, is a real one and must be recognized as an influence in all U.S. thinking involving foreign policy. The prospect of the strengthening of that trend causes grave concern to those in the United States who can best be described as neo-realists, who attempt to take the long view of world affairs and the role of the United States, and who take the trends in relations among nations as given facts of the real world, a world in which the United States must continue to live. Among this group, there is concern that the sacrifice of the non-seabed provisions of the treaty to the benefit of the ephemeral gains for a presently nonviable industry is a shortsighted policy. They are concerned that the United States can protect these other interests only at high political and economic costs, if at all, in the role as a nonsignatory. Particularly, they are concerned that the rejection of the treaty is a step away from the rule of law.

The United States has been traditionally perceived as advancing the rule of law in international affairs. It has supported negotiated solutions to problems and it has supported peaceful conflict resolution. If there is, in the rejection of the treaty, a shift in policy in this regard, then that fact is not only a cause for concern but it is puzzling as well. The history of conservatism in the United States certainly reflects a desire to maintain a prominent role for the United States in world affairs. It reflects a view that the United States must negotiate from strength, militarily as well as economically. But it also reflects a strong attitude in favor of law and order, and that attitude continues to be reflected in the fact that most political campaigns in the United States are structured to address this problem.

These are two fundamental prongs of traditional conservatism in U.S. domestic politics, and it is strange to see them divorced in foreign policy levels. Clearly, the United States believes it can protect its ocean interests by a projection of economic and military strength. But it is strange, in the view of the history referred to, that it does not see the advantage of achieving rules of international law that solidify these national goals.

With the United States rejecting a significant portion of the treaty, the preservation of the remainder is no small task. If the United States acts in total consistency with the rights and duties provided for in the non-seabed portions of the Convention, it is not at all clear that the rest of the world will be willing publicly to announce that it will accord to the United States those rights as a matter of law. If, on the other hand, the United States exceeds the authority allocated to states by those provisions, there is no reason to expect other countries, including our allies, to act within the restraint of the treaty, and process of expanding jurisdiction may accelerate all over again, only this time, in a much more extensive zone with much more important consequences.

The role of the United States in the immediate future, therefore, must be perceived as one of a stabilizer. The President has announced his intention to assume that role in the oceans. Whether the power and prestige of the United States in the world community is still strong enough to permit it to play this role successfully remains to be seen. There is no doubt that there are those in the world who will seek to portray U.S. actions in exactly the opposite light. Nonetheless, the President's policy for the oceans announced to date is the only course he could take to prevent the undermining and eventual destruction of the treaty provisions universally deemed beneficial. There is no other course for the present.

10.
The Unfinished Business of the Law of the Sea Conference

JONATHAN I. CHARNEY

DESPITE THE SUBSTANTIAL EFFORT at the Third United Nations Conference on the Law of the Sea (UNCLOS III) to resolve issues related to the Law of the Sea, it was inevitable that the product of that negotiation would not contain solutions to all the outstanding issues. If the Law of the Sea Convention were to enter into force many issues would be resolved among the state parties.[1] Nevertheless, there would still remain a number of significant issues that would not be resolved by a binding Law of the Sea Convention.

The Law of the Sea Convention and the preceding international negotiations have had a significant impact on the state of relevant international law. The impact of the Convention on future developments of that law will depend on state adherence to the Convention and state practice. It is clear, however, that regardless of the path taken by the international community, questions arising from UNCLOS III negotiations will not be resolved for a long time.

These unanswered questions are divisible into four categories. First, the Conference did not consider a number of issues that reasonably might have been included within the scope of a complete review of the Law of the Sea. Some of those issues will demand resolution in the foreseeable future. The second relates to the actual contents of the Law of the Sea Convention. Even though the Convention does address a large number of subjects it does not provide a definitive resolution of all issues relating to the Law of the Sea. Rather, in many areas it provides only a framework for future resolution of unresolved issues. In others, the Convention text is ambiguous, requiring further developments and interpretations.

Third, it appears likely that in the near future the Law of the Sea Convention will not obtain the adherence of all the participants at the Conference. Some major states have decided for reasons of substance, either to refuse to participate or to withhold participation for some time. Other states may not join due to their disinterest.[2] It is also possible that the Convention will never enter into force.[3] Under these circumstances questions arise as to the status of various rules found in traditional international law and those found in the Convention. To some extent the UNCLOS III negotiations and the LOS Convention will affect a change in the rules of international law applicable to states not party to the Convention. The scope of that change is not yet known.

Fourth, the UNCLOS III negotiations provided a forum at which issues of international law and relations having importance beyond the boundaries of the Law of the Sea were both directly and indirectly addressed. UNCLOS III provided a convenient opportunity for the international communtiy to wrestle with a number of those issues. As a consequence, the UNCLOS III deliberations will have an impact on a wide variety of non Law of the Sea issues in international law and relations.

It is apparent from this list of four categories of unresolved issues that the adoption of the LOS Convention cannot be viewed as a completed act, even for a short period of time. Furthermore, as new uses of the oceans develop and nations' interests change the law will have to be adjusted to accommodate new demands placed on ocean law. Thus, a complete review of the unfinished business of the Law of the Sea Conference would be impossible. Even a comprehensive review of the known outstanding issues would present an overwhelming task. In fact, much of the Law of the Sea literature that will appear in the next few years is likely to focus, in whole or in part, on the unfinished business of the Conference regardless of the fate of the Convention.[4]

Rather than attempting to present a detailed catalogue of the individual outstanding issues, this paper will approach the unfinished business of the Conference at a level of generality that will review the four categories of outstanding issues. Specific examples will be used to illustrate the type of questions found within each category. From this review, the reader should be able to locate the outer boundaries of the legacy of UNCLOS III. By identifying those limits the scope and direction of future work will, thus, be identified.

The Convention Avoids Certain Related Issues

In selecting the agenda for the Law of the Sea Conference the participating delegates opted for one that permitted a rather complete review of the international Law of the Sea.[5] Many commentators have faulted the delegates for undertaking such a comprehensive negotiation.[6] Perhaps a piecemeal approach would have permitted a more complete resolution of the issues brought to the negotiations. Despite the effort to include all Law of the Sea issues, there are a number of issues that were avoided by the Conference, even though the international community had knowledge of the issues and the oportunity to place them on the agenda of the Conference. It is difficult to determine why these issues were avoided. Three factors may have dominated the apparent consensus to avoid them. First, the issues appeared to be remote, not requiring early resolution. Second, the issues were before other international forums. Third, the issues were known to be so explosive that they would not be negotiable at a universal forum and, if raised, might thwart all efforts to negotiate other issues. Perhaps the most significant issues not dealt with at the Conference relate to the polar regions and military uses of the oceans.

The questions relating to Antarctica were not addressed at the Conference. Disputes concerning the legal status of the continent and the various claims of national jurisdiction raise serious questions of international law and relations.[7] Furthermore, the legal status of the ocean areas adjacent to the continent is in dispute. If, as many argue, the continent is not part of the territory of any sovereign state, questions arise as to whether the regimes of the continental shelf, the territorial sea or the Exclusive Economic Zone (EEZ) exist in the oceans adjacent to Antarctica. Even if one were to conclude that these regimes did not apply to Antarctica, it still would not be clear whether the exploration and exploitation of the nonrenewable resources of those ocean areas is open to all states or reserved until sovereignty is established or an international regime is in force for the area.[8] These issues had been held in abeyance by the parties to the Antarctic Treaty,[9] but recently the Antarctic Treaty members have moved forward to develop a fisheries convention and currently they have under negotiation a mineral resource convention.[10] Some states not party to those negotiations have objected to the use of the Antarctic Treaty forum and recently have brought the matter to the United Nations General Assembly.[11] Nevertheless, no nation strongly pressed the issue at the Law of the Sea Conference where all ocean regimes were under negotiation.

Jurisdiction over the Arctic Ocean also remains an outstanding issue with virtually all nations that front on the Arctic asserting conflicting claims.[12] While some view the question in terms of the traditional zones of national jurisdiction in the seas (territorial sea, EEZ, and continental shelf), others maintain that different rules apply because it is an ice-covered area.[13] Due to the small number of contesting states, the fact that some of the major world powers are at odds on the question, and the difficulty of the issue, no serious effort was made to place this issue on the Conference agenda. Recently, the question of Arctic jurisdiction has received increased attention.[14]

The conduct of military activities at sea was not on the Conference agenda. Nevertheless it was insinuated into many aspects of the negotiations. It was rarely directly addressed in the open discussions or in the Convention text. No direct consideration was given to arms control at sea even though it is a major aspect of the arms control debate.[15] One leg of the United States triad (land, sea, and air) is sea-based and the Soviets are similarly reliant on the use of the seas for military purposes.[16] Many Third World coastal states find these uses threatening. While the emplacement of weapons of mass destruction (that is nuclear weapons) on the seabed is prohibited, other military uses of the seas, including seabed emplacements, are not covered by similar agreements.[17]

The major powers regularly engage in various black box operations in which items other than vessels are placed on the seabed or in the water column for military purposes.[18] While there are provisions in the text that may ambiguously address these operations, issues arising from these activities were largely avoided.[19] It appeared to be generally understood that the major powers would not allow arms control issues to be negotiated at this universal conference and the other countries could not muster sufficient unity to be assured that they could force a resolution of the military issues. Furthermore, arms control has been a subject on the agenda of other negotiating forums at which the necessary representation and expertise have been present.[20]

Artificial earth satellites have significant importance in ocean surveillance, communication for purposes of navigation, and marine scientific research.[21] Nevertheless, the relationship of satellites to ocean law is not addressed in the LOS Convention. Similarly, the potential establishment of major installations at sea, particularly beyond zones of national jurisdiction, such as living habitats, was not directly addressed although it is likely that such activities will be attempted in the not so distant future.[22]

Certainly, other ocean issues were ignored by the Conference. In all probability, the fact that no immediate problem was presented or the matter was under consideration at another forum permitted the Conference to avoid them. The next generation of negotiators may not be permitted that luxury.

The Scope of the Convention Text

Even those items that were on the agenda of the Conference were not fully settled. The Law of the Sea Convention is perhaps the largest and most complicated written international agreement that has been put before the international community.[23] As a consequence, it is bound to present to those states that become parties to the Convention many questions that will require resolution. No matter how exacting the negotiators may have been, there are ambiguities in the written language that will require resolution.

In fact, precise draftsmanship was not always the goal of the negotiators at UNCLOS III. Thus, rather than resolving intractable substantive issues they often chose to paper over those issues by use of ambiguous language which the parties to the Convention would have to resolve at a later date by negotiation or international dispute settlement.

Two examples of this intentional ambiguity suffice to illustrate this strategy. Considerable controversy arose over the resolution of conflicts between the rights claimed by the coastal state in the EEZ and those claimed by foreign states which have traditionally used ocean areas within 200 nautical miles of foreign states for nonresource related activities.[24] Rather than spelling out a rule that expressly determines states rights and duties, the Convention presents a pattern of cross-references to the articles in the text and a rather ambiguous principle for resolution.[25]

Similarly, it became impossible for the negotiators to resolve a dispute over the rule for delimiting ocean boundaries between states that are opposite or adjacent to each other. The resulting text is a classic example of intentionally ambiguous treaty language.[26]

Other issues that could not be properly resolved at the Conference were referred to individual nation-states to resolve with other interested states. Thus, the Convention calls for international coordination and compromise in a large variety of areas.[27] Some of these will quickly give rise to international negotiation, i.e., fisheries,[28] rights of land-locked states,[29] and states' uses of enclosed or semi-enclosed seas.[30] Other issues, i.e., transfer of technology,[31] are less likely to receive early and productive consultations.

Often issues presented to the Conference required the application of specific expertise to a large variety of circumstances that may change over time. Rather than attempting to spell out rules applicable to each circumstance, the negotiators chose to refer such matters to international organizations now in existence or expected to be created in the future.[32] This technique was used extensively in the context of the chapter on the marine environment.[33] It was also used when there remained a fundamental difference of views on the substantive issues. Thus, a large number of issues relating to the development of deep-seabed resources were referred to the Preparatory Commission and organs of the international seabed authority becauses they could not be resolved at the Conference.[34]

Attempts to implement the Convention will cause other issues to surface. Some issues could not have been predicted. For example, much of the substance of the Convention represents a substantial change in the Law of the Sea. These changes were often produced by the diplomatic brain power present at the Conference aided by support personnel having a wide range of expertise and experience. While on paper the Convention text may appear to present good solutions to outstanding issues, implementation is likely to identify unforeseen difficulties. In fact, this potential was given recognition by the negotiators who provided for a rather simple amendment procedure when a change in the Convention's deep-seabed regime is required and the parties are in general agreement on the proposed solution.[35] The same interests required that provisions be made for other types of amendments to the Convention and for a review conference.[36]

Serious questions will arise when and if the deep-seabed portions of the text are implemented. While the Convention provisions on this subject are largely fashioned to establish a dynamic international organization capable of managing deep-seabed mining, there is a high probability that problems will arise. The organization designed in the Convention is extremely complex. It would be a miracle, indeed, if all the various provisions regulating this organization would mesh as well in practice as they might in theory.

Furthermore, the organization was designed at a time when the activities that are to be the subject of the organization's attention had never taken place. Deep-seabed mining of commercial quantities of any deep-seabed natural resource has not yet occurred and may not occur for many years to come.[37] Thus, the system was designed to address hypothetical activities. When and if the industry is fully operational, its requirements and the requirements of the organization that regulates its activities may vary substantially. As a consequence, the Convention will have to be adjusted.[38]

Finally, it is certain that in the future mankind will discover new uses of the oceans not foreseen during the negotiations or foreseen but ignored. Those new uses may not be adequately accommodated in the Convention text and thus would call for adjustments in the text. One such issue has already been raised in the context of the mining of resources of the deep seabed other than manganese nodules. It has been recently observed that deposits of polymetallic sulfides may present a substantial opportunity for ocean mining.[39] Unfortunately, their composition, distribution, and location may not have been adequately accounted for in the deep-seabed mining portions of the Convention.[40]

While not always causing serious international concern, important questions arise in the context of the domestic implementation of the rules found within the Convention. Many states have domestic law that is not compatible with the substance of the Convention, and steps may have to be taken to adjust domestic law to conform to the requirements of the Convention.

The classic example of this issue arises with those states which have claimed territorial seas in excess of 12 nautical miles.[41] A number of states claim 200-mile territorial seas. Those claims may exceed the jurisdiction permitted by the Convention in the 200-nautical mile EEZ.[42] There are more subtle circumstances in which domestic implementation requires attention. The Convention requires specific procedures for the release of fishermen,[43] the enforcement of judgments,[44] the protection of the privileges and immunities of certain organizations and individuals,[45] and the payment of various fees and charges,[46] among others. While these demands on domestic legal systems may not be unusual, they will require attention and changes may face resistance from affected domestic constituencies.

It is apparent from this review of the Law of the Sea Convention that matters directly addressed by the Convention have not been completely resolved. The Convention may represent a successful negotiation of a large number of law of the sea issues. Nevertheless, the nature of the subject matter made it inevitable that many issues would remain for future resolution.

Questions of Customary Law

It is virtually certain that the Convention will not receive the unanimous participation of states.[47] A significant number of states of varying international power may not join the Convention.[48] It is even possible that the Convention will never enter into force. Consequently, the public international Law of the Sea outside of the Convention will continue to play an important role in international ocean affairs. An understanding of the current and future rules of general international law requires that the UNCLOS III negotiations and the Convention be taken into account. In fact, international lawyers, particularly those in academia, have already focused on the question of how the Conference and the Convention may have already affected general international law.[49] It presents a fascinating fundamental issue of how public international law is made and changed.

Opinions on what impact the Conference and Convention have had and will have on the law vary significantly. There are those who argue that the history of the negotiations, the adoption of the Convention, the signature of 131 states, resolutions of international organizations, and state practice have caused many if not all of the norms found in the Convention to merge into international law binding on all nations.[50] At the other end of the spectrum, there are those who would argue that the product of negotiations could only bind states party to the agreement upon its entry into force.[51] Between these two extremes are those who, in varying ways, would consider the record of the Conference and the text of the Convention as some evidence of new international law or even a source of that law. These observers would pick and choose among the provisions of the Convention, taking into account the specific history of the subject, the nature of the negotiations and state practice.[52] The use to which UNCLOS III and the Convention would be put would change as state behavior changes.

This debate will continue for some time. While it will be difficult to reach a consensus among experts, the debate will cause the international community to focus on the international law legacy of UNCLOS III. Individual nations will be constrained to tailor their statements and behavior in order to influence the outcome of this debate.

It should be clear, however, that there is no significant dispute that much of the substance of the Law of the Sea Convention codifies existing norms of international law. Thus, there is no question that a state has the right to claim a territorial sea, a continental shelf or a contiguous zone, and the freedom to run a ship on the high seas.[53] On the other hand, serious questions exist as to the exact nature and scope of other extended resource zones in the oceans such as the EEZ, the right to mine the deep-seabed, and the scope of the right to navigate through various zones of the national jurisdiction of coastal states.[54]

Regardless of the fate of the Law of the Sea Convention the contents of the customary international Law of the Sea will remain an important and difficult issue. While the negotiations may have helped to develop agreement on certain rules of law, new demands on the oceans and new national interests have encouraged efforts to change the traditional law. The answer to the queston of how many of the proposed changes have or will merge into customary Law of the Sea will have to await the passage of time and the efforts of interested experts and government officials.

Broad Issues of International Law and Relations

The Law of the Sea Conference was unique; however it was not isolated from major movements in international law and relations. In fact, because of timing of the Conference (beginning in 1972) and the universal participation of nations in the negotiations, it became the testing ground for many major international issues which have importance beyond the Law of the Sea. One can debate the merits of the approaches taken by the Conference. Nevertheless, the experience of the Conference and the precedent of the Convention have significance beyond the scope of the Law of the Sea. Accordingly, one category of the unfinished business will require the international community to study the negotiations in order to assess the impact of UNCLOS III on issues of more general international importance.

While there are many topics worthy of study, a few stand out as particularly deserving of close attention.

has obtained the support of environmentalists, industrialists and diplomats alike and has already influenced the development of the international law of the environment in areas outside of the Law of the Sea.[82]

The Common Heritage of Mankind

During the course of the Law of the Sea negotiations the United Nations adopted the Agreement Governing the Activities of States on the Moon and Other Celestial Bodies (Moon Treaty) and commended it to member states for their adoption.[83] The promulgation of that treaty created an uproar from a number of persons who have expressed an interest in the commercial development of outer space. They protested that the Moon Treaty accepted the principle of the "common heritage of mankind" and, as a consequence, carried with it all of the obstacles to development alleged to be present in the regime for the deep-seabed.[84] Regardless of whether or not the Moon Treaty ever enters into force, the application of the common heritage doctrine to outer space is an objective of many third world advocates and others. There is thus a direct link between the substance of the deep-seabed portions of the Law of the Sea Convention and the fate of that Convention to the issues involved in the law for outer space.[85]

The same issue has arisen in the context of Antarctica. The role of the common heritage doctrine in these common spaces will be affected by the results of the regime for the deep-seabed in a number of ways. First, the deep-seabed regime may have given substance to the general doctrine of the common heritage. Second, the success or failure of the deep-seabed regime may determine the role that doctrine will play in other common spaces.

General International Law Development

As mentioned above, a major issue raised by UNCLOS III and the Law of the Sea Convention is the impact that it will have on general rules of international law.[86] That issue has two aspects. The first, addressed above, concerns the substantive result of that debate, e.g., which rules will mature into public international law. The second is more fundamental. It concerns the method by which new law is created. Major divisions exist in the international community concerning the appropriate evidences and sources of international law. Some rely largely on state practice conducted over time pursuant to a sense of legal obligation.[87] Others, seeking a more flexible rule, would find more rapid change in law through the adoption of resolutions by major international organizations and the conclusion by consensus or majority vote of Convention texts negotiated at large-scale international negotiations.[88]

The Law of the Sea Conference and the LOS Convention have fallen into the middle of that debate. In the course of resolving the substantive issues arising from UNCLOS III the international community will inevitably have to address the broader question of how international negotiations affect general international law. It will be informative to study this debate for clues about how the international community develops new international law. One justice on the International Court of Justice (ICJ), Judge Oda, has already insinuated himself into this debate in a dissenting opinion.[89]

The Role of Functional International Organizations

Perhaps one of the most dramatic developments at the Law of the Sea Conference was the construction of a major international organization designed to manage and conduct resource development for the international community. If successful, it would become financially self-supporting, independent of contributions of nation-states. It would, in fact, distribute revenues to the international community and perhaps play an independent role in international affairs. The success or failure of this effort will have profound effect on international organization. It will provide a fertile source of data for those studying theories of international organization. For example, the difficulty of the negotiations up to this point and the dim prospects for the success of the deep-seabed regime may not bode well for those who strongly advocate a functionalist approach to world order.[90] Certainly this issue will warrant attention.

Conclusion

One might conclude from this review of the unfinished business of the Law of the Sea Conference that the Conference has created more issues than it has resolved. Perhaps that is true. It would not be appropriate, however, thereby to conclude that the LOS Conference was a mistake. It appears to me that the crisis in the Law of the Sea had to be addressed by the international community. The decision to convene the LOS Conference was reasonable. Due to the complexity of the issues and perhaps the unfortunate timing of the Conference, it was unavoidable that a large number of issues would not be resolved.

An international negotiation of major issues such as those present in the Law of the Sea could not have produced a resolution of all issues. The substance of the unfinished business might have been different had other procedures been used, or the dynamic interaction of the Conference participants differed. Nevertheless, it is not yet clear that any different approach would have produced a result in which the quantity and general nature of the unfinished business would have been substantially different. In this imperfect and everchanging world one can be assured that so long as there is an international community neither the international Law of the Sea, nor major issues of international law and relations will ever be finally resolved.

The history of international agreements and the pace of change in international society require that no international agreement of a magnitude comparable to the Law of the Sea Convention will remain in force for long. One can almost be certain that within 20 to 40 years this Convention, even if it were to enter into force for the vast majority of states, will be replaced by new law. That law will reflect the economic and political realities of that age. It is thus clear the task of fashioning the Law of the Sea will always be unfinished.

NOTES

The author wishes to thank Michael Russell, J.D. 1984, Vanderbilt University School of Law, for his assistance.

1. Third United Nations Convention on the Law of the Sea, opened for signature December 10, 1982, UN Doc. A/Conf. 62/122 (1982). Hereinafter cited as LOS Convention.

2. Countries, in addition to the United States, which did not sign because of concerns over the deep-seabed mining provisions include the Federal Republic of Germany and the United Kingdom. See *United Nations Law of the Sea Bulletin*, (February 1985), 4:2–6. See also Nine-Year United Nations Conference on Law of the Sea Ends with Signing of Convention by 119 Delegations, UN Dep't Pub. Info. Rep., No. SWA/514, December 10, 1982. Statement by the President, July 9, 1982, in Convention on the Law of the Sea, Weekly Comp. Pres. Docs. (July 12, 1982), 18:887–88. Law of the Sea Convention, Survey of

Current Affairs (January 1983), 13(1):24, 26 (British reason for abstaining from signing the Convention.) The 15 states which have not signed the LOS Convention include Albania, Federal Republic of Germany, the Holy See, Israel, Jordan, Kiribati, Peru, San Marino, South Africa, Syria, Tonga, Turkey, United Kingdom, United States, and Venezuela. There were 155 states that did sign the Convention. See *LOS Bulletin*.

3. See Gamble, "Post World War II Multilateral Treaty-Making: The Task of the Third United Nations Law of the Sea Conference in Perspective," *San Diego Law Review* (1980), 17:527. Although the Convention attracted 155 signatories, as of February 1985, it claimed only 13 ratifications since it was opened for signature. The countries which have ratified the Convention include: the Bahamas, Belize, Cuba, Egypt, Fiji, Gambia, Ghana, Ivory Coast and Jamaica, Mexico, Philippines, Senegal, the United Nations Council for Namibia, and Zambia. See *LOS Bulletin*. Many years passed before the 1958 Law of the Sea conventions entered into force: the Convention on the Territorial Sea and the Contiguous Zone done on April 29, 1958, entered into force on September 10, 1964; the Convention on the Continental Shelf done on April 29, 1958, entered into force on June 10, 1964; the Convention on the High Seas done on April 29, 1958, entered into force on September 30, 1962; and the Convention on Fishing and Conservation of the Living Resources of the High Seas done on April 29, 1958, entered into force on March 20, 1966. See generally 1 S. Lay, R. Churchill, and M. Nordquist, eds., *New Directions in the Law of the Sea* (Dobbs Ferry, N.Y.: Oceana, 1973).

4. See, e.g., Oxman, "Customary International Law in the Absence of Widespread Ratification of the United Nations Convention on the Law of the Sea," W. Ostreng, ed., Law of the Sea Institute, Honolulu (paper presented at Oslo, July 16, 1983); Clingan, "Freedom of Navigation in a Post-UNCLOS III Environment," *Law and Contemporary Problems* (1983), 46:107; Charney, "The Law of the Deep Seabed Post UNCLOS III," *Oregon Law Review* (1984), 63:19; Charney, "The United States and the Law of the Sea After UNCLOS III: The Impact of General International Law," *Law and Contemporary Problems* (1983), 46:37; hereinafter cited as Charney, "U.S. and Law of the Sea After UNCLOS III"; Oda, Sharing of Ocean Resources—Unresolved Issues in the Law of the Sea," *New York Law School Journal of International and Comparative Law* (1981), 3:1.

5. See Organization of the Second Session of the Conference and Allocation of Items: Report of the General Committee, U.N. Doc. A/Conf. 62/28 (1974), Third United Nations Conference on the Law of the Sea, *Official Records* (1975), 3:57; 1–2 Official Records, Third U.N. Conference on the Law of the Sea, summary records (1975). See also United Nations Conference on the Law of the Sea: Informal Single Negotiating Text, U.N. Doc. A/Conf. 62/WP. 8/Parts I–III (1975), reprinted in *International Legal Materials* (1975), 14:682; U.N. Doc. A/Conf. 62/WP. 9/Rev. 2 Pt. IV (1976); Charney, "Technology and International Negotiations," *American Journal of International Law* (1982), 76:78; Miles, "An Interpretation of the Caracas Proceedings," in F. Christy, T. Clingan, J. Gamble, G. Knight, and E. Miles, eds., *The Law of the Sea: Caracas and Beyond* (Cambridge: Ballinger, 1975), p. 39; Miles, "An Interpretation of the Geneva Pro-

ceedings: Part 1," *Ocean Development and International Law Journal* (1976), 3:187; Haight, "Law of the Sea Conference—Why Paralysis?" *Journal of Maritime Law and Commerce* (1977), 8:281; Charney, "The International Regime for the Deep Seabed: Past Conflicts and Proposals for Progress," *Harvard Journal of International Law* (1976) 17:1; Hollick, "LOS III: Prospects and Problems," *Columbia Journal of Transnational Law* (1975), 14:102; Krueger, "Where Are We on the Law of the Sea?" *San Diego Law Review* (1976) 13:552; Stevenson and Oxman, "The Third United Nations Conference on the Law of the Sea: The 1975 Geneva Session," *American Journal of International Law* (1975), 69:763.

6. See, e.g., Hollick, LOS III; Stevenson and Oxman, "The Third United Nation Conference," p. 797. One 1974 newspaper editorial predicted: "These issues and many others are so complex, and the stakes are so high, that it is unlikely that the conference will agree on a final treaty. Perhaps the best that can be expected is agreement on a new and refined agenda for another conference that seems certain to be necessary." *Los Angeles Times*, June 24, 1974 (editorial).

7. See generally Bilder, "The Present Legal and Political Situation in Antarctica," in J. Charney, ed., *The New Nationalism and the Use of Common Spaces 167–205*. See also Frank "The Convention of the Conservation of Antarctic Marine Living Resources," *Ocean Development and International Law* (1983), 13:291.

8. See Sollie, "Polar Seas: Issues Not Dealt with in the Law of the Sea Convention: Reasons and Problems," *Proceedings of the Law of the Sea Institute* (1983), paper presented at the Seventeenth Annual Conference of the Law of the Sea Institute, July 13–16, 1983, Oslo, Norway.

9. Antarctic Treaty, December 1, 1959, 12 U.S.T. 194, T.I.A.S. No. 4780, 402 U.N.T.S. 71. The Antarctic Treaty has sixteen consultative parties: Argentina, Australia, Belgium, Brazil, Chile, Federal Republic of Germany, France, India, Japan, New Zealand, Norway, Poland, South Africa, Union of Soviet Socialist Republics, United Kingdom, and United States. Sixteen additional states are Non-Consultative Parties: Bulgaria, China, Czechoslovakia, Cuba, Denmark, Finland, German Democratic Republic, Hungary, Italy, Netherlands, Papua New Guinea, Peru, Romania, Spain, Sweden, and Uruguay. For discussion of the Antarctic Treaty regime, see F. Auburn, Antarctic Law and Politics (1982), and Charney, ed., *The New Nationalism*. The resource potential of Antarctica is discussed in Zumberge, "Potential Mineral Resource Availability and Possible Environmental Problems in Antarctica," Charney, p. 115, and in Pontecorvo, "The Economics of the Resources of Antarctica," Charney, p. 155.

10. Convention on the Conservation of Antarctic Marine Living Resources," reprinted in *International Legal Materials* (1980), 19:837. See Sollie, "Polar Seas," pp. 5–6; Barnes, "The Emerging Convention on the Conservation of Antarctic Marine Living Resources: An Attempt to Meet the New Realities of Resource Exploitation in the Southern Ocean," in Charney, ed., *The New Nationalism*, p. 239. For a discussion of a regime for mineral exploitation in Antarctica, see Charney, "Future Strategies for an Antarctic Mineral Resource Regime: Can the Environment Be Protected?" in Charney, ed., *The New Nationalism*, pp.

206–38. See also F. Auburn, *Antarctic Law and Politics* (London: Murst 1982); B. Mitchell, *Frozen Stakes: The Future of Antarctic Minerals*, (Nottingham: Russell Press, 1983).

11. See Report of the Secretary General, Question of Antarctica, U.N. Doc. A/39/583 (1984). See "U.N. Urges a Study of Antarctica," *New York Times*, December 1, 1983, p. 6; "U.N. Launches Debate on Antarctica," *Washington Post*, December 1, 1983, p. A33. See also Pinto, "The International Community and Antarctica," *Miami Law Review* (1978), 33:483–85; Sollie, 11.

12. See, e.g., Sollie, "Polar Seas," pp. 9–10. The five bordering countries are the United States (Alaska), the Soviet Union, Canada, Denmark (Greenland), and Norway (Jan Mayen and Svalbard/Spitsbergen). See Sollie, p. 2. See also Pardo, "The Convention on the Law of the Sea: A Preliminary Appraisal," *San Diego Law Review* (1983), 20:489, 494 and n. 22. See generally, Pharand, "The Arctic Resources in International Law," in R. Girardot, H. Ridder, M. Srin, and T. Schiller, eds., *New Directions in International Law* (Ardsley-on-Hudson, N.Y.: Transnational Publishers, 1982), p. 257.

13. See Sollie, "Polar Seas," pp. 7–9; Alexander, "The Ocean Enclosure Movement: Inventory and Prospect," *San Diego Law Review.* (1983), 20:561, 574–75.

14. See, e.g., NOTE, "Delimiting Continental Shelf Boundaries in the Arctic: The United States-Canada Beaufort Sea Boundary," *Virginia Journal of International Law* (1981), 22:221; McRae, "Arctic Waters and Canadian Sovereignty," *International Journal* (1983), 38:476.

15. See Dore, "International Law and the Preservation of the Ocean Space and Outer Space as Zones of Peace: Progress and Problems," *Cornell International Law Journal*, (1982), 15:1; Treves, "Military Installations, Structures, and Devices on the Seabed, *American Journal of International Law* (1980), 74:808; Editorial NOTE, "The Seabed Arms Limitation Treaty: A Significant Development in Arms Control and Disarmament," *Journal of International Law and Economics* (1971), 6:157; Gorove, "Toward Denuclearization of the Ocean Floor," *San Diego Law Review* (1970), 7:504; Zedalis, " 'Peaceful Purposes' and Other Relevant Provisions of the Revised Composite Negotiating Text: A Comparative Analysis of the Existing and the Proposed Military Regime for the High Seas," *Syracuse Journal of International Law and Commerce* (1979), 7:1; Borgese, "Role of the International Seabed Authority in the 1980s," *San Diego Law Review* (1981), 18:395.

16. Although submarine-launched nuclear missiles compose one leg of the United States defense triad, their actual firepower surpasses that of the air and land forces combined. See Tierney, "The Invisible Force," *Science 83* (November 1983), 4:73, 77–78. See also Barnaby, "Strategic Submarines and Antisubmarine Warfare," in E. Borgese and N. Ginsburg, eds., *Ocean Yearbook* (1978), 1:376; Wilkes, "Ocean-Based Nuclear Deterrent Forces and Antisubmarine Warfare," in E. Borgese and N. Ginsburg eds., *Ocean Yearbook* (1980), 2:226.

17. See Goldblat, "Review of the Seabed Treaty," in E. Borgese and N. Ginsburg, eds., *Ocean Yearbook* (1978), 2:270; see also Treves, "Military Installations"; Purver, "The Control of Strategic Anti-submarine Warfare," *International Journal* (1983), 38:409.

18. For example, the sound surveillance system (SOSUS) is a series of microphones placed on the seabed and sonobuoys suspend microphones and sonar in the water column used to track vessels in the oceans. See Tierney, "The Invisible Force," pp. 73, 74–75; Wilkes, "Ocean-Based Nuclear Deterrent Forces," pp. 232–34. See generally Allen and Polmar, "The Silent Chase: Tracking Soviet Submarines," *New York Times*, January 1, 1984, S6 (magazine), p. 12 (description of antisubmarine warfare).

19. E.g., LOS Convention, arts. 88, 141. See Dore, pp. 19–24; see also Pardo, "The Convention on the Law of the Sea," pp. 494–95 and n.23.

20. The general legal issues of arms control have also been extensively debated. See, e.g., Bailey, "Nonmilitary Areas in U.N. Practice," *American Journal of International Law* (1980), 74:499; "The Future of Strategic Arms Control in the Wake of Salt II," *Proceedings of the American Society of International Law* (1980), 74:212; Vlasic, "Disarmament Decade, Outer Space, and International Law," *McGill Law Journal* (1981), 26:135; Mondale, "Criteria for a Comprehensive Strategy for Nuclear Arms Control," *Journal of Legislation* (1983), 10:1; Levinson, "Lawyers Can, But Law May Be Unable to Contribute to Nuclear Weapons Debate," *Nova Law Journal* (1982), 7:137. See generally U.S. Arms Control and Disarmament Agency, Arms Control and Disarmament Agreements (1982); Review of Administration Initiatives on Strategic, Theater, and Conventional Arms Control, Briefing of the Subcommittee on International Security and Scientific Affairs of the Senate Comm. on Foreign Relations, 97th Cong., 1st Sess. (1981).

21. See, e.g., Menon, "International Maritime Satellite System," *Journal of Maritime Law and Commerce* (1976) 8:95; Jasani, "Ocean Surveillance by Earth Satellites," in E. Borgese and N. Ginsburg, eds., *Ocean Yearbook* (1980), 2:250.

22. For a discussion of floating nuclear power plants, see Kindt, "Offshore Siting of Nuclear Power Plants," *Ocean Development and International Law Journal* (1980), 8:57; and Moris and Kindt, "The Law of the Sea: Domestic and International Considerations Arising from the Classification of Floating Nuclear Power Plants and Their Breakwaters as Artificial Islands," *Virginia Journal of International Law* (1979), 19:300.

23. Arvid Pardo described the LOS Convention as "[t]he most ambitious example of global negotiations under United Nations auspices" and as "certainly one of the most—if not the most—exhaustive and complex documents ever drafted by an international conference." Pardo, "The Convention on the Law of the Sea," p. 489. Also, the late Under Secretary General of the United Nations for the Law of the Sea observed that "[n]ever in the history of treaty-making has such a large and varied number of countries signed a convention on the day it was opened for signature." Zuleta, "The Law of the Sea After Montego Bay," *San Diego Law Review* (1983), 20:475, 476.

24. See Pardo, "An Opportunity Lost," in B. Oxman, D. Caron, and C. Burderi, eds., *Law of the Sea: U.S. Policy Dilemma* (San Francisco: Institute for Contemporary Studies, 1983), pp. 16–17. Aguilar, "The Patrimonial Sea or Economic Zone Concept," *San Diego Law Review* (1974), 11:579; Alexander and Hodgson, "The Impact of the 200-Mile Economic Zone on the Law of the Sea," *San Diego Law Review* (1975), 12:569; Pollard, "The Exclusive Economic Zone—

The Elusive Consensus," *San Diego Law Review* (1975), 12:600; Clingan, "Emerging Law of the Sea: The Economic Zone Dilemma," *San Diego Law Review* (1977), 14:530; Oxman, "An Analysis of the Exclusive Economic Zone as Formulated in the Informal Composite Negotiating Text in T. Clingan, ed., *Law of the Sea: State Practice in Zones of Special Jurisdiction* (Honolulu: Law of the Sea Institute, 1982), p. 57; Oxman, "The Third United Nations Conference on the Law of the Sea: The 1976 New York Sessions," *American Journal of International Law* (1977), 71:247, 259–68. See also Oxman, "The Third United Nations Conference on the Law of the Sea: The Tenth Session (1981)," *American Journal of International Law* (1982), 76:1, 14–15.

25. LOS Convention, arts. 58, 59. See Clingan, "Freedom of Navigation," pp. 113–17; Oxman, "The Third United Nations Conference on the Law of the Sea: The 1976 New York Sessions," *American Journal of International Law* (1977), 71:247, 259–68; Pardo, "An Opportunity Lost," pp. 15–17.

26. See LOS Convention, arts. 74, 83. See also Pardo, "An Opportunity Lost," pp. 15–16. This issue has been the subject of extensive litigation. See, e.g., "The Tunisia/Libya Continental Shelf Case, 1982" I.C.J. (February 24, 1982), p. 18; the Case Concerning Delimitation of the Maritime Boundary in the Gulf of Maine Area (Canada v. United States) (1984) I.C.J. Rep. 246.

For a review of the boundary provisions in the LOS Convention, see Hedberg, "Critique of Boundary Provisions in the Law of the Sea Treaty," *Development and International Law Journal* (1983), 12:337.

27. Reference is made to "Co-operation" in the following contexts in the Convention:

bilateral: 66(4); 269(e)

international: 64(1): 65; 69(3)(d); 70(4); 94(7); 100; 108(1); 108(2); 109(1); 117; 118; 123; 129; 143(3); 150; 151(1)(a); 160(2)(j); 226; 235; 242; 244; 268(2); 270 303(1)

international organizations 64(1); 123(d); 144(2); 151(10); 169(1); 197; 199; 200; 201; 202; 243; 266(1); 269; 271; 272; 273; 278; 303(1); A2/3(2)

subregional, regional or global: 41(5); 43; 61(2); 61(3); 61(5); 64(1); 66(3)(b); 66(4); 98(2); 118; 119(1)(a); 119(2); 123; 129; 132; 197; 200; 201; 202; 269; 270; 276(2)

The Law of the Sea, United Nations Convention on the Law of the Sea, with Index of Final Act of the Third United Nations Conference on the Law of the Sea (1983), p. 200.

28. See LOS Convention, arts. 61–68 (EEZ), 116–19 (high seas). In a recent article, Judge Oda has explored the difficulties likely to arise as the fishery provisions are applied in light of the many ambiguities in the convention text. He focused particularly on the ambiguous obligation to cooperate. Oda, "Fisheries under the United Nations Convention on the Law of the Sea," *American Journal of International Law* (1983), 77:739.

29. See LOS Convention, arts. 124–32.

30. See LOS Convention, arts. 70, 122–23.

31. See LOS Convention, arts. 266–78.

32. Reference is made to "International Organizations" in the following contexts in the Convention:

appropriate: 64(1); 65; 143(3)(b); 297(3)(d); A8/3(e)

competent: 22(3)(a); 41(4); 41(5); 53(9); 60(3); 60(5); 61(2); 61(5); 119(2); 197; 198; 199; 200; 201; 202; 204(1); 205; 207(4); 208(5); 210(4); 211(1); 211(2); 211(3); 211(5);

211(6)(a); 212(3); 213; 214; 216(1); 217(1); 217(4); 217(7); 218(1); 220(7); 222; 223;
238; 239; 242(1); 243; 244(1); 244(2); 246(3); 246(5); 246(5)(d); 248; 249(1); 251;
252; 252(b); 253(1)(b); 253(4); 253(5); 254(1); 254(2); 254(3); 254(4); 256; 257; 262;
263(1); 263(2); 263(3); 265; 266(1); 268; 269; 271; 272; 273; 275(1); 275(2); 276(1);
278; 297(1)(c); A2/3(2)

co-operation with States: 123(d)

co-operation with the Authority: 143(3)(b); 151(10); 162(2)(f); 163(13); A3/13(9)(b);
A4/13(2)(a); R1/5(d)

development and transfer of marine technology: 266(1); 268; 269; 271; 272; 273;
275(1); 275(2); 276(1); 278

living resources management: 61(2); 61(5); 64(1); 65; 72(2); 119(2)

marine scientific research: 238; 239; 242(1); 243; 244(1); 244(2); 246(3); 246(5);
246(5)(d); 247; 248; 249(1); 251; 252; 252(b); 253(1)(b); 253(4); 253(5); 254(1);
254(2); 254(3); 254(4); 256; 257; 262; 263(1); 263(2); 263(3); 265

obligations under this Convention: A9/4; A9/4(1); A9/4(3); A9/4(6); A9/6(1)

protection and preservation of the marine environment: 197; 198; 199; 200; 201;
202; 203; 204(1); 205; 207(4); 208(5); 210(4); 211(1); 211(2); 211(3); 211(5); 211(6)(a);
212(3); 213; 214; 216(1); 217(1); 217(4); 217(7); 218(1); 220(7); 222

responsibility and liability: 139(1); 139(2); 139(3); 263(3)

signature of the Convention: 305(1)(f); A9/2

use of the term: A9/1

The Law of the Sea, with Index and Final Act, (1983), p. 208.

33. *Ibid.*

34. See Resolutions of the Third United Nations Conference on the Law of the Sea, Working Paper 2, June 4, 1982; LOS Convention, arts. 133–191 and Annexes III and IV. For a discussion of some of the issues to be addressed by the Preparatory Commission, see Zuleta, "The Law of the Sea After Montego Bay," pp. 483–87.

35. LOS Convention, art. 313.

36. LOS Convention, arts. 155, 312–16. The Convention provides for "a general and systematic review" every five years of the operation of the deep-seabed regime. *Ibid.*, art. 154. A conference will be convened 15 years after the initial commercial production of deep-seabed resources to review certain issues relating to the deep-seabed regime. *Ibid.*, art. 155.

37. See Pardo, "An Opportunity Lost," p. 23. For a pessimistic review of the future potential of deep-seabed mining, see Goldwin, "Common Sense v. 'The Common Heritage,' " in Oxman, Caron, and Buderi, eds., *Law of the Sea*, pp. 59, 62–66. See also Statement by the President, July 9, 1982, p. 888; Statement by Marne Dubs, in D. Johnston and N. Letalik, eds., *The Law of the Sea and Ocean Industry: New Opportunities and Restraints* (Honolulu: Law of the Sea Institute, 1984), p. 4.

38. See Charney, "The International Regime for the Deep Seabed"; Charney, "Law of the Sea: Breaking the Deadlock," *Foreign Affairs* (1977), 55:598.

39. See "Outer Continental Shelf: Notice of Jurisdiction of the Department of the Interior Relating to Minerals Other Than Oil, Gas, and Sulphur, 47 Fed. Reg. 55, 313 (1982), clarified at 48 Fed. Reg. 2450 (1983).

40. See Pardo, "An Opportunity Lost," pp. 496–97; Charney, "The Law of the Deep Seabed Post UNCLOS III," pp. 41–46.

41. See State Dept., Bureau of Intelligence and Research, "Limits in the

Seas," No. 36, R. Smith ed. and comp., *National Claims to Maritime Jurisdiction* ed. (Washington, D.C.: GPO, 1981).

42. See Charney, "Exclusive Economic Zone and Public International Law," *Ocean Development in International Law* (1984) 15:233.

43. See LOS Convention, art. 292.

44. See *ibid.*, art. 296(1); Annex VI, arts. 33, 39; Annex VII, art. 11.

45. *Ibid.*, arts. 177–83; Annex IV, art. 13 (privilege and immunity of the Enterprise).

46. *Ibid.*, arts. 160(2)(e), 171(a).

47. See notes 2 and 3 and accompanying text.

48. See note 2 and accompanying text.

49. See note 4. It is beyond dispute that the negotiations have already affected state behavior. Perhaps the best example can be found in the context of the Exclusive Economic Zone. The Zone was a creation of the Conference that was subject to substantial agreement by 1977. As a result, many nations established their own EEZs or comparable zones of jurisdiction which were patterned in large part after the Convention text then under consideration at UNCLOS III. For a discussion of the public international law of the sea and development of the exclusive economic zone, see Charney, "Exclusive Economic Zone"; Clingan, "Freedom of Navigation," pp. 113–17. The Conference may also set in motion changes in the law that go beyond the Convention text. Express recognition of limited coastal nations' rights in expanded ocean zones adjacent to their coasts may blossom into greater coastal state jurisdiction despite Convention terms that were designed to foreclose such expansions. This phenomenon of expanding jurisdiction is commonly referred to as "creeping jurisdiction." See Charney, "The United States and the Law of the Sea After UNCLOS III," p. 44. At risk will be commercial and military navigation and overflight and marine scientific research, the very interests that stimulated the UNCLOS III negotiations.

Part V of the Restatement of the Foreign Relations Law of the United States (Revised) makes extensive use of the Conference and the Convention to find customary international law. See Tentative Draft Numbers 3 (1982) and 5 (1984).

50. See note 4; and Sohn, "The Law of the Sea: Customary International Law Developments," *American University Law Review* (1985), 34:271.

51. The Islamic Republic of Iran made the following declaration when it signed the Convention: "Notwithstanding the intended character of the Convention being one of general application and of law making nature, certain of its provisions are merely product of *quid-pro-quo*, which do not necessarily purport to codify the existing customs or established usage (practice) regarded as having an obligatory character. Therefore, ... only states parties to the Law of the Sea Convention shall be entitled to benefit from the contractual rights created therein." LOS Bulletin, supra note 2 at 21. See also Zuleta, supra note 23, at 477–81.

52. For a rule by rule analysis, see Oxman, "Customary International Law," pp. 16–23; Charney, "The United States and the Law of the Sea After UNCLOS III." For a discussion of the pick and choose issue, see Harlow, COMMENT, *Law and Contemporary Problems* (1983), 46:125. See also Restatement, note 49.

53. LOS Convention, arts. 2 (territorial sea), 13 (Contiguous Zone), 76 (con-

tinental shelf), 87 (high seas). See Charney, "The United States and the Law of the Sea After UNCLOS III," pp. 44–48.

54. LOS Convention, arts. 56 (EEZ), 150–53 (deep-seabed mining), 37–45 (transit and innocent passage). See Charney, "The United States and the Law of the Sea After UNCLOS III"; Charney, "Exclusive Economic Zone."

55. See Third United Nations Conference on the Law of the Sea: Rules of Procedure, U.N. Doc. A/Conf. 62/30/Rev. 1 (1974); hereinafter cited as Rules of Procedure; Declaration incorporating the "Gentleman's Agreement" made by the President and endorsed by the Conference at its 19th meeting on June 27, 1974, U.N. Doc. A/Conf. 62/30/Rev. 1 (1974) (appendix). See also Buzan, "Negotiating by Consensus: Developments in Technique at the United Nations Conference on the Law of the Sea," *American Journal of International Law* (1981), 75:324; Charney, "Technology and International Negotiations"; Beesley, "The Negotiating Strategy of UNCLOS III: Developing and Developed Countries as Partners—A Pattern for Future Multilateral International Conferences?" *Law and Contemporary Problems* (1983), 46:183.

56. See Charney, "Technology and International Negotiations."

57. See Arnold, "The Common Heritage of Mankind as a Legal Concept," *International Law* (1975), 9:153; Danzig, "A Funny Thing Happened to the Common Heritage on the Way to the Sea," *San Diego Law Review* (1975), 12:655; Finlay and McKnight, "Law of the Sea: Its Impact on the International Energy Crisis," *Law and Pol. International Business* (1974), 6:639; Saffo, "Common Heritage of Mankind: Has the General Assembly Created a Law to Govern Seabed Mining?" *Tulane Law Review* (1979), 53:492; Borgese, "The New International Economic Order and the Law of the Sea," *San Diego Law Review* (1977), 14:584; Adede, "The Group of 77 and the Establishment of the International Sea-Bed Authority," *Ocean Development and International Law Journal* (1979), 7:31; Juda, "UNCLOS III and the New International Economic Order," *Ocean Development and International Law Journal* (1979), 7:221.

58. See United Nations General Assembly, Declaration on the Establishment of a New International Economic Order, G.A. Res. 3201, 6th Spec. Sess., Supp. (A/9559), May 1974. See also Juda, "UNCLOS III and the New Economic Order."

59. See note 57 for a discussion of the arguments that the United States should not join the LOS Convention because of the presence of NIEO ideology in the Convention, see Burke and Brokaw, "Ideology and the Law of the Sea," in B. Oxman, D. Caron, and C. Buderi, eds., *Law of the Sea: U.S. Policy Dilemma* (San Francisco: Institute for Contemporary Studies, 1983), pp. 3, 5–7. Bandow, "UNCLOS III: A Flawed Treaty," *San Diego Law Review* (1982), 19:475. See also Gamble, "The Third United Nations Conference on the Law of the Sea and the New International Economic Order," *Loyola International and Comparative Journal* (1983), 6:65.

60. The Reagan administration objected to the deep-seabed regime because many provisions would be incompatible with the theory of the free market. Similarly, the administration objected to the transfer of technology provisions and to the decision-making system in the deep-seabed authority, among others. President's Statement of July 9, 1982, supra note 2, 887–88; see also Brandow, "UNCLOS III," pp. 477–81.

61. President's Statement of July 9, 1982.

62. See, e.g., COMMENT, Law of the Sea: The Scope of the Third-Party, Compulsory Procedures for Settlement of Disputes," *American Journal of International Law (1977)*, 71:305; COMMENT, "Dispute Settlement Mechanisms in the Draft Convention on the Law of the Sea," *Denver Journal of International Law and Policy* (1981), 10:331; Gaertner, "The Dispute Settlement Provisions of the Convention on the Law of the Sea: Critique and Alternatives to the International Tribunal for the Law of the Sea," *San Diego Law Review* (1982), 19:577; Adede, "The Basic Structure of the Disputes Settlement Part of the Law of the Sea Convention," *Ocean Development and International Law Journal* (1982), 11:125; Sohn, "Problems of Dispute Settlement," in E. Miles and J. Gamble eds., *Law of the Sea: Conference Outcomes and Problems of Implementation* (Cambridge: Ballinger, 1977), p. 223. See also Sohn, "The Role of Arbitration in Recent International Multilateral Treaties," *Virginia Journal of International Law* (1983), 23:171; Sohn, "Peaceful Settlement of Disputes in Ocean Conflicts: Does UNCLOS III Point the Way," *Law and Contemporary Problems* (1983), 46:195; Jacovides, COMMENT, *Ibid.*, p. 201; Grzybowski, COMMENT, *Ibid.*, p. 205.

63. See LOS Convention, arts. 186–91, 279–296, Annexes V–VIII.

64. See Buhl, "The European Economic Community and the Law of the Sea," *Ocean Development and International Law Journal* (1982), 11:181; Treves, "The EEC and the Law of the Sea: How Close to One Voice?" *Ocean Development and International Law Journal* (1983), 12:173. See also Frank, "Antarctic Marine Living Resources," pp. 310–11. See generally, Stein, "The European Community in 1983: A Less Perfect Union?" *Common Market Law Review* (1983), 20:641.

65. See Buhl, "The European Economic Community," Treves, "The EEC and the Law of the Sea," and Gaja, "The European Community's Participation in the Law of the Sea Convention: Some Incoherencies in a Compromise Solution," *Italian Yearbook International Law* (1983), 5:110.

66. See LOS Convention, art. 305.1(f) Annex IX, art. 4.

67. See Holden, "Management of Fisheries Resources: The Experience of the European Economic Community," paper presented at the OECD extended meeting of the Committee for Fisheries on the Management of National Fishing Zones (1983).

68. LOS Convention, art. 305.1, Annex IX.

69. See Kassim, "The Palestine Liberation Organization's Claim to Status: A Juridicial Analysis Under International Law," *Denver Journal of International Law and Policy* (1981), 9:1, 20–21 (PLO); M. Rajan, "The Expanding Jurisdiction of the United Nations" (SWAPO) (Dobbs Ferry, N.Y.: Oceana, 1982), p. 74.

70. See Rules of Procedure, Rule 63, p. 15; LOS Bulletin, p. 10.

71. LOS Convention, arts. 140, 160.2(f)(i).

72. LOS Convention, arts. 161.8(d), 161.8(e), 162.1(o)(ii).

73. LOS Convention, art. 305(1); see LOS Bulletin, p. 10.

74. LOS Convention, art. 305(1)(f), Annex IX; see LOS Bulletin, p. 10.

75. See generally H. Chiu, The Capacity of International Organizations to Conclude Treaties, and the Special Legal Aspects of the Treaties Concluded (1966).

76. See generally Barston, "The Law of the Sea: The Conference and After,"

Journal of World Trade Law (1983), 17:207, 209; COMMENT, "The Future of United States Deep Seabed Mining: Still in the Hands of Congress," *San Diego Law Review* (1982), 19:613, 624–25 (miners influence Congress and congressional intent may be incorporated in informal working papers presented at UNCLOS). For mining industry testimony before Congress, see, e.g., Law of the Sea Conference: Hearings Before the House Subcommittee on Domestic and International Scientific Planning, Analysis and Cooperation of the Comm. on Science and Technology, 95th Cong., 1st Sess., passim (1977).

77. LOS Convention, arts. 187(c), 187(d), Annex III.

78. See generally, Charney, "Transnational Corporations and Developing Public International Law," *Duke Law Journal* (1983), p. 748.

79. Declaration of the United Nations Conference on the Human Environment, U.N. Doc. A/Conf. 48/14 and Corr. 1, reprinted in *International Legal Material,* (1972), 11:1416. See J. Schneider, *World Public Order of the Environment: Towards an International Ecological Law and Organization* (Toronto: University of Toronto Press, 1979).

80. See Stevenson and Oxman, "The Preparations for the Law of the Sea Conference," *American Journal of International Law* (1974), 68:23–28; Smith, "Innocent Passage as a Rule of Decision: Navigation v. Environmental Protection," *Columbia Journal of Transnational Law* (1982), 49:71; Schneider, "Prevention of Pollution from Vessels; or, Don't Give Up the Ship," in Charney, ed., *The New Nationalism,* pp. 14–17.

81. See, e.g., LOS Convention, arts. 194, 197–218, 222, 223, 226.2, 243, 244, 251, 266.1, 268–73, 276–78. See Vallarta, "Protection of the Marine Environment and Scientific Research in the Oceans in a Post-UNCLOS III Environment," *Law and Contemporary Problems* (1983), 46:147.

82. See "Protection of the Global Heritage," (remarks by Ian Brownlie), *American Society of International Law Proceedings* (1981) 75:32, 36–39.

83. Treaty of Principles Governing the Activities of States in the Exploration and Use of Outer Space, including the Moon and Other Celestial Bodies, done January 1967, reprinted in *International Legal Materials* (1979), 18:1434.

84. See "Space Law's Business Impact," *New York Times,* December 2, 1981. See also The Moon Treaty: Hearings Before the Subcommittee on Science, Technology, and Space of the Senate Committee on Commerce, Science, and Transportation, 96th Cong., 2d Sess. (statement of Marne Dubs, Chairman, American Mining Congress Committee on Undersea Mineral Resources, and Vice President, Kennecott Development Corp.), pp. 133–36.

85. See Nesgros, "The Proposed International Sea-Bed Authority as a Model for Future Outer Space International Regime," *Annals of Air and Space Law* (1980), 5:549; NOTE, Extraterrestrial Law on the Final Frontier: A Regime to Govern the Development of Celestial Body Resources," *Georgetown Law Journal* (1983), 71:1427. See also Matte, "The Law of the Sea and Outer Space: A Comparative Survey of Specific Issues," in Borgese and N. Ginsburg, eds., *Ocean Yearbook* (1982), 3:13; and Williams, "International Law and the Exploitation of Outer Space: A New Market for Private Enterprise," *International Relations* (1983), 7:2476, 2478.

86. See notes 4 and 51 and accompanying text.

87. See Thirlway, International Customary Law and Codification (1972), pp. 80–81. See also North Sea Continental Shelf Cases *(W. Germany v. Denmark; W. Germany v. Netherlands)* I.C.J. (1969), pp. 37–38.

88. See M. Bedjaoui, "Towards a New International Economic Order," (1979), pp. 138–42; South West Africa Cases *(Ethiopia v. So. Africa; Liberia v. So. Africa)*, I.C.J. (1966), pp. 291–93 (Judgment of July 18) (J. Tanaka, dissenting). See, generally, Kerwin, "The Role of United Nations General Assembly Resolutions in Determining Principles of International Law in United States Courts," *Duke Law Journal* (1983), p. 876.

89. Judge Oda has argued that certain aspects of the LOS Convention have already been incorporated into general international law. Case Concerning the Continental Shelf *(Tunisia v. Libya)*, 1982 I.C.J. 143, para. 23, 120, 125, 129 (J. Oda, dissenting).

90. See E. Haas, *Beyond the Nation-State: Functionalism and the International Organization,* (Stanford: Stanford University Press, 1964).

Index

AALCC (Asian African Legal Consultative Committee), and EEZ, 135–36, 141

Abstaining states, 58n35

Abundance, historic period, 3

Adjudicatory mechanisms, 45; *see also* Conflict resolution mechanisms

Advantaged states, 154

AFERNOD (Association Française pour l'Etude et la Recherche des Nodules), 92–93, 103–4, 108, 115, 118–20, 121n3

Afghanistan, 154

Africa: continental shelf, 132; and LOS negotiations, 132–48; *see also* names of countries

Agreement Governing the Activities of States on the Moon and Other Celestial Bodies, 251

Aguilar, Andres, vii, xiii

Albania, 152, 254n2

Alexander VI, Pope, 3

Algeria, 150, 152

Allott, P., 39

Ambiguities in LOS Convention, 242–45

American International Law, 164

American Mining Congress, 114

Amoco, 108

AMR, 107

Antarctica, 240, 251; exclusive economic zone, 71

Antarctic Treaty, 240, 255n9

Antigua, 196n1, 198n17

Arab states, and continental shelf provisions, 191

Arbitration agreement for seabed mining conflicts, 86, 92, 105, 117–20

Archipelagic sealane passage, 210–11

Archipelagic states, 165; Latin American countries and, 190–91; Indonesia, 201–2; Malaysia, 204; navigational issues, 207

Archipelagic waters, 68, 70; military ships in, 76

Arctic Ocean, jurisdiction, 241

"Area, the," 68, 75

Argentina, 154, 169, 172–75 passim, 195, 196n1, 198n17, 255n9; coastline, 152; jurisdictional claims, 165–66, 171; draft treaty articles, 182

Arms control issues, 241

Artificial earth satellites, 241–42

ASEAN countries: and LOS Conference, 205; and U.S. position, 214–15; ratification of Convention, 213

Asian African Legal Consultative Committee (AALCC), and EEZ, 135–36, 141

Asian-African states, jurisdictional claims, 150–51

Assembly, Seabed Authority proposal, 183

Assets, 13

Association Française pour l'Etude et la Recherche des Nodules (AFTERNOD), 92–93, 103–4, 108, 115, 118–20, 121n3

Australia, 34, 152, 154, 255n9

Austria, 154

Bab el Mandeb, 70

Bahamas, 165, 190, 196n1, 198n17, 254n3

Barbados, 154, 176, 177, 196n1, 198n17

Barbuda, 196n1, 198n17

Belgium, 152, 157n45, 255n9; nodule consortium participation, 106

Belize, 196n1, 198n17, 254n3

Bello, Andres, *Principles of International Law*, 159–60

Bhutan, 154

Bilateral research programs, 80–82

Billiton, 108

Bolivia, 154, 165, 169, 171, 174, 175, 192–

Bolovia (Continued)
   93, 195, 196n1, 198n17; draft treaty
   articles, 182
Boskalis, 108
Botswana, 151, 154
Boundaries, delimitation of, 242
Brazil, 154, 165, 171–75 passim, 195,
   196n1, 198n17, 255n9, coastline length,
   152; draft treaty articles, 182
British Petroleum, 107
Bulgaria, 152, 255n9
Burma, 150, 152, 154; joint proposal, 169
Burundi, 151, 154
Business firm, development of, 3–4
Business Week, "The Death of Mining,"
   87
Byelorussian SSR, 154
Bynkershoek, 127

Cables, laying of, 178
Cambodia, 150, 152
Cameroon, 150, 152
Canada, 152, 154; management of assets,
   13; rearrangement of fishing effort,
   26, 27; and exclusive zone decision, 34;
   nodule consortium participation, 106,
   107; and LOS negotiations, 225, 226
Capital, European, and oceanic expan-
   sion, 2
Caracas, Venezuela, LOS session, 185
Caribbean countries, 192, 196n1, 198n17
Carter, Jimmy, 226
Carter administration and LOS negotia-
   tions, 227
Castaneda, Jorge, 187, 190, 223
Central African Republic, 151, 154
Ceylon (Sri Lanka), 150, 152, 154; Pearl
   Fisheries Ordinance, 155n13
Chad, 151, 154
Charney, Jonathan I., vii, xii, 14
Charter of Economic Rights and Duties
   of States, 79
Chile, 137–38, 154, 165, 169–75 passim,
   196n1, 198n17, 255n9; exclusive fishing
   rights, 32; jurisdiction claims, 56–
   57n6, 166–67, 170; coastline, 152;
   Seabed Committee draft, 182–84
China, 152, 255n9; jurisdiction claims,
   150
Clarion/Clipperton region, 92–93, 105,
   119
Clingan, Thomas A., Jr., vii–viii, xiv–xv

Closed seas, 192, 224
Coastal state authority, 11–14, 44–50,
   260n49; and continental shelf resources, 16–17; and rearrangement of
   fishing efforts, 26–27; and redistribution of wealth, 28; Truman Proclamation, 31–32; exclusive fishing rights
   claims, 32; military concerns, 36; and
   freedom of the seas, 37–38; over foreign research, 68–69; of developing
   countries, 135–36; and traditional
   freedoms, 220–21; see also Exclusive
   economic zones
Coastal states: claim to continental
   shelf, 31–32; rights of, 46–47, 233;
   Latin American, 180, 188; Seabed
   Committee draft of rights, 182–83
Coastal zone management programs, 81
Coastline lengths, 152–53
Cobalt, 87, 89
Cod wars, 32
Colombia, 154, 165, 169, 171–77 passim,
   196n1, 197–98n12, 198n17; coastline,
   152; joint proposal, 169; draft treaty
   articles, 180–81; Seabed Committee
   draft, 182–84
Commerce, freedom of, 13–14, 127
Commercialization of deep-seabed min-
   erals, 109–10
Committee on the Peaceful Use of the
   Sea Bed and Ocean Floor, see Seabed
   Committee
Common heritage principle, 50–51, 111,
   172, 208–9, 231, 251; legal aspects,
   52–55; and technological advances,
   55–56; Santo Domingo Declaration,
   179; Latin American countries and,
   193; Reagan and, 230; negotiations,
   233–34
Common property problem, 17–18, 32–
   33; Georges Bank resources, 22–24
Communication, freedom of, 127
Complexity of LOS Convention, 38–43
Concessions system, 184
Conciliation mechanisms, 45, 48, 49; see
   also Conflict resolution mechanisms
Conference on the Exploitation and
   Conservation of Marine Resources in
   the South Pacific, 166
Conflicting interests, reconciliation of,
   43–50
Conflict resolution mechanisms, 248; of

nodule consortia, 108, 114, 117–20; LOS provisions, 45, 48, 49, 76, 145; LOS negotiations, 187, 194
Conflicts in deep-sea mining, 87, 105
Congo, 150, 152
Conservation of resources, 6–7, 170; coastal state obligations, 46
Conservation zones, U.S. establishment of, 163
Conservatism, in U.S., 235–36
Consolidated Gold Fields, 107
Consortia, see Nodule consortia
Contiguity, and exclusive economic zones, 36–38
Contiguous zone convention, 170
Continental shelf, 31, 71, 129–32, 138, 170, 221; manganese nodules, 54; beyond 200 miles, 74–75; African views, 143; claims to, 161–67; Venezuelan proposal, 176; Santo Domingo Declaration, 178–79; draft treaty articles, 181; negotiations, 191, 208; resource exploitation, 201; U.S. and, 211
Continental states, Latin American, 165
Control of oceans, before seventeenth century, 3; see also Coastal state authority
Convention on Fishing and Conservation of the Living Resources of the High Seas, 254n3
Convention on the Continental Shelf, 254n3
Convention on the High Seas, 254n3
Convention on the Territorial Sea and the Contiguous Zone, 254n3
Copper, 87, 89
Corfu Channel, 58n25
Corporación Venezolana del Petroleo, 184
Corporate form, seventeenth century, 3–4
Costa Rica, 154, 165, 169, 171, 176, 177, 196n1, 198n17; coastline, 152
Costs of mining operations, 98–99
Council, Seabed Authority proposal, 183
Council of Ministers, and LOS negotiations, 142
Creeping jurisdiction, 37–38, 49, 223–24; military concerns, 61–62
Cuba, 154, 165, 171, 190, 196n1, 196n2, 198n17, 254n3, 255n9; coastline, 152

Customary law: rights of innocent passage, 44; and LOS Convention, 40–43, 49, 56, 245–46; seabed status, 51–52; and EEZ, 147
Cyprus, 150, 152
Czechoslovakia, 154, 255n9

Dahomey, 150, 152
DCON, 108
Declaration of Principles of 1970, 52, 54
Declaration of the Latin American States on the Law of the Sea, 174
Deep Ocean Mining Company, 107
Deep Seabed Authority, see Seabed Authority
Deep-seabed mineral resources, 8, 85–121
Deep-seabed mining, xiii; LOS negotiations, 15–16; U.S. approach, 224–25; problems of, 243–44
Deep-seabed regime: and common heritage issues, 251; and free market theory, 261n60; see also Seabed Authority
Deepsea Ventures, 92, 107
Defense Department, U.S., and LOS treaty, 230
Delimitation of ocean boundaries, 242
Demand pull investment model, 2–3
Democratization of international lawmaking, 33
Demonstrated hydrocarbon resources, 27–28
Denmark, 152, 255n9
Department of Economic and Social Affairs, United Nations, 89
Detection devices, military use, 35
De Vattel, 127
Developing countries: and exclusive economic zones, 34–35; and marine research, 78–81; and deep-seabed mining, 111, 209–10; and freedom of the seas, 135; coastally disadvantaged, 153
Diminishing returns, of fisheries, 6–7
Disadvantaged states, 153–54
Dispute settlement machinery, see Conflict resolution mechanisms
Distribution of wealth, 28n1
Djalal, Hasjim, viii, xiii
Domestic laws, and LOS Convention, 41, 49, 196, 244
Dominica, 196n1, 198n17

Dominican Republic, 154, 165, 170–71, 174, 176, 177, 195, 196n1, 198n17; coastline, 152

DORD (Deep Ocean Resources Development Company), 92–93, 104–5, 108, 115, 118–20, 121n3

Dubs, Marne A., viii, xiii

Due regard principle, 44–45

Dutch East Indies Company, 4, 56n1, 30, 126

Earth satellites, issues of, 241–42

Eastern bloc investment in fishing fleets, 7

East Germany, *see* German Democratic Republic

Economic activity, overseas structure, 2

Economic factors: oceanic expansion, 1–2; in ocean resource development, 8; in LOS negotiations, 13; of deep-seabed mining, 16, 54, 94–95, 98–99, 101–2, 120

Economic limits of open ocean system, 5

Economic organization, seventeenth century, 3–4

Ecuador, 137–38, 154, 165, 169–75 passim, 191, 195, 196n1, 198n1; jurisdictional claims, 32, 57n6, 166–67, 170, 171; coastline, 152; draft treaty articles, 182; Seabed Committee draft, 182–84

EEC (European Economic Community), 248–49

EEZs, *see* Exclusive Economic Zones

EFJ (Extended Fisheries Jurisdiction), 17–19; and Georges Bank, 21; and transfer of wealth, 25–26; and world catch of fish, 20

Egypt, 152, 254n3

El Salvador, 152, 165, 171–77 passim, 195, 196n1, 198n17; Seabed Committee draft, 182–84

Enclosed seas, 192, 224

Energy companies, and coastal state control, 16–17

Energy production, from ocean, 55

England, *see* United Kingdom

Engo, Paul, 226–27

ENI, 107

Enterprise, The, Seabed Authority proposal, 183–84, 209, 212–13, 226

Environmental concerns, 48–49, 199; and exclusive economic zones, 35; and military concerns, 61; Santo Domingo Declaration, 179

Environmental law, international, 250–51

Equatorial Guinea, 152, 154

Equity, relevance of, 45

Ethiopia, 150, 152

European Economic Community (EEC), 248–49

Evensen, Jens, 187, 226

Evensen group, 227

Exclusive economic zones (EEZs), 32–34, 56–57n6, 128–32, 192, 260n49; navigational rights, 44–45; legal status controversy, 46; and scientific research, 47–48, 65–67, 71–74; environmental concerns, 48–49; military concerns, 61; African interests, 134–41; revised draft articles, 148–50; Latin American countries and, 189–90; negotiations, 207–8, 223–24; U.S. and, 211; conflicts of, 242

Exploitability criteria of continental shelf, 130–31, 201

Exploitation of common resources, 32–33; Seabed Committee draft, 182

Exploitation of weak nations, 125

Exploration of seabed, 100; French, 104

Extended Fisheries Jurisdiction, *see* EFJ

Extension of Land, 131–32

Federal Republic of Germany, 153, 157n45, 233, 253n2, 255n9; and seabed mining, 53, 86, 92; support of marine science, 68; and LOS treaty, 85; nodule consortium participation, 106, 107

Fiji, 154, 254n3

Financial arrangements, and LOS Treaty, 115

Finland, 152, 255n9

Fisheries, 6–7, 224; East coast, 13; income redistribution, 19; resource utilization, 20–21; depletion of, 133, 159–60; U.S. interests, 200; Antarctic, 240; ambiguities in LOS Convention, 258n28

Fishermen, in U.S., 18

Fishing disputes, U.S.-Japanese, 8

Fishing effort, rearrangement of, 26

Fishing fleets, Eastern block investment, 7

Fishing grounds, value of, 27

Fishing jurisdiction claims, 150–51

Fishing rights: of coastal states, 32; Santo Domingo Declaration, 179

Fish price, and value of Georges Bank, 25

Fish stock, management of, 17–18, 20

France, 152, 157*n*45, 233, 255*n*9; mining license application, 86, 92; ocean mining ventures, 103–4; and LOS Treaty, 115

Freedom of access, and deep-sea mining, 115

Freedom of the seas, 3–4, 13–14, 30–38, 43, 58*n*25, 126–27; threats to, 15; and coastal state jurisdiction, 37–38; and relevant equity, 45; Latin American states and, 160, 173–74; in patrimonial seas, Venezuelan proposal, 176; Santo Domingo Declaration, 178; Indonesian views, 202; and EEZ, 207

Free enterprise, and seabed resources, 211–12, 261*n*60

Gabon, 150, 152

Gambia, 150, 152, 254*n*3

Geneva Conference, 1958, 31, 128–32, 169–70; and LOS Convention, 39–40

Geneva Conference, 1982, 187–96; *see also* Law of the Sea Conference; Law of the Sea Treaty

Genoa, 125

Geographical contiguity, and territorial acquisition, 36–37

Geographically disadvantaged countries, 190, 140; and exclusive economic zone, 34, 143–45; and continental shelf concept, 191; Singapore, 203; resource issues, 207–8

Geographic distribution of fish populations, 20

Geography, and income distribution, 12–13

Georges Bank, 21–27, 28*n*3

German Democratic Republic, 152, 255*n*9; investment in fishing fleets, 7; rearrangement of fishing effort, 26

Ghana, 150, 152, 254*n*3

Global issues of ocean use, 8, 43

Grandfather rights for pretreaty seabed investors, 112

Great Britain, *see* United Kingdom

Greece, 152, 154

Greenland, increase in catch, 27

Grenada, 196*n*1, 198*n*17

Grotius, Hugo, 3, 126, 56*n*1, 202; *Mare Liberum*, 4, 30

Group of 11, 232

Group of 77, 19, 164, 194, 225, 234; and EEZ, 143–44; Latin American countries and, 193; and LOS negotiations, 226; African control, 231–32

Guam Doctrine, 199–200

Guatemala, 165, 169, 171, 174–77 passim, 195, 196*n*1, 198*n*12, 198*n*17; coastline, 152; Seabed Committee draft, 182–84

Guinea, 150, 152

Guinea Bissau, 152

Gulf of Paria, Venezuelan claims, 161

Gunboat diplomacy, 50

Guyana, 152, 175, 177, 182–84, 196*n*1, 198*n*17

Haiti, 152, 154, 165, 171, 176, 177, 196*n*1, 198*n*17

Harris (Australian ambassador), 187

Hibernia oil field, 27–28

High seas, 68, 75; EEZ status, 46, 61, 207, 223; convention adopted, 170; Santo Domingo Declaration, 179; draft treaty articles, 181; Latin American countries and, 191–92

Holy See, 254*n*2

Honduras, 152, 165, 171, 174, 177, 196*n*1, 198*n*17; ocean sovereignty claim, 137

Humboldt current, 168

Hungary, 154, 255*n*9

Huxley, Thomas, 6

Hydrocarbon resources, 8, 27, 31–32; coastal state control, 16–17

Hypothetical resources, 27

Iceland, 152, 154; "cod wars," 32; preferential fishing rights, 33; fisheries case, 43

ICES (International Council for the Exploration of the Seas), 6

ICNT (Integrated Composite Negotiating Text), 227

Idealism in Law of the Sea negotiations, 12–13

Identified hydrocarbon resources, 27

Ideological arguments in deep-seabed mining negotiations, 111–12

Implementation problems, 243

Implied consent for scientific research, 75, 77

Income distribution problems, 11, 12–14; and deep-sea mining, 15–16; and coastal state control of resources, 17–19

India, 152, 154, 255n9; mining license application, 86, 93; ocean mining ventures, 106; and arbitration agreement, 120; jurisdictional claims, 150; and LOS negotiations, 226

Individuals, and extended fisheries jurisdiction, 18

Indonesia, 70, 152, 154, 215; jurisdictional claims, 150; joint proposal, 169; LOS concerns, 201–2, 204; ratification of Convention, 213

Industrialization, worldwide, 5

Industrialized states, coastally disadvantaged, 153

Inefficiency of Georges Bank production, 22–25

Inferred hydrocarbon resources, 27

Informal Consultative Meeting of Foreign Ministers of the Countries of the Caribbean, 176–77

Inland waters, world catch, 28n2

Innocent passage, 44, 210; of military ships, 61, 76; in territorial seas, 70, 176, 181; and Latin American jurisdictional claims, 167; in international straits, 200

Integrated Composite Negotiating Text (ICNT), 227

Intent of treaty, 42

Inter-American Conference, Caracas, 1954, 168

Inter-American Conference, Montevideo, 1933, 160

Inter-American Council of Jurists, 168

Inter-American Specialized Conference on "Preservation of Natural Resources: Continental Shelf and the Waters of the Sea," 169, 170, 177

Inter-American system, 164, 168

Interference with commerce, protection against, 13–14

Intergovernmental Oceanographic Commission, 80

Intergovernmental organizations, 250

Internal waters, 68, 69

International bureaucracy, LOS administration, 115

International changes, post World War II, 161

International control of seabed mining, 36, 54; see also Seabed Authority

International Council for the Exploration of the Seas (ICES), 6

International Court of Justice, 45; Iceland Fisheries Case, 43

International dispute settlement systems, see Conflict resolution mechanisms

International distribution of income, 11

International environmental law, 250–51; see also Environmental concerns

International law, 220, 251–52; and LOS Convention, 245–46; 264n89

International Law Commission, 169

International law-making, democratization of, 33

International negotiations, 247

International Nickel Company, 107

International organizations, 252

International regime for seabed development, see Seabed Authority

International revenue sharing plan, 12

International seabed, Santo Domingo Declaration, 179

International Seabed enterprise, see Seabed Authority

International straits, 58n25, 68, 70, 210–11; rights of passage, 41, 44; states bordering, 165; U.S. proposals, 171, 221; Latin American countries and, 190; and territorial seas, 200; Indonesian views, 202; Singapore and, 203; Strait of Malacca, 203, 204

Investment in fishing fleets, by Eastern bloc, 7

Investment opportunities, overseas, 2

Investment pull model, 4

Iran, 150, 152, 260n51

Iraq, 150, 153

Ireland, 153, 154

Islands, regime of, 192

Island states, Latin American, 165
Israel, 67, 153, 254n2
Italy, 153, 154, 157n45, 255n9; nodule
  consortium participation, 106, 107
Ivory Coast, 150, 152, 254n3

Jamaica, 154, 175, 176, 177, 196n1, 198n17,
  254n3; coastline, 153; draft treaty
  articles, 182; Seabed Committee draft,
  182–84
Japan, 86, 153, 154, 157n45, 233, 255n9;
  and fisheries agreement, 18; rearrangement of fishing effort, 26; South
  Pacific whaling, 32; support of marine
  science, 68; mining license application, 86, 92; ocean mining ventures,
  104–5; nodule consortium participation, 106, 107; and LOS Treaty, 115;
  jurisdictional claims, 150
Joint proposal, First Geneva conference,
  169–70
Jordan, 150, 153, 254n2
Juridical continental shelf, 74
Juridical regions of ocean, 68
Jurisdictional rights: and rights of passage, 44; in exclusive economic zone,
  146

KCON (Kennecott Consortium), 86, 92–
  93, 107, 108, 118–19, 121n1
Kennecott Corporation, 107, 108
Kenya, 151, 152; Revised Draft Articles
  on the Exclusive Economic Zone, 141,
  148–50
Kiribati, 254n2
Kissinger, Henry, 224–25, 226
Knowledge, valuation of, 5
Korea, jurisdictional claims, 151
Kuwait, 151, 153

Labor, and oceanic expansion, 2
Laing, Austin, 11
Land-based minerals, production costs,
  99
Landlocked countries, 81, 154; Asian-
  African, 140, 151; and EEZ, 143–45;
  Latin American, 165; rights of, 190,
  192; and continental shelf concept,
  191; resource issues, 207–8
Laos, 154
Latin American countries, 164, 196nm1, 2;

and continental shelf, 130; ocean
  sovereignty claims, 136–37; patrimonial sea proposal, 140; and LOS negotiations, 158–98
Lauterpacht, H., 36
Law of the sea, traditional, 197n5
Law of the Sea Conference, 1973–82,
  xii–xiii, 169–72, 184–96, 206, 219–20;
  organizational structure, 222; see
  also Geneva Conference, 1958
Law of the sea negotiations, 10–14; exclusive economic zone proposal, 134–
  48; U.S. and, 219–37
Law of the Sea Treaty, xi–xv, 9, 29, 38–
  43, 187–96; and fishery resource utilization, 20; and transfer of wealth,
  25; and coastal state authority, 28; and
  exclusive economic zones, 33–34, 44–
  50; structure of, 38–43; and scientific
  research, 67–83; rejection by U.S., 85,
  233–37; and deep-seabed mining,
  110–21; signers, 157n45; unresolved
  questions, 238–53
Lebanon, 151, 153
Legal aspects of deep-seabed mining,
  87
Legal relations, in LOS Convention, 38
Legal status of EEZs, 61
Lesotho, 151, 154
Liberia, 152, 151, 154
Libya, 151, 152
Licensing of seabed mining, 59n38, 86
Liechtenstein, 154
Likeminded states, cooperation of, 121
Lima, Peru, LOS meeting, 174
Limits of open ocean system, 5–6
Lissitzyn, O., 220
Living resources: coastal state control,
  17; sharing of, 46–47
Lockheed Corporation, 107–8
Long distance pulse fishing fleets, 7
Luxembourg, 154

Madagascar, 152, 154
Malagasy Republic, 151
Malawi, 151, 154
Malaysia, 151, 152, 154; LOS concerns,
  204
Maldive Islands, 152, 154
Mali, 151, 154
Malone, James L., 114, 230

Malta, coastline length, 152

Management of fish populations, 20; of Georges Bank, 22–24

Manganese, in deepsea nodules, 89

Manganese nodules, 52, 81, 87–89; on continental shelf, 54; economics of mining, 94–95; technology of mining, 95–102

Mare Liberum, Grotius, 4, 30, 56n1, 126

Marine conservation movement, 6–7

Marine research, 47–48, 61, 65–84, 208

Maritime powers, rise of, 30

Maritime states, and exclusive economic zone principle, 33–34

Marshall, Alfred, 6

Mauritania, 151, 152

Mauritius, 151, 152, 154

Menchaca, Aramburu, 167

Mercantile economic organization, 4

Metallgesellschaft, 107

Mexico, 154, 165, 169, 171, 174–77 passim, 196n1, 198n17, 254n3; anchoveta fishery, 20; rearrangement of fishing effort, 26; coastline, 152; and LOS negotiations, 169, 180–84, 226

"Mexico Principles on the Legal Regime of the Sea," 168–69

Military activities, and marine research, 76–77

Military concerns, 240, 241; and LOS negotiations, 10–11, 13–14, 16, 60–62; and exclusive economic zones, 35–36

Mineral resources, deep-sea, 8, 88–95

Mineral rights, of deep-seabed, 50–56

Mine sites: estimated number, 90; size of, 91; conflicts, 105, 108, 117–20

Mining, *see* Deep-seabed mining

Mining industry, depression in, 87–88

Mining interests, U.S., and LOS negotiations, 227–28, 230

Mining licenses, applications for, 92–93

Mining rights, licensing, 59n38

Mitsubishi Corporation, 107

Monaco, 152

Mongolia, 154

Montevideo Declaration on the Law of the Sea, 172–73

Moon Treaty, 251

Morocco, 151, 152; joint proposal, 169

Multinational research programs, 80–82

Muscat and Oman, 152

Namibia, 154, 254n3

Namier, 43

Nationalism, and exclusive economic zones, 34–35

National liberation organizations, 249–50

National Oceanic and Atmospheric Administration (NOAA), 81, 92, 109

National Science Foundation, deep-sea drilling program, 96

National security issues, 112–13

Nations, new, and limits on open ocean system, 5

Nation states, and railroad development, 5

Natural prolongation of land, 131–32

Nauru, 154

Naval power, 35–36

Naval vessels, and environmental pollution control, 61

Navigation, freedom of, *see* Freedom of the seas

Navigational issues, superpowers and, 206–7

Negotiations, international, 247; *see also* Law of the Sea negotiations

Neo-isolationism, in U.S., 236

Nepal, 154

Netherlands, 152, 255n9; support of marine science, 68; nodule consortium participation, 106, 107

New Guinea, 255n9

New International Economic Order (NIEO), 247

New nations, and limits on open ocean system, 5

Newport News Shipbuilding, 107

New World, Spanish exploitation, 3

New Zealand, 152, 154, 255n9

Nicaragua, 152, 165, 171–77 passim, 196n1, 198n17

Nickel, 87, 89, 225; production and consumption, 93–94

NIEO (New International Economic Order), 247

Niger, 151, 154

Nigeria, 151, 152

Nixon, Richard M., 12, 52–53, 199

Njenga, Frank, xiii

NOAA (National Oceanic and Atmospheric Administration), 81, 92, report on deep-seabed mining, 109

Nodule consortia, 86, 100–1, 103, 106–10, 114, 118–19

Nodule mining: economics of, 94–95; technology of, 95–102

Nonparties, 58n35, 253n2; rights of, 40, 41, 210–11; status of, 49–50

Nonstate entities, 249–50

Noranda Mines, 107

North Central Pacific Ocean, Clarion/Clipperton region, 92–93, 105, 119

North Korea, 152

North/South economic issues, 111

North Vietnam, 152

Norway, 152, 154, 255n9; South Pacific whaling, 32

OAU (Organization of African Unity): and LOS negotiations, 141–46; and EEZ development, 147–48

Obligations of coastal states, 46–47; in exclusive economic zones, 164

Ocean boundaries, delimitation of, 242

Ocean Economics and Technology Office, 89

Ocean fish, world catch, 17–18

Ocean Management, Inc. (OMI), 86, 92–93, 107, 108, 118–19, 121n1

Ocean Minerals Company (OMCO), 86, 92, 107–8, 118–19, 121n1

Ocean Mining Associates (OMA), 86, 92, 107, 118–20, 121n1

Ocean mining consortia, see Nodule consortia

Ocean mining ventures, 103–10

Ocean Policy Committee, 1981 study, 82–83

Oceans, role in economic development, 1–3

Ocean science, and LOS Treaty, 64–84

Ocean space: twentieth-century utilization, 5; uses other than mining, 55

Ocean transportation newtork, 4

Oda, S. (International Court judge), 252

Office of International Marine Science Cooperation, 82

Offshore drilling rigs, 7–8

Offshore oil technology, 96

Oil companies, and mineral holdings, 88

Oil spills, 35

OMA (Ocean Mining Associates), 86, 92, 107, 118–20, 121n1

Oman, 154

OMCO (Ocean Minerals Company), 86, 92, 107–8, 118–19, 121n1

OMI (Ocean Management, Inc.), 86, 92–93, 107, 108, 118–19, 121n1

Open ocean system, 2–4; limits of, 5–6

Opportunity, historic period, 3–4

Organization of African Unity (OAU), and LOS negotiations, 141–46

Organization of American States, 164

Overflight rights, 6; of territorial sea, 173–74; Santo Domingo Declaration, 178

Overseas investment, 2; sixteenth-century expectations, 3

Ownership of ocean, 3

Pacific Ocean, 215

Pakistan, 151, 152

Palestine Liberation Organization (PLO), 249–50

Panama, 152, 154, 165, 169, 171–77 passim, 195, 196n1, 198n17; LOS negotiations, 182–84

Papua, 255n9

Paraguay, 154, 165, 171, 174, 192–93, 195, 196n1, 198n17

Parallel system of seabed resource development, 194, 209, 224–25

Pardo, Arvid, 172, 199, 257n23

Participation in LOS Convention, 245–46, 260n51

Patrimonialist Latin American countries, 180, 189

Patrimonial sea proposal, 140, 176, 178–79, 181

Pearl Fisheries Ordinance of Ceylon, 155n13

Peru, 137–38, 154, 165, 169, 172–75 passim, 195, 196n1, 198n17, 254n2, 255n9; anchoveta fishery, 20; exclusive fishing rights, 32; jurisdictional claims, 57n6, 166–67, 170, 171; coastline, 152; LOS negotiations, 182–84

Philippines, 70, 151, 152, 154, 254n3; LOS concerns, 205; ratification of Convention, 213

Pioneer investors in seabed mining, 86, 115, 116, 209–10, 232–33; France, 104;

Pioneer investors (Continued)
    Japan, 104–5; USSR, 105; India, 106
Pioneer mining areas, 91
Pipelines, Santo Domingo Declaration, 178
PLO (Palestine Liberation Organization), 249–50
Pohl, Galindo, 187
Poland, 152, 255n9; investment in fishing fleets, 7; rearrangement of fishing effort, 26
Polar regions, issues of, 240–41
Political aspects: of continental shelf resources, 16; of deep-sea mining, 16, 55, 111–14; of freedom of the seas decisions, 33–34; of coastal state authority, 49; of Russian ocean mining ventures, 105
Political limits of open ocean system, 5
Pollution of oceans, 133–34; coastal state authority, 48–49
Polymetallic nodules, see Manganese nodules
Polymetallic sulfide deposits, 89, 244
Pontecorvo, Giulio, viii–ix, xii
Portugal, 152, 154; sovereignty of seas, 4, 125–26
Portuguese vessel, captured by Dutch East Indies Company, 56n1
Preferential rights of coastal states, 33
Preparatory Commission, xii, xiii, 85–86, 116, 121, 214; U.S. and, 234
Preparatory phase for UNCLOS III, 175–84
Presussag, 107
Pretreaty seabed investors, rights of, 112
Price of fish, and value of Georges Bank, 25
Price of minerals, 87
Principles of International Law, Bello, 159–60
Private industry, and LOS Treaty, 111–12, 114–17
Procedural innovations, xv
Processing costs for manganese nodules, 99
Processing technology for manganese nodules, 100
Production, overseas organization of, 2
Production allotments of LOS Treaty, 115

Production costs: Georges Bank fisheries, 24; deep seabed mining, 95
Protectionism: in exclusive zone decision, 33–34; of coastal states, 49
Provisional Understanding, 86–87, 114, 115–16; see also Arbitration agreement
Prudhoe Bay, 28
Publication of scientific results, 75–76, 79
Pulse fishing fleets, 7

Railroads, development of, 5
Ratification of LOS Convention, xii, 67–68, 186, 213, 254n3
Reagan, Ronald, 83–84n10; and LOS Treaty, 85, 113–14, 213, 229–30, 233–35
Reagan Administration: and LOS Convention, xv; and Third World demands, 248; and deep-seabed regime, 261n60
Rearrangement of fishing effort, 26
Recovery of manganese nodules, 91
Redistribution of income: and LOS Treaty, 15; and coastal state control, 17–19
Redundancy in Georges Bank fishing effort, 22–24
Regulation of passage: and environmental protection, 35; and relevant equity, 45
Relative scarcity, historic period, 3
Republican platform, 1980, 112–13
Res communis status of seabed, 51–52
Research, marine, 47–48, 61, 65–84, 208
Res nullius status of seabed, 51–52
Resolution II, LOS treaty, 91–92, 103
Resolution 13, 168
Resolution, 84, 168
Resource issues, U.S. position, 221–22
Resource orientation of LOS, 161
Return rate of overseas investment, 2
Revenue-sharing proposal, 12, 53–54, 224; U.S. and, 211
Revised Draft Articles on the Exclusive Economic Zone, 148–50
Revised Single Negotiating Text (RSNT), 225, 226
Richardson, Elliott L., ix, 228
Richardson proposal of 1970, 12
Rights, in exclusive economic zone, 146
Rights of transit, 58n25; and jurisdic-

tional rights, 44; of nonparties to LOS Convention, 50
Rio Tinto Zinc, 107
Risks, financial, of seabed mining development, 101–2
Romania, 152, 255n9
Roosevelt, Franklin D., 168
Ross, David A., ix
Royal Dutch Shell, 108
Rules of Procedure for LOS Conference, 185
Rwanda, 151, 154

Sailing vessels, technical advances, 4
Saint Kitts and Nevis, 196n1
Saint Lucia, 196n1, 198n17
Saint Vincent and the Grenadines, 196n1, 198n17
Salzgitter, 107
San Marino, 154, 254n2
Santiago Declaration on the Maritime Zone, 166
Santo Domingo Declaration, 177–81, 189
Satellites, artificial, issues of, 241–42
Saudi Arabia, 151, 152, 169
Scarcity, relative, historic period, 3
Schachter, Oscar, ix–x, xiv–xv
Scientific knowledge, valuation of, 5
Scientific marine research, 47–48, 61, 65–84; issues of, 208
Seabed: sovereignty claims, 51–52; Santo Domingo Declaration, 179; see also Common heritage principle
Seabed Authority, 36, 51–54, 75, 143, 183–84; Santo Domingo Declaration, 179; decision-making structure, 228–29; organization of, 243–44; proposal, 183; review of operations, 259n36
Seabed Committee, 175, 180–84, 199, 221, 222; revenue-sharing proposal, 12; EEZ proposal, 141; draft submitted to, 182–84
Seabed exploration, technology of, 100
Seabed mineral resources, 88–95; rights to, 50–56; Latin American countries and, 193
Seabed mining, xiii–xiv, 208–9; exclusive rights, 52; licensing, 59n38, 86; U.S. and, 211–14; see also Seabed Authority
Sea Grant, 81
Second Committee, 185–87, 222–23, 233

Secretariat, Seabed Authority proposal, 183
Secret negotiations, 225–26
Sedco, Inc., 107
Self-defense, naval activity, 60–61
Semi-enclosed seas, 192, 203–4, 224
Seminar of African Experts, Yaounde, Cameroun, 138–40
Semiprivate firms, seventeenth century, 4
Senegal, 151, 152, 254n3
Seventeenth-century economic organization, 3–4
Seventh Inter-American Conference, 1933, 160
Sharing of living resources, 46–4
Sierra Leone, 142, 151, 152
Signers of Geneva Convention, 195–96
Singapore, 151, 152; LOS concerns, 203
Sixteenth-century view of oceans, 3
Slave trade, 133
Socialism, and exclusive economic zones, 34
Somalia, 142, 151, 152, 154
SOSUS (Sound surveillance system), 257n18
South Africa, 152, 154, 254n2, 255n9
Southeast Asian countries, and LOS Convention, 199–216
South Korea, 152, 154
South Vietnam, 152, 154
South West Africa People's Organization (SWAPO), 249–50
Sovereignty claims, beyond territorial sea, 161; see also Exclusive economic zones; Territorial seas
Soviet Union, see USSR
Spain, 3, 125–26, 152, 154, 255n9
Specialized Conference of the Caribbean Countries, 169, 170, 177
Speculative resources, 27
Spontaneity of marine research, 78
Sri Lanka, 150, 152, 154; Pearl Fisheries Ordinance, 155n13
Standard Oil Company of Indiana, 108
Standard Oil Company of Ohio, 107
State behavior, and LOS negotiations, 260n49
Steam trawlers, 5, 6
Strait of Gibraltar, 70
Strait of Malacca, 203, 204

Straits states, and LOS negotiations, 206–7; *see also* International straits
Submarine-launched nuclear missiles, 256*n*16
Submarines, 35; rights of passage, 61
Sudan, 151, 152
Suffering, creative power of, 134
Sun Company, 107
Supertankers, pollution by, 133–34
Supra national organizations, 248–49
Suriname, 196*n*1, 198*n*17
SWAPO (South West Africa People's Organization), 249–50
Swaziland, 151, 154
Sweden, 152, 255*n*9
Switzerland, 154
Syria, 152, 151, 254*n*2

Taiwan, 152
Tanzania, 151, 152
Taxation questions, 117
Technological advances, xii, 2, 4–6, 8, 160; and coastal state authority, 31; and exclusive economic zones, 34–35; military, 35–36; and common heritage principle, 55–56
Technology of deep-seabed mining, 95–102, 120–21; of AFERNOD, 104
Tenneco, 107
Tenth Inter-American Conference, Caracas, 1954, 168
Territorialist countries, 233; Latin American, 180, 189, 195
Territorial seas, 68, 69–70, 127, 128–29, 138; rights of passage, 44; military ships in, 76; breadth claimed, 150–51; joint proposal, 169–70; claims greater than twelve miles, 171; and 200-mile limit, 173; Venezuelan proposal, 176; Santo Domingo Declaration, 177; draft treaty articles, 181; Latin American countries and, 189; and international straits, 200; U.S. proposal, 221
Thailand, 151, 152; LOS concerns, 203–4
Thermal energy conversion, 55
Third United Nations Conference on the Law of the Sea (UNCLOS III), *see* Law of the Sea Conference; Law of the Sea Treaty
Third World issues, 247–48
Three-mile limit, 128–29

Togo, 151, 152
Tonga, 154, 254*n*2
Tordeseillas, treaty of, 3, 125–26
Torry Canyon accident, 199
Traditional Law of the Sea, 197*n*5
Tramp steamers, 5
Transfer of technology, 102, 115; U.S. and, 212
Transitional period in ocean development, 5–7
Transit rights, 44, 61
Transnational corporations, 250
Transportation network, 4
Travaux preparatoires, 42
Treaty adherence, and transit rights, 44
Treaty of Tordeseillas, 3, 125–26
Trinidad and Tobago, 152, 165, 174–77 passim, 190, 196*n*1, 198*n*17; Seabed Committee draft, 182–84
Truman Proclamation,. 16, 31, 57*n*6, 129–30, 161–64
Trusteeship proposal, 221–22
Tuna war, 32
Tunisia, 151, 152
Turkey, 67, 151, 152, 254*n*2; amendment to LOS Convention, 195
200-mile limit, 137–38, 167–68, 173

Uganda, 151, 154
UNCLOS III, *see* Law of the Sea Conference; Law of the Sea Treaty
Undiscovered resources, 27, 28
UNESCO, 80
Union Miniere, 107
Union of South Africa, 152, 154, 254*n*2, 255*n*9
Unitary system, 209; Latin American countries and, 184, 193–94
United Arab Republic, 151, 169
United Kingdom, 125, 153, 154, 157*n*45, 233, 253–54*n*2, 255*n*9; and freedom of the seas, 30; "cod wars," 32; and LOS treaty, 85; seabed mining license, 86, 92; nodule consortium participation, 106, 107
United Nations, 36, 161; international law-making conferences, 33; Charter of Economic Rights and Duties of States, 79; Department of Economic and Social Affairs, 89; *see also* Geneva Conference, 1958; Law of the Sea

Conference; Law of the Sea Treaty;
Seabed Committee
United Nations charter, and naval activity, 60
United Nations General Assembly: and
seabed minerals, 50–51, 172; and developing states, 220; Seabed Committee, 221
United States, 27, 67, 153, 154, 171,
157n45, 254n2, 255n9; and LOS Convention, xiii–xv, 40, 44, 45–46, 49–50,
85, 200–1; revenue-sharing proposal,
12; management of assets, 13; and
EEZ, 16–17, 33–34, 147; Georges Bank
catch, 22, 23; continental shelf claims,
31, 129–30, 161–64; "tuna war," 32;
and seabed mining control, 54; military concerns, 60–62; support of marine science, 68; and IOC, 80; marine
scientific research, 81–83; ocean mining ventures, 92–93, 106–10; and LOS
negotiations, 112–14, 219–37; ocean
mining prospects, 121; Guam Doctrine, 199–200; LOS negotiations
(Asian view), 206–16; and Third World
demands, 248
Unpredictability of permission for marine research, 77
Unresolved disputes, 49
Upper Volta, 151, 154
Uruguay, 165, 169, 171, 172, 174, 175, 195,
196n1, 198n17, 255n9; coastline, 153;
draft treaty articles, 182; Seabed Committee draft, 182–84
User fees, for ocean transit, 15
USSR, 152, 154, 171, 255n9; investment
in fishing fleets, 7; and fisheries
agreement, 18; rearrangement of fishing effort, 26; military concerns, 60–
62; support of marine science, 68; and
LOS treaty, 85, 200–1; mining license
application, 86, 93; mine site conflicts,
87, 105, 108, 120; and LOS negotiations, 206–8

US Steel, 107
Utilization of fishery resources, 20–21

Value: of Georges Bank, 24–25; of continental shelf hydrocarbons, 27, 28
Vargas Carreno, Edmundo, 176, 177
Vatican City, 154
Venezuela, 67, 165, 169, 171, 174–77 passim, 195, 196, 196n1, 197n12, 198n17,
254n2; coastline, 153; sovereignty
claims, 161; LOS negotiations, 176,
180–82, 195; state enterprise, 184; and
island provisions, 192
Venice, 125
Viet Nam, 151

Warships, marine research by, 76–77
Weak nations, exploitation of, 125
Wealth, redistribution of, 17–19
Weapons, on ocean bed, 35
Weather, and mining operations, 98
Western Europe, overseas investment,
sixteenth century, 3
Western Samoa, 153
Western technology, transfer to new
nations, 5
West Germany, see Federal Republic of
Germany
Whaling industry, and EEZs, 56–57n6
World catch of ocean fish, 17–18; biological limits, 19–21; rearrangement of,
26; value of, 27, 28n6
World nickel production capacity, 93–94
World War II, and EEZs, 56–57n6

Yemen, 151, 153, 154
Yugoslavia, 153

Zaire, 152
Zambia, 151, 154, 254n3
Zimbabwe, 151, 154